God Bless
Ivan E Nancy
Philip
4/06

The design and
origin of Birds

© Day One Publications 2006
First printed 2006

ISBN 1-84625-002-1

9 781846 250026 >

ISBN 1 84625 002 1

British Library Cataloguing in Publication Data available

Published by Day One Publications
Ryelands Road, Leominster, HR6 8NZ
☎ 01568 613 740 FAX 01568 611 473
email—sales@dayone.co.uk
web site—www.dayone.co.uk
North American—e-mail—sales@dayonebookstore.com
North American—web site—www.dayonebookstore.com

Designed by Steve Devane and printed by Gutenberg Press, Malta

'Even the stork in the heavens knows her appointed times; and the turtledove, the swift and the swallow observe the time of their coming' Jeremiah 8:7.

Contents

B irds have played an important part in human history and have always been respected and loved for their beauty and amazing flying skills. Philip Snow has produced a unique book which expertly describes and illustrates the design, life and beauty of birds.

Stuart Burgess, BSc (Eng), PhD, CEng, FIMechE, FRAeS
Professor of Design & Nature, Head of Department of Mechanical Engineering
University of Bristol

Foreword

P hilip Snow has long been a person I have a great admiration for, not just because of his evident knowledge of birds, but because of his great artistic abilities (his paintings and drawings of birds are a great inspiration to many), and his clear personal testimony of conversion to Christ after going through some very difficult times in his life. In this very readable book, Philip covers the whole area of bird design and structure, their superb flight characteristics, and then considers their origin. By his sheer precision of detailed description, he leaves one with a sense of overriding awe concerning the amazing ability of birds, whether it be their superb wing structure, the beauty of bird song and courtship displays, or their staggering feats of migration. Even the most determined evolutionist will have to ask the question, 'Could they possibly be the accidental side-effect of a random explosion and blind evolution? Could they really have evolved their wonderful aerial lifestyle and unique, warm-blooded design by unguided chance?' In the closing chapter 'Birds in religion, myth and art', Philip Snow shows that in every age, people have wondered about these masters of the sky. Most of us will come away from this book with a deep fascination with the wonder of flight, and some will be challenged with the strong evidence that all of nature bears testimony to the Master Designer.

Prof. Andy C. McIntosh, DSc, FIMA, C.Math, FEI, C.Eng, FInstP, MIGEM, FRAeS
Professor of Thermodynamics and Combustion Theory
Energy and Resources Research Institute School of Process, Environmental and Materials Engineering,
University of Leeds
LEEDS
United Kingdom
LS2 9JT

B irds are one of the world's most beautiful and inspiring creations, so it is not unusual that they have been studied, used, loved and painted by so many different peoples. The Bible first wrote of their migrations, and used the eagle as one of the 'four living creatures', symbolizing at least one of God's attributes—far-sightedness. This was probably because God was 'above' or outside his created time/space, although, of course, still occasionally intervening on our behalf. This is enforced every time I see an eagle soaring effortlessly over some beautiful wild place, its superior vision missing nothing below, behind—*or in front of me*. Only God sees and declares 'the end from the beginning' (Isaiah 46:10)

The earliest cultures ate them, hunted them and with them, and even revered them. Thus they also mythologized, and misused them, as symbols of their own aggression or expansionist policies. Many empires and countries like Rome, Russia, and later the USA, Germany, France and Iraq use birds, especially eagles, as their national symbols. Birds have been carved and painted on caves, rocks, temples, and associated with pyramids and religions, art and literature, sport and farming, war and peace, life and death and even heaven and hell. Eagles have long stood for higher, spiritual things, while conversely, serpents typify lower, craftier and rebellious ideas. Thus 'the Eagle and the Serpent' are at war in us all, still—our earthly old creation fighting our spiritually born-again, new creation. That explains not only our angst but also all the images and ideas, found worldwide, about gods or eagles conquering serpents or dragons. These are very potent images found in most cultures, and are originally based on Genesis 3, where the Lord Jesus Christ is prophesied to be temporarily 'bruised' before finally crushing the head of the original serpent, or Satan (see chapter 7).

Birds have also inspired and instructed our own efforts at flight, from propellers to jets and rockets, but perhaps most beautifully in silent and graceful gliders. We can see the broad principles of bird flight put to practical use every time an airliner approaches the runway, when the rear and forward wing flaps are lowered to create more lift as the aircraft reduces speed. This is but a crude emulation of a bird's supreme mastery of the air, with its concave wing and raised alulae (the 'little wing' at the 'thumb'), which prevents stalling at low speeds. We can only begin to approach that sort of effortless flight in our dreams ... at the moment.

The natural grace and immaculate design of birds is incontestable, even to evolutionists, but it is saddening to hear the oft-repeated claim that they have only 'accidentally' developed from reptiles, themselves but random developments from green slime. Genetic mistakes, or copying errors in DNA, are held to be responsible for turning chance chemicals into Peacocks—or 'Goo into You' as Bible-believing scientist Ken Ham says. Many of us enjoy TV programmes on the life of birds, graced with the usual high standard of close-up photography that so aids our appreciation and understanding. However, more discerning viewers will have great problems with the evolutionary bias of the commentator. There are many wild theories on bird 'evolution' (see chapter 6), although they are usually outside the strict guidelines of science. Real science is acceptable when it sticks to its own limitations and rules of observation, ideas and testing, but it is woefully inadequate when it comes to speculating on unobserved and supposedly distant phenomena like origins. Sadly, evolution is now applied to just about everything from the beginning of the universe and life to the development of religion. However, random 'Big Bangs' and endless blind mistakes can be tested—and the result is not evolution of complexity or improvement—but devolution and destruction.

Although flight is incredibly expensive in terms of energy requirements, it has supposedly 'accidentally' evolved at least four times and in very different forms. That is a remarkable claim, especially when all the major changes needed to turn one kind of creature into another are looked at. And as usual, the 'first' (lowest in the fossil record) creatures always had perfect flight from the beginning—'ancient' insects and Pterosaurs are still the most sophisticated fliers known. It is beyond rational belief that our incredibly beautiful, complex variety of birds, insects, bats and extinct flying reptiles could be just the 'inevitable' side-effect of chance chemical evolution. Evolutionists claim that the miracle of life only accidentally came from non-life, when the first so-called 'simple cell' somehow got together in a 'chemical soup'. It would then have to rapidly and blindly develop DNA and all the highly specialised methods of keeping itself going by replication or reproduction, and then only by endless genetic mistakes.

Leaving aside the many huge problems with all that, well before trilobites, tuna or terns could appear—does a Blue Tit or a chickadee really look like an accident to you? Could it possibly be assembled in all its exquisite, delicate yet successful form just because some 'selfish gene' needed to reproduce itself? Our most prominent evolutionist, Richard Dawkins, constantly presents that sort of unverifiable nonsense as science, and the majority of the media, public and other academics lap it up. The big question is: why?—when none would deny that a much simpler computer or car needed a designer. One of the aims of this book is to show that the complexity, beauty, adaptability, variety and flying abilities of birds could not possibly be accidental. They, like all creatures, are here to teach us. As the Bible states: 'For since the creation of the world [God's] invisible attributes are clearly seen, being understood by the things that are made, even His eternal power and Godhead, so that they are without excuse' (Romans 1:20).

Of all creations, the bird is perhaps the most beautiful and remarkable, and therefore the most unlikely to be written off as the result of blind evolution. They number among the most spectacularly coloured or shaped of any creature. Even their huge range of coloration depends upon incredibly complex design factors, and at least four separate sources. Birds are found virtually everywhere on earth, from the coldest polar regions to the hottest deserts, the highest mountains or flattest farmlands and grasslands, in the wettest swamps or deepest oceans, the thickest woods, in hedgerows, ditches, ponds, lakes, rivers, or even the tidiest parks, car parks or gardens. Most of us can enjoy watching their elegant flight and entertaining feeding habits every day, as long as it is not a Herring Gull pilfering our ice-cream, or Black Kites stealing picnic sandwiches. We can also savour their liquid song and great variety of colours and patterns. Although most of us will never see an Australian Lyrebird in the flesh perform its incredible display of mimicry, we can watch it at a very good second hand, thanks to TV and video. The performance of this exotically-tailed bird includes not only other birds' songs, but also uncanny and exact copies of mechanical sounds like camera shutters, motor-drives, chain saws and car alarms. However, you do not need to go to distant lands to hear such mimicry—our very own starlings or mockingbirds are pretty good too. They effectively copy man-made sounds, like ambulance sirens or other birds' calls and songs, among their own repetitive rooftop chatter. The fact that two or more rival male birds can deliberately sing elaborate and highly technical duets together is just another example of the real life of birds (see chapter 1).

Every single part of a bird is a marvel of intricate and precise design, many of them unique to birds alone. One of the smallest hummingbirds weighs little more than 0.05 oz (1.5 gm), while the huge Ostrich tips the scales at 345 lb (156 kg), yet they both have the same sort of structure, even though one flies and the other runs. When we think of birds, flight is the first thing that springs to mind, and the flying abilities of many of them are truly amazing. Sooty Terns are claimed to fly for up to ten years, only rarely alighting, while others like Ruppell's Vulture soar at heights up to 37,000ft (11,000m), in air so thin that it would kill us. Peregrines can dive at over 175mph (280kph) without blacking out, or Woodcocks can fly as slowly as 5mph (8kph) without falling from the sky. The Horned Gemstar Hummingbird beats its wings up to 90 times per second, while circling Andean Condors barely move their 10ft (3m) wings for hours on end. African Queleas (seed-eating weaverbirds) can form flocks so dense they can blot out the sun—with 32 *million* recorded in one Sudanese flock alone!

Bird vision is also legendary, probably up to eight times sharper than human vision in some raptors (birds of prey). Woodcocks can see even more than a full circle, including above, without moving, while the Tawny Owl must turn its head around nearly 360°, as its eyes are fixed looking straight ahead. Some birds can correct light distortion under water, see ultra-violet and fluorescent light, or hear the slightest sound beneath thick layers of grass or snow. Western Grebes and Storm Petrels 'walk' and dance on water, while Emperor Penguins can 'fly' underwater to depths of around 1,500ft (480m), staying down for as long as 18 minutes, three times deeper and longer than the world human free-dive record. The way birds construct their huge variety of nests or migrate long distances by 'instinct' has also baffled scientists for centuries. Birds can use infrasound, echolocation, electromagnetism and built-in altimeters. All of these behaviours are even more mysterious if you consider, like evolutionists, that they have only arisen by chance or accident.

How does a young Blackpoll Warbler 'know' that it must first fly the *wrong* way, eastwards, to get to South America from Canada, after its parents have already left? How does it work out that it must fly out over the Atlantic towards Africa, at a precise time to catch higher winds that only then allow it to turn south, then relax and fly on down to Brazil with minimum effort? How could it 'read' that information written on microscopic molecules of sugar and water called DNA—and who first wrote it? It all had to be pre-coded to work first time or not at all: a drowning warbler is of no use to the future of its species. And how can that code of mere sugar or water 'think', reason or instruct the young bird? And every code requires a coder ...

Bible writers like Job and Solomon, as well as Paul, told us to 'look to creation' for instruction—and specifically birds. They are just one part of the whole exciting web of life (ecology) that is there to both delight, intrigue and educate us—and that we were instructed to look after. It seems that generally we have not done very well on any of these points. The aim of this book is to help us understand how we can do better, and the role that creation plays in our science, history, religion and daily lives, and even our future. It describes how birds were wonderfully designed right from the beginning, but with built-in information so that they can adapt to their many changing environments. Such miraculous design could not possibly have come about by a 'tornado rushing through a junkyard', as the well-known evolutionist Sir Fred Hoyle said as he ridiculed current theories of 'natural' development.[1] I can think of no better example of Creation than birds to 'instruct us'; from the most exotic to the common garden birds we can enjoy every day.

General bird facts
• There are claimed to be about 9,000 bird 'species' in the world.
• All birds lay eggs.
• They can live up to 80 years or more.
• All have feathers, beaks and wings. Only the extinct flightless giant Moa is claimed not to have had wings.
• Birds are the only creatures that have feathers. See chapter 6 for the controversial claims about 'Feathered Dinosaurs'.

- Most birds can fly but some do not—they seem to have deliberately lost flight, or are in the process of losing it.
- They can use infrasound, echolocation, electromagnetism and built-in altimeters.
- Birds are warm-blooded.
- Birds are very intelligent—brighter than apes.
- Birds have always provided materials and inspiration for mankind.

Let us now look at these facts in greater detail, remembering that our human knowledge is frequently subject to change, and many reconstructions from fossils, etc., should be understood as imaginative guesswork. Likewise, our knowledge of the universe must be seen as very limited.

Notes

1 Dawkins then ridiculed Hoyle, by claiming that over time and countless other accidents, anything can 'evolve'. We shall see if Dawkins's 'faith' is misplaced, as even he recently admitted his belief in all the missing links was 'a matter of faith' (Jonathan Miller, BBC4, 11:2004).

Birds: general design, structure and functions

The Bible tells us in its very first verse (Genesis 1:1), 'In the beginning God created the heavens and the earth'. The rest of the chapter then gives the order of creation. Birds were one of the first forms of life to be made, and in fact the very first flying creatures. Much of this is in direct contradiction to evolutionary ideas of the origins of life, which also claim that birds only evolved by trial and error from some kind of reptilian ancestor. We shall look in detail at these amazing claims throughout this book.

This most remarkable class of creatures, called *aves* (Latin for birds), is chock full of special design features. Flight and feathers are the most obvious differences from all other creatures, even including other fliers. Only birds have feathered wings and the luxury of 'hands' (feet) completely free to do other things, unlike bats, butterflies or pterosaurs. To propel themselves through, or ride on, the air requires perfect *aerodynamics* (or the effects of motion of solid bodies through the air), and that usually means slender rounded bodies and long wings. But even then, there are always exceptions that once more demonstrate amazing variety and construction—not blind accident. Birds do have slightly less variation in form than some other creatures, because there are many problems associated with flight. Birds had perfect flight from the beginning, as both Genesis 1:20 and the fossil record show, despite the ideas of evolutionists. The fossil record is not a record of development of complexity, for it shows very sophisticated flight and perfect aerodynamics in other creatures as well—also from the 'earliest', lowest levels. As God said to Job, 'Does the hawk fly by your wisdom …? (Job 39:26). Fortunately not, as all human inventions are still incredibly cumbersome compared with all the immaculate designs required for real flight.

Such aerodynamics reaches perfection in birds. Whether they stoop (swoop on prey) or hover, glide or soar, flap or bound through the skies or

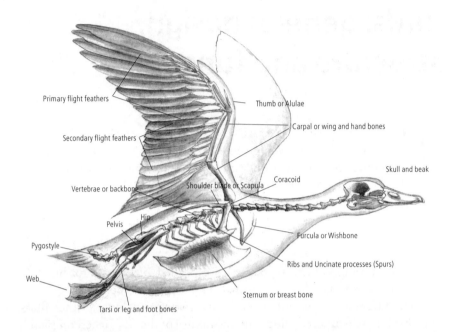

Fig. 1: SIMPLIFIED SKELETON OF A DUCK.

even 'fly' beneath the waves, birds are indeed brilliant. Even when they are flightless or mainly ground dwelling, they still exhibit superb engineering. Yet their most famous and distinctive feature, flight, obviously requires a very light and specialised airy skeleton.

Because they need to be both light and yet strong, bones and feather shafts are thin walled and hollow, but stiffened inside with thin struts or trusses.

It is no coincidence that our first aeroplanes had hollow wings with such struts between, as well as inside them. It is the wing bones that naturally need more of these struts for added strength, whereas the leg bones of say, a Grey Heron, are largely hollow. However, there are some birds that do not have completely hollow bones, like the deep-diving cormorants. Birds can even breathe through their bones! As flight is very expensive in terms of energy needs, breathing and digestion must also be superbly designed.

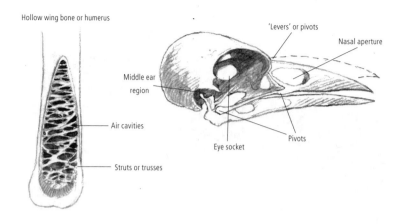

Hollow wing bone or humerus

Air cavities

Struts or trusses

'Levers' or pivots

Nasal aperture

Middle ear region

Eye socket

Pivots

Fig. 2: (left) BONE STRENGTHENING STRUTS.
Fig. 4: (right) SKULL BONES OF A JACKDAW, SHOWING THE 'PIVOTS OR LEVERS' THAT MOVE THE UPPER MANDIBLE.

Another important difference from other creatures is found in the general skeleton. The bones of birds are heavily fused together in areas like the spine, shoulder and hip, which reduces weight by doing away with the need for ligaments and cartilage in individual joints. The shoulder (pectoral) girdle is especially important for flight and is firmly joined to both the spine and breastbone (sternum). Then the 'wishbone' (furcula), famously seen on birds like chickens, braces the wings apart on all flying birds. Two main, all-important wing bones strongly attach to both the main bones of the pectoral girdle (coracoids) and the tendons of the two pairs of large breast muscles, which work the wings up and down—one contracts as the other stretches in a unique 'rope and pulley' system.

Even the large breastbone (sternum), needed to carry these heavy flight muscles, is wafer thin. Birds have the advantage of walking and running as well as flying, so their legs are also rather special. What looks like a knee to us is actually an ankle, for the upper foot bones are elongated and fused to form the lower leg bone.

Skulls are also very light but strong and, unlike reptiles, fully filled by

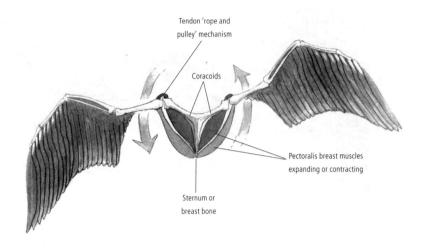

Tendon 'rope and
pulley' mechanism

Coracoids

Pectoralis breast muscles
expanding or contracting

Sternum or
breast bone

Fig. 3: HOW THE BREAST MUSCLES WORK THE WINGS UP AND DOWN.

their large brains and eyes. Birds' skulls are capable of very subtle and delicate movements—just watch how a huge eagle carefully tears up tiny bits of meat to feed to its little chick. Unlike mammals, many birds can move the upper beak (mandible) as well as the lower by a complex system of levers.

Again there are exceptions, and some waders only move the tip of the upper mandible, to feel about in the mud for food. Excellent vision is also common in birds, especially in 'raptors' (birds of prey) such as the Peregrine Falcon, whose eyes are as large as a human's, although its skull is naturally but a fraction of the size of ours. Another intriguing design fact has recently emerged: some birds that bury lots of nuts in the autumn actually regrow and enlarge, annually, parts of the brain concerned with memory. It should be obvious to us all that a bird's absolute mastery of the air also requires large back-up systems. Whether 'intelligence' or 'instinct'—everything from feathers to muscles, nerves to skeleton, sight to brain, must follow strict instructions and work precisely together. For instance, man-made gliders would find it very difficult to fly effortlessly into the teeth of a gale, as many seabirds (and even bumblebees) do.

Naturally, such splendid design also needs exact *timing* mechanisms for all the trillions of precise, electrochemical reactions. One of the ways they are regulated, as in us, is by the Pineal Gland, or 'Third Eye'. This little 'eye' is buried beneath the skin, and operates through the external eyes to measure light levels and regulate melatonin. Another 'supernatural' function is the detection of infrasound, used to 'hear' the air in thermals, and anticipate approaching bad weather. Other aspects of a bird's ear are also special, including the ability to detect very delicate differences in air (barometric) pressure. This 'altimeter' enables bird to fly at precise heights, and in accurately gauged, vertical bands, often unique to their species (see chapter 3).

The ribcage is also specialised. Some of the ribs are strengthened by 'uncinate processes', or hook-like spurs of bone lying across the next rib, which strengthens the whole cavity. These also help to lessen pressure on the lungs of diving birds like guillemots. Only the screamers, which are South American birds vaguely like pheasants, do not have them, nor Archaeopteryx (see chapter 6), but both birds are 'modern' fliers.

Birds naturally depend upon their feathers, and we will see just how beautifully designed, suited and lightweight they are, too. Barn Owls or Kittiwake gulls, which spend a lot of time riding the winds above meadows or sea, weigh hardly anything at all: a mere 12 oz (350 gm) in the case of a Kittiwake. Also the 2.5lb (1.2kg) Frigate Bird's skeleton is only 4 per cent of body weight; and even the feathers weigh more.

Before we move on to those marvels lets look at another unique function of the skeleton—breathing. A bird's lungs and respiratory system are just so well designed—there is no other word for it. It is very different from ours, or the reptiles they are claimed to descend from, consisting of so much more than lungs. Firstly, it is a one-way system; secondly, the air goes almost all around the body through many large air sacs and even many of the hollow bones; and thirdly most of the air is exchanged in one breath. The air first goes straight through the lungs to the rear air sacs, and only then comes back through the lungs to be absorbed.

These need to be beautifully designed, to rapidly absorb the maximum amount of oxygen by flowing against huge numbers of tiny blood vessels. All are vital functions, as birds need to obtain maximum oxygen and get rid

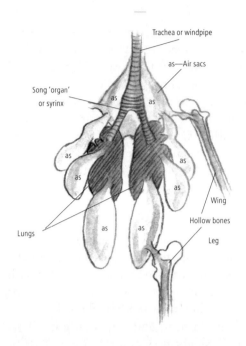

Trachea or windpipe

as—Air sacs

Song 'organ' or syrinx

as

as

as

as

as

as

Wing

Hollow bones

Lungs

as

as

Leg

Fig. 5: SIMPLIFIED RESPIRATORY SYSTEM.

of maximum carbon dioxide as quickly as possible, as well as keep buoyant. It is indeed the best 'air-cooled engine of any animal'. No dinosaur could possibly breathe like that because its lungs are completely different, making any 'evolution' impossible (see chapter 6).

There is another rather special purpose for the respiratory system— singing. When many birds breathe out, they can vibrate beautifully designed membranes at the top of the 'bronchi' (two breathing tubes meeting in the trachea, or wind pipe) and 'semi-ring' muscles round the outside. This arrangement can produce unlimited sounds. We need lips to whistle, but birds do not, and the quality and variety of sound seems to depend upon the numbers of bronchial 'rings' the bird has. Hence the 'Oscines' or 'true Songbirds' are said to be the most 'evolved' birds because they have the most semi-rings. Tell that to a crane or Whooper Swan, which have specially designed coiled trachea for their wonderful, far-carrying bugling. Other amazing features of bird song are covered in great detail in Stuart Burgess's book *Hallmarks of Design* (see bibliography).

Although the ability to sing is physically built in, most birds learn to refine it, and their wonderful mimicry confirms that. When Common Starlings were exported to America, they rapidly learnt local sounds previously unknown to them. Singing both delights us and communicates many different messages to other birds, as well as various alarm calls and quiet contact among themselves. Although it is usually the males that sing, certain pairs will indulge in perfectly timed antiphonal duets, like the 'call and response' of plantation blues or Gaelic psalmody. Such timing and pitch is remarkable, especially when it is done without visual contact. It recalls the incredible synchrony within flocks of flying birds. Certain African shrike pairs not only produce the most amazing counterpoint singing, they will even duet perfectly with another rival couple. Birds like the American Song Sparrow have literally hundreds of songs to which they can always return, and always pitch perfect. Not only will birds duet or compose perfect quartet pieces, they can also indulge in impromptu trios. Listen carefully to three Common Blackbirds on adjacent territories singing, and you will sometimes hear them passing around instant variations upon each other's song. This is all put down to pure functionality by evolutionary biologists—rival males advertising their territory. That is true, but there is little evolutionary advantage in such incredible vocal ornamentation, or in the tail of a peacock. Some 3,000 years ago King Solomon so valued their outstanding beauty that he especially imported peacocks from the East (1 Kings 10:22).

'Sexual selection', as Darwin called the development of such incredible ornaments as the peacock's tail, or complex song, involves elaboration way beyond mere existence. It clearly requires much more energy, and increases exposure to danger. Such superb design cannot be put down to massive numbers of evolution's 'chance mistakes'. Scientists now think that individual song actually advertises the best and most distant genes, at least in Sedge Warblers, to prevent incest, inbreeding and other inherited problems.[1] This only adds to our confidence in creation, and knowledge about how genetics and other inheritance devices always protect against the weakening of life's lines, yet spread the variety as far and wide as possible. This is the superb concept of 'more-from-less' that will continually crop up—design and 'speciation' from lessening amounts of information, and always 'top down'. This is apparently how we have such superb variety in birds like finches or birds of paradise, which can still interbreed to produce further and new colour variations—yet without any new genetic information (see chapter 6).

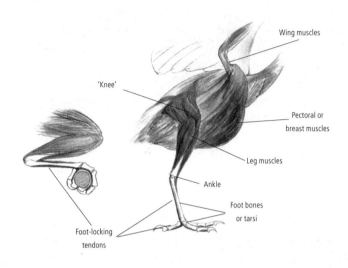

Fig. 6: MAIN MUSCLE GROUPS AND FOOT LOCKING MECHANISM.

Mention must be made of another special feature here, allied to both respiration and circulatory systems. Some South American hummingbirds can turn down their 'central heating' during very cold nights and more or less die. They can live with highs and lows of 40°C to −13°C. Only one bird is known to hibernate completely for the five winter months—the nightjar-like Poorwill, which also endures similar temperatures to the hummingbirds, in North American deserts.

The *muscles* of a bird are, as one would expect, also admirably suited for the job. Because of the superb lightweight design of the rest of the body they can afford to be quite heavy, especially the vital breast (pectoral) muscles. In an energetic flier like the pigeon they may make up nearly half of the entire body weight though 15–20 per cent is normal for most birds.

The aforementioned two pairs of pectoral muscles are also unique to birds, working the wings. They need to be strongly attached to both the sternum and the first wing bone (humerus), so the bones have extra large and flared ends. Note how the leg muscles are also quite large, particularly at the top. This naturally centres most of the body weight around the heavy pectoral muscles and helps balance the bird. Having the heaviest muscles compactly arranged in the middle means that they must also operate the limbs by long tendons. Thus the ends of the powerful wings and legs are both light and yet have maximum flexibility. The colour of muscle also demonstrates function—whiter if less well used, or redder if well supplied with blood for sustainable powered flight or running. That is why chickens, now bred to be as heavy as possible and for flightlessness, have whiter breast meat, but redder legs. Birds that only need short bursts of flight generally have whiter breast muscles, like the ancestors of domestic hens. Domestic duck breast meat is darker because their recent ancestors flew more than Jungle Fowls, the probable ancestors of all domestic hens.

Flying, walking and swimming—no other creature has such design of form, bone and muscle, allowing it to do all of these, but even individual birds have difficulty doing all three well. In particular, diving birds have legs that are superb for swimming but are weaker for walking, as they are placed well to the rear. Most *legs* are held firmly against the bird's side in the middle of the body, even when their actual hipbones are set further back. Because many birds spend a lot of time on the ground, balance can be maintained by this unique arrangement. The Secretary Bird has such long and powerful legs that it can stamp snakes to death, and a kick from an Ostrich could cause serious injury. As roughly two thirds of all bird families are 'passerines' (perching/song birds), they need another special design feature: *locking feet*. When a passerine settles on a branch and relaxes, its weight causes the ankle to bend and tighten a long tendon. This elastic tendon stretches from the tibia to the end of the toes, behind the ankle joint, causing the toes to curl and grip tightly, as illustrated. This ingenious arrangement also allows raptors to grasp their prey firmly—Eurasian Sparrowhawks have been observed to nearly drown when hooked into feisty Moorhens. It is fascinating to watch how a Black-winged Stilt or Greater Flamingo folds up its ridiculously long pink legs to sit on the nest, or how a Harrier Hawk's double-jointed 'knee' (ankle) allows it to winkle lizards out of holes or from between rocks. The next time you watch a Black-headed Gull or blackbird pattering its feet up and down you will know it is imitating rain to make worms come up. The Little Egret waggles its bright yellow feet about under water to fascinate or disturb fish. The Louisiana Heron drags its feet across the water while in flight to imitate smaller fish, in order to lure bigger fish out, and there are many more wonderful examples.

As you might expect, even bird's feet are fascinating, varied and perfectly suited for all the different environments. They are all based upon an amazingly intricate design blueprint with additional extras for specialisation. Whether using two, three or four toes, long or short, fat or thin, webbed, lobed, scaled, feathered or fringed—all do their varied jobs well. Feet are almost as important to birds as their wings, helping them to move about efficiently whether on the ground, snow, mud, water, or up in the trees on fine branches. Some of the main sorts of feet are illustrated below. They must be able to perch, grasp, run, wade, paddle, scratch, dig and even fight.

Most birds walk or run around when on the ground, or hop, or alternate between walking and running or walking and hopping. Many smaller birds will hop when on the ground presumably because they are used to hopping from branch to branch in the trees. The majority of them will have the most common type of bird foot, like the crow with three toes forward and one back.

This is the best design for perching on branches, rocks, ground or cables. Birds that run a lot will usually have the rear toe smaller, and some waders have little more than a bump. Some, like game birds or waders, especially the Roadrunner and the Ostrich, can run very fast indeed. The Ostrich's long, powerful legs with only two wide toes make it the fastest runner of any bird. Game birds, like partridges or pheasants, will also run for cover rather than expend energy flying.

Water birds have their own special needs and designs. They vary from the fully webbed feet of wildfowl, gulls and auks to the partially webbed feet of some waders, or the 'lobed' feet of grebes, coots and phalaropes. Other large birds like the pelicans, gannets or cormorants go even further and have webs between all four toes. Diving birds such as penguins, divers (USA—loons[2]), auks (puffins, etc.) and wildfowl need powerful webbed feet to propel them, though some will also use their wings to 'fly'

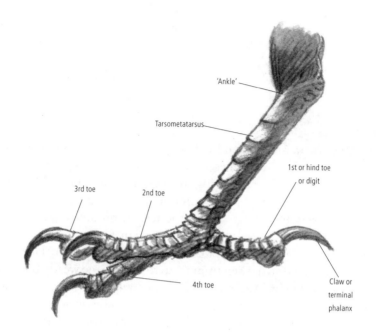

Fig. 7: COMMONEST FOOT and TOE ARRANGEMENT—CROW.

Fig. 8: OSTRICH.

underwater. Streamlined seabirds like the gannets or boobies that dive into the water for their food also do this, and have very large webbed feet further to assist underwater propulsion. By contrast, kingfishers that only dive into the shallows for fish and rely mainly on their long beaks and wings underwater, have strange, partially joined toes ('syndactyl').

These are obviously useful for digging, as other tunnel nesters, like bee-eaters, share them. Many water birds will use three main toes with the rear (first or reversible) toe reduced, as they rarely use them for perching in trees, though they can.

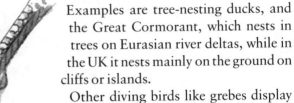

Examples are tree-nesting ducks, and the Great Cormorant, which nests in trees on Eurasian river deltas, while in the UK it nests mainly on the ground on cliffs or islands.

Other diving birds like grebes display yet another ingenious trait—each toe has individual 'paddles' or lobes on each side. These provide a much bigger area for thrusting through the water, but fold back for maximum slimness to reduce friction when the foot is brought forwards. The dumpy Eurasian Coot's foot is similar, but scalloped like Victorian lace. They

Fig. 9: TYPICAL WEBBED WILDFOWL FOOT.

help to keep its head down when tipping up to browse the weedy bottom of shallow lakes, or diving. Waders usually have long legs to walk around in the shallows or on mud, sand or grass. Like many other ground birds, and seabirds and wildfowl, the rear toe is either raised, smaller or not present. Their toes, and others like herons, are often long and slender for spreading their weight evenly on soft surfaces. Avocets and flamingos, and others, have partially webbed toes on their elegant blue (or pink) legs.

Lily-trotters or jacanas, tropical birds similar to moorhens, have the most extraordinary feet. Their toes are extremely long and thin to help spread their weight when walking across floating lily pads.

By complete contrast, although also for weight spreading, North America's Ruffed Grouse grow scaly fringes or 'snowshoes' on their feet in the winter, to help them walk across the snow. Ptarmigan and Snowy Owls of the sub-Arctic have white, fluffy feet, even

Fig. 10: PARTIALLY FUSED 'SYNDACTYL' FOOT OF A COMMON KINGFISHER (FEET NOT TO SCALE).

feathered underneath for reducing heat loss. Many waders and waterfowl commonly stand on one leg for this reason, also probably to brace them upright while asleep, having a similar sort of locking tendon to the passerines. Ground birds such as gamebirds, guineafowl or domestic hens that dig or scratch about, generally have stubbier and blunter claws than passerines, also due to wear. The Mallee Fowl of Australia must be the champion digger—it spends most of the year excavating a huge hole in which to bury its eggs. Then it must constantly adjust the earth covering to regulate the temperature with its precise, thermometer beak, to keep the eggs at a constant temperature. Such marvellous qualities can only indicate special creation, for once again, what 'evolutionary' use are eggs buried in earth too cold or hot to hatch them? 'Trial and error' is not good enough. The only real question is, how much variety was built into life to begin with? The answer will possibly help us decide the extent of the original biblical 'Kinds' (remember any creature will only breed 'after its kind', Genesis 1:21). Such inbuilt adaptability also allows beaks and claws to grow longer easily when required, to be regulated by wear and use. Thus larks and pipits that spend a lot of the time on the ground have the rear claw very long. This is thought to help them balance on the windy plains or open grasslands that they prefer.

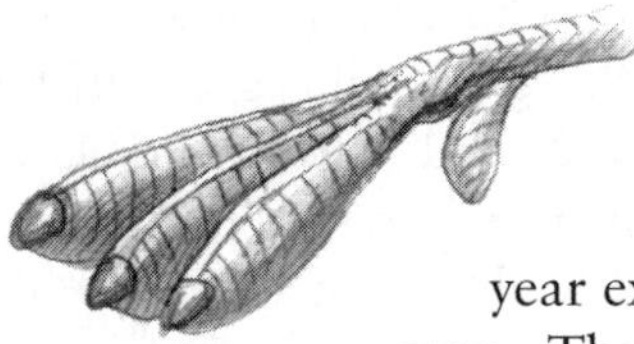

Fig. 11: 'LOBED' FOOT OF A GREBE.

The massive Philippine, Crowned and Harpy Eagles have great curved feet and massive hooked claws, essential for rapidly killing and carrying off heavy loads. Their prey includes monkeys, always agile and powerful creatures. Job 39:27,29 tells of mighty eagles that 'nest on high' from where 'it spies out the prey'. This probably refers to the very widespread Golden Eagle (*Aquila chrysaetos*), which can carry red foxes and small

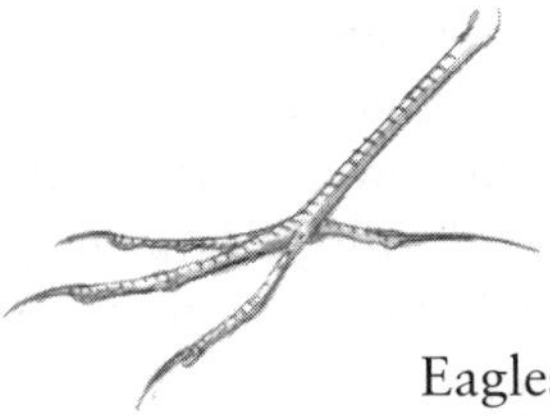

Fig. 12: LILYTROTTER, OR JACANA.

lambs, though it must be pointed out that they are usually dead to begin with. Most birds of prey have very strong feet and curved claws which vary according to their favoured food (used here of the raptors or 'Falconiformes' like eagles, hawks and falcons, etc., or owls, though other birds like shrikes take live prey. You could argue that robins, thrushes and tits are also 'birds of prey', though they do not have the hooked beaks and claws that typify raptors.) Falcons like the Peregrine, and especially hawks like the sparrowhawks, have long slender toes and razor sharp claws for catching birds in the air, or even grabbing them from cover. They will often also have a 'tomial tooth', or similar, near the front of the beak for dispatching, if the bird or other creature is not killed outright by the feet. Again, there are always exceptions and variations, for the smaller Red-footed Falcons or American Kestrels that eat lots of insects, have smaller feet and talons. The larger Northern Goshawk also takes mammals, and its feet are stronger and toes thicker. They have especially deadly and long rear talons for penetrating, gripping and crushing, like the Peregrine and most eagles. A more generalised raptor like the Common Buzzard has stubbier

feet capable only of subduing the smallest rabbit or liveliest worm. In fact, such feet are not dissimilar to a large crow or raven's, but have a much stronger grip. There are three particularly unusual raptors with weaker feet: Honey Buzzards dig up wasps' nests, Palm-nut Eagles prefer palm fruit, and the majority of vultures who very rarely need to kill anything. (Although known to most as the Palm-nut Vulture (Gypohierax angolensis), I personally see this African bird as one of the fish-eagles, which it so much more resembles in looks and habits.)

Fig. 13: GOLDEN EAGLE.

The Osprey or Fish Hawk also has unique eagle-like feet, well equipped with short spikes underneath to retain its grasp on slippery fish. American Bald Eagles have such feet too, as they often feed on salmon, although the fish are often dying after spawning. Like other birds that eat potentially oily or slimy fare, many fish-eagle's legs are not feathered towards the bottom, in particular the Osprey's long blue limbs.

The weakest feet of all belong to birds like the Common Swift, which can spend years in the air without landing at all! Then they only do so to nest on tall buildings or cliffs, and consequently need only small weak feet, with all four toes pointing forward to cling on briefly, though they can shuffle about on the flat. Another variation is two toes forward, two back (zygodactyl), as in woodpeckers, parrots, cuckoos and barbets, although this is usually for great strength or holding food. Some birds can move the fourth toe to either the front or rear, depending upon function. Owls and ospreys can, while the fluffy mousebirds of southern Africa turn their first toe backwards to help them hold food like berries.

Like feet, beaks (also called bills) must serve an even greater variety of purposes. They can crush, hammer, drill, stab, tear, plaster, roof, entwine, knot, drill, filter, spoon, suck, sift, grasp, carry food, fight and signal. The bowerbird even uses its beak as a paintbrush! The Common Eider duck and Eurasian Curlew can neatly remove crabs' legs, finches can hull (remove the shell) from seeds, weaverbirds and tailorbirds can weave the most wonderful nests, and ovenbirds can 'bake' their nests (see chapter 5). The design of the beak will often tell you what a bird eats—it is then hardly surprising that there are so many different ones. Parrots and others use theirs to help them climb, and virtually all birds need them to preen their feathers. Beaks are mainly made of bone and attached to the skull, with a thin outer sheath of keratin (the same sort of horny substance as nails or scales). Since this is always growing, the act of feeding wears it down. You can sometimes see zoo or falconer's birds with too-long bills, which usually means not enough roughage in their food. Once again, such versatile growth can easily adapt to differing foodstuffs and conditions, and negate the evolutionary idea that such adaptation is based on random accidents. The whole outer sheath of the bill can be shed, especially if it is enlarged for display purposes, and even the whole beak regrown if injured. It is the colourful outer part that is shed by the Atlantic Puffin, and some parrots, at the end of the breeding season.

Pelicans and toucans also grow various brightly hued plates on the sides of their beaks during breeding, making them individually recognisable.

Fig. 14: ATLANTIC PUFFIN, WINTER, and RIGHT, WITH SUMMER BEAK SHEATH.

Most beaks are hard, apart from those of the waterfowl, which are often soft and leathery with only the tip or 'nail' hard. There is a sensitive waxy 'cere' around the base of beaks of raptors, which is usually yellow and encircles the nostrils. The nostrils themselves will also vary greatly, from small slits near the base of the bill to large open ones standing proud on the top. A good example is the American Turkey Vulture's beak, probably because it seems to rely more upon scent than African/Eurasian vultures, which soar over much more open terrain and utilise their excellent sight. Many beaks will have cutting edges of some sort, or even teeth-like serrations in the case of 'sawbill' diving ducks like the Red-breasted Merganser.

(The illustration compares its teeth with the diver-like fossil bird, *Hesperornis regalis:* see chapter 6). We have already seen how the two mandibles can move independently, and in some parrots this skill serves to crack hard nuts.

A bird will always have the best beak for its commonest food—and if not it will personally shape it to suit, as 'Darwin's' Finches and our own Great

Tits and Oystercatchers still do, showing no new genetic information, and thus no evolution. Let us look at a selection of beaks, both small and great. The first type is the *slenderest* one, typically an insect eater's beak.

As most migrate, this means they have masses of insects and almost endless summer to feast in. The Bible mentions migration (Jeremiah 8:7), and we will look at

Fig. 15: 'TOOTHED' BILL OF RED BREASTED MERGANSER, and BELOW, THE EXTINCT *'HESPERORNIS REGALIS'*.

the reasons for it in chapter 6). Wrens, treecreepers, Wallcreepers, bee-eaters, Hoopoes, hummingbirds, sunbirds, swallows, nightjars, flycatchers, pipits, and wagtails (and dippers) all have this kind of bill. However, not all insect-eaters need to travel, and manage to find enough insects or nectar wherever they are, whether searched out in the vegetation, bark, rocks, soil, flowers, in the air, or underwater. In the winter, beautiful little Wallcreepers come down from high Eurasian cliffs on their flashing scarlet wings, to creep about on old buildings. They see little difference in hunting for spiders lurking in the highly decorated crannies of say, Vienna Cathedral—and perhaps the strains of Mozart percolating up also sooth them and discerning birders?! Many warblers also feast on small fruits like elderberries in the autumn. The marvellous hummingbirds and sunbirds also have very thin beaks, specifically planned for sipping nectar from flowers. The length and curve of the bill will usually denote the depth of the flower, with the Sword-billed Hummingbird having the longest beak per body length of any bird, 4in (10cm) longer than its tiny body!

Fig. 16: MACAW BILL.

The beaks of tits are also fairly slender, and fall between this group and the next, as they tend to be stubbier. This allows many of them to feast on caterpillars in the summer, even timing their broods precisely to their cycles, and increasingly turn to seeds and peanuts we provide in the winter. This has quickly led to the beak of the Great Tit becoming thicker in the winter, but reverting to thinner in summer, yet more proof that such superficial changes are rapid and built-in, not blind 'evolutionary' accidents. It is worth mentioning in passing that some English Great Tits have further upset evolutionary ideas by forming separate breeding groups of larger and smaller birds, yet still living close by each other and flocking together in winter. It was wrongly thought that only distant, isolated birds could 'evolve' in this way, Note, however, that they are still Great Tits.

Fig. 17: TYPICAL SMALL INSECT EATER'S BILL—WHITETHROAT.

The commonest beak is the passerine (perching/song bird) type. It is the most generalised for eating a selection of foodstuffs from insects and fruits

Fig. 18: A SELECTION OF HUMMINGBIRD BEAKS, SWORD-BILLED AT TOP,
and BELOW, SHOWING VERY FINE TONGUE.

to carrion. Blackbirds and other thrushes have them, as do chats, starlings, todys, orioles and many larger birds like rollers, bulbuls, birds of paradise, gulls and crows. Blackbirds can pull out worms, or Song Thrushes swing snails with theirs to crack the shells.

As they increase in size, bright turquoise European Rollers catch large grasshoppers with theirs, gulls eat just about anything, and ravens use them to break open carcasses. Such beaks take advantage of the glut of insects in summer and fruits and berries in autumn. All these birds increasingly rely on our contribution of bird food, such as suet or oat flakes. This sort of beak can naturally overlap with other types, as for instance in a carnivorous shrike's beak, which also has a small, sharp 'tooth' like a raptor's.

The *seed-crushing* beak is the next type. Finches, and fairly similar families of birds are common in one form or other worldwide, and have this kind of beak. These are generally stout, conical and ideal for cracking seeds. Some finches also have special grooves and 'anvils' for holding and crushing, with the Hawfinch's the most astounding of all. This 5oz (130gm) bird can crush hard cherry or olive stones, using a pressure of at least 30lb/sq in (10kg/sq cm).

Fossil finches have been found with even larger beaks, which must have also meant very powerful neck, skull and jaw muscles indeed. The parrot's bill must be mentioned here, even though it looks very different. The lower mandible fits neatly into the larger, curved upper and the whole structure is wonderful for crushing or shelling nuts, or manipulating food, along with the feet. New Zealand's Kea parrot exhibits another use of this bill—eating flesh and drinking blood! Probably because of the sudden availability of many sheep (some with maggoty sores) when European settlers arrived in the early 19th century, the Keas took to their flesh and were almost exterminated by shepherds.

Fig. 19: PASSERINE-TYPE BILL—COMMON BLACKBIRD.

The most noticeable design feature of the seed-eating finches, buntings, weavers and sparrows is the sharply angled 'commissure', or line where the two mandibles join near the base of the bill. Other finches like crossbills have the upper mandible overlapping the lower, at the tip, ingeniously used for levering out conifer seeds from cones. These lovely little birds are somewhat parrot-like, not only because of such beaks, but also their bright red or green colouring and habit of hanging upside down in the tree tops. The largest billed ones are called Parrot Crossbills and feed on the hardest cones of pines. Then come the slightly smaller billed Scottish Crossbill which depends upon Scots Pine, and lastly the Common and Two-barred Crossbill (USA: Red and White-winged) which live on the seeds of softer and smaller spruce and larch cones. Naturally there can be a lot of overlap, and some of the divisions owe more to the twitcher's or taxonomist's desire for more 'species' to tick off or arrange in man-made lists. (Twitchers,

Fig. 20:THE POWERFUL BILL OF THE HAWFINCH, SHOWING THE ANGLED 'COMMISSURE' AT THE BASE OF THE BILL.

Tickers or Listers want to record as many species as possible, so can spend inordinate amounts of time inventing them. As stated elsewhere, as a species is usually defined by its inability to breed with another, similar, species, it should rule out birds like Parrot and Scottish Crossbills as separate species. Taxonomists seriously study and classify all creatures, but again their evolutionary ideas often cause them to invent as many species as possible, or classify large and small fossils of the same creature as different species. They may, of course, be just adult and offspring or male and female.) Exquisite goldfinches, along with other finches such as the Twite and Linnet, have smaller, finer bills associated with extracting the seeds of plants like teasel, dandelion and various 'weeds' and grasses.

Some birds are expert users of 'tools', including a Galapagos Finch, which wields fine sticks for winkling grubs out of wood. The New Caledonian Crow has gone much further. It has been seen to deliberately bend a piece of wire to do this more efficiently! Straight pieces of wire were specially supplied to aviary birds for testing, but this behaviour has not yet been observed in wild birds. Once again, the speed with which birds learn things is astounding, and cannot be put down to random accident.

Very long and specialised *fruit eating* beaks are found on the hornbill family, which include the toucans, barbets, and for obscurer reasons, the honeyguides. These extraordinary structures enable them to feed high up in the trees and reach fruits on slender branches otherwise out of reach. As with other fruit or seedeaters they will take advantage of high-protein insect food in season, especially for their nestlings. Hornbills are famed for the strange 'casque' chambers on the tops of their heads or beaks, toucans similar, but with long, multi-coloured and banana shaped beaks.

Each bird will have its own recognisable colour patterns, as will males and females. The problem of weight is well taken care of. These fantastic beaks and casques are only possible because they are usually full of air chambers in light spongy tissue, or braced with slender struts like their hollow bones. Male hornbills also have the strange habit of using their beaks to cement up the nest hole with mud. This makes it impossible for the female to leave once she is brooding the eggs, and she endures this voluntarily. Fortunately he does remember to feed her regularly through the little hole, and once again this is behaviour that could not have evolved. To us, it simply represents God's provision of huge and enjoyable variety, because there are many other birds happily eating fruit without such enormous beaks. Many of the wonderful, outlandish designs and displays of birds have little evolutionary survival power. However, toucan's bills do stand out well in the dark jungles where they live, and are therefore useful for signalling to each other.

The *stabbing/fishing* beak is also very common, especially on birds associated with water. It can be seen on birds as diverse as darters, divers, grebes, gannets, auks, terns, waders, kiwis, heron types, kingfishers, and also, in a very specialised form, woodpeckers. As always, there will be considerable overlap with other types of beak. This one is dagger-like,

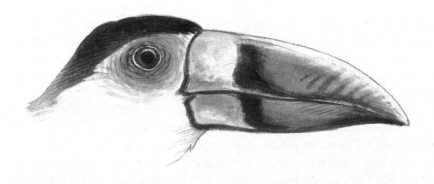

Fig. 21: THE COLOURFUL BILL OF THE CUVIER'S TOUCAN.

slender and sharp, though used more often for grabbing than stabbing (although I once caught a flatfish with a perfect heron beak-shaped hole straight through it, just missing the vital organs and backbone, and the hole had healed well!). Darters or anhingas ('snakebirds') certainly spear fish or frogs in the Florida Everglades or Africa and Asia, using a slender dagger beak and a powerful 'coiled' spring of a neck. The sea and diving birds mentioned all usually grab their fishy prey underwater, whether diving from the air or the surface, deeply or shallowly, by chase or surprise.

Rhos On Sea Go[

S[

Chef's Home M[

Seaf[

Creamy Garlic M[

Egg[

Pa[

Bacon and[

Wader's beaks are mostly long and can be curved, and often show the depth of their food items in the ground. They range from the very long Eurasian Curlew's down-turned beak, or slightly upturned Black-tailed Godwit's, through the medium length of the sandpipers, to the very short Ringed Plover's or Sanderling's. Curlews probe deeply in mud or soil for invertebrates (creatures without backbones) like worms and grubs, or seek out small crabs among seaweed. By contrast, plovers and similar waders walk or run around picking up tiny invertebrates or little crustaceans (crabs, shrimps, waterfleas, etc.) by the tide line. Sanderlings are particularly endearing as they scoot along the beach like little clockwork toys, retreating and advancing with the waves. Oystercatcher's beaks come in two types—stabber or hammerer! They shape them personally either to winkle out the mussel or cockle from the open shell, or to hammer open the closed shell. Individuals will often be observed with either blunter or sharper beaks—though it is not clear whether they have either one or the other permanently. Tortoiseshell-coloured Turnstones justify their name by expertly flipping them over, or tossing aside seaweed in their quest for little invertebrates like sandhoppers.

Farming methods have increasingly led to the loss of boggy and 'unimproved' areas in fields, the traditional 'snipey ground' beloved of so many probing waders that also feed inland. It also means loss of vital nest sites for the likes of our Northern Lapwings, Redshank, snipe and curlews, as well as others like herons, Corncrake and larks, etc.

Fig. 22: TYPICAL FISH-EATER'S BILL— GREAT CRESTED GREBE.

Woodcock prefer damp woodlands to dibble in and flock into the UK or southern USA for our winter, while the sub-Arctic phalaropes usually drop in only on migration. These delightful and tame little birds spin like tops on the water to stir up the bottom for food, or stalk flies on loch shores, snatching them in their very fine beaks. Only the Red-necked

Fig. 23: WADER'S PROBING BILL—EURASIAN CURLEW.

Phalarope breeds in the UK, in the Hebrides or far Shetland Isles. Few waders actually prefer dry ground, one being the strange nocturnal Stone Curlew, which nests only in the East Anglian region of the UK. Its beak is more like a generalised insect eater's. The finer curved bill of the Cream-coloured Courser is used to grab insects as it dashes about dry and sandy grasslands in Africa or Asia. Collared Pratincoles are another strange 'wader' that prefer dry ground, yet look like falcons or giant swifts as they energetically hawk for flies over Eurasian marshes, grabbing them in short decurved beaks. Such birds are still fairly familiar as they fly north on migration.

There are a small number of other waders, which include the oddest and most extreme of curved bills. Avocets use their thin and sharply up-curved beaks to sift small invertebrates from the shallows by scything them rapidly back and forth. The Wrybill of New Zealand has the only bill I know of that is bent to one side (always to the right)—clearly useful for poking under beach stones for food. Spoon-billed Sandpipers sift out small insects and larvae from the water with side-to-side movements, not dissimilar to the much larger heron-like, spoonbill's methods and beak.

Woodpeckers deserve special mention for their absolutely amazing *chisel* beaks and long tongues—once more displaying wonderful complexity and the strongest possible case for creation. As they both drum loudly on, and dig into, often-hard trees, very specialised structures indeed are required. We could not begin to imagine the forces generated by such

Fig. 24: EXTRAORDINARY BILL and TONGUE OF A GREEN WOODPECKER, WITH ITS SHEATH ORIGINATING IN A NOSTRIL!

head-banging—some 250 times greater than astronauts are subjected to on lift-off. The 'rate of fire' when hammering is twice as fast as some machine guns, so the skull is particularly well reinforced with bone, very strong muscles and excellent shock absorbers, far superior to any man-made ones. Unlike other birds, its bony underbeak is not joined to the skull but separated off by these spongy shock absorbers. The sort of juicy grubs and insects preferred live deep in trees or underground, so the *tongue* must be very long, and up to three times as long as the beak.

It is so long that it must be stored somewhere else when not in use, as the beak is obviously not long enough, and this unbelievable tongue stretches up behind the skull and down to the front where it is anchored and coiled in the right nostril. Clearly impossible to 'evolve' by endless genetic mistakes and time, around the skull—the bird could starve until it eventually emerged! The tongues of various woodpeckers are either especially sticky for snaring insects like ants, or have barbs for hooking them, or grubs, out. Even that function requires beautifully designed additional organs, for unseen detection deep inside wood or ground. Like the feather-filter covered slit nostrils, which are just right for breathing without choking on the sawdust generated by all that head-banging. Everywhere we look in this amazing creation, even though it is no longer 'very good' as it was originally designed, we see the designer hand of God, and further evidence of Irreducible Complexity.[3]

Waterfowl beaks come next. They are usually softer than others and flattened from side to side, tending to be flatter or spoon shaped at the tip,

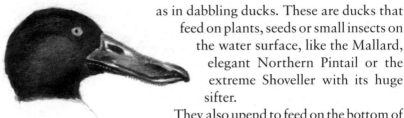

as in dabbling ducks. These are ducks that feed on plants, seeds or small insects on the water surface, like the Mallard, elegant Northern Pintail or the extreme Shoveller with its huge sifter.

They also upend to feed on the bottom of lakes, pools and rivers, or graze on land upon plant matter. A goose's beak is usually deeper, presumably as they crop far more grass than dabbling ducks. Wigeon also crop more plant matter; hence their beak is also shorter and stockier. Many ducks also have 'lamellae' to filter food out of the water—like the brush-like or very fine comb-like hanging plates on the side of the shoveller's beak. Geese have small tooth-like serrations for grass cutting, a habit that makes them unpopular with many farmers when they alight on fields in large winter flocks. The lamellae can also be clearly seen in a good view of a flamingo or Asian Open-bill Stork. It is not altogether surprising that our Creator has also seen fit to use similar but stronger lamellae ('whalebone') on the Bowhead Whale, whose head and mouth looks very like a flamingo's beak.

Fig. 25: DABBLING DUCK BILL—SHOVELLER, SHOWING THE 'LAMALLAE'.

As for the sorts of storks that filter through often murky water with their curved and powerful bills, slightly open, their reaction times on feeling prey are among the very fastest of any creature. Snap!

Diving ducks have already been mentioned in their endless task of deep diving for small fish or invertebrates and shellfish. They range across fresh and salt water, from the common Tufted Duck and Pochard to goldeneye, and 'sawbills' like the Common Goosander or Smew. Marine ducks include Black Scoters, Common Eiders whose powerful beaks pluck and crush mussels from the seabed, and the pretty Long-tailed Duck (USA—Old Squaw), one of the very few waterfowl to change dress completely in the summer. Diving ducks' beaks tend to be shorter and stubbier then dabblers, with eiders especially different looking. The male King Eider has a bumpy, designer orange bill to complement its sky-blue head, while the Common Eider has a very strong, triangular bill with an arrow head of white 'lores' (feathers between eye and bill) echoing it.

There is only one resident swan in the UK, although many 'Arctic' Whooper and Tundra Swans visit in the winter. The impressive sight of these bugling flocks has become a popular spectacle at Wildfowl Trust reserves like Slimbridge and Martin Mere. They are all largely vegetarian and exist on waterweeds, seeds or by cropping grasses with a beak that is roughly a cross between that of a goose and a duck. The Mute Swan has the distinctive extra of a decorative black knob at the base of its bright orange bill, larger in the male and on both in the summer. Despite its name, it is not completely 'mute', as it regularly 'huffs and snorts' its feelings, unlike clamorous Arctic swans.

Fig. 26: FLAMINGO SIFTING INVERTEBRATES FROM SHALLOW WATER.

The beaks of a few other waterbirds are also very distinctive. The very strange skimmer is the only bird to have the lower mandible longer than the upper. This is excellent for its unique method of fishing. It looks like a large tern, but unlike a tern it patrols tropical inshore waters or lakes at dusk with its lower mandible zipping through the water. When its bill feels a fish or shrimp it suddenly snaps shut and quickly swallows it. Not only does this method work wonderfully well, but also it seems to attract other fish. This sort of action probably produces a line of silvery bubbles, like the wake of a small fish. The similar behaviour of the Louisiana Heron has already been noted.

Pelicans alone have *fishing 'nets'* for a beak, although other birds also have expandable 'gular' (throat) sacs (the piratical Frigate Bird distends his bright red sac into a large balloon for display). Brown Pelicans are a common sight in North and South American coastal waters, diving spectacularly for fish on sharply folded wings—or robbing rod fishermen

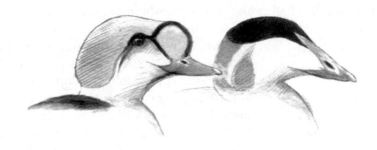

Fig. 27: KING and COMMON EIDERS.

of their catch. Fish are actually stunned by the bird's broad breast hitting the water, before the 'bag' opens wide to engulf fish and water alike, then strains the water out and it rises with the fish.

By contrast, White Pelicans of Eurasia and the Americas fish far more sedately in semi-circular groups in shallow waters, all dipping their heads in together. The fish are only temporarily kept in the Pelican's pouch, by the way—'its beak holds more than its belly can' only initially, if at all!

The final oddity in this group belongs to the Whale-headed or Boatbill Stork of tropical African swamps. It can gulp down huge lungfish whole with its massive 'Shoebill' (another appropriate name for it).

The last group includes some of the most famous beaks of all—those of the *meat eaters,* or raptors. They are all characterised by hooked tips, which combined often with a notched 'tooth' and prominent, shading eyebrow can make them look appropriately ferocious. God ironically asked Job if he could command such fierce creatures (Job 39:27). Their appearance is somewhat softened by the waxy 'cere' around the bill's base and nostrils, often yellow or red, and matched by the eye-ring. Most raptors kill their food with either beak or feet, or a combination of the two, so both beak and feet are well equipped with strong, sharp hooks. The hooked tip of the beak is mostly used for tearing up meat, and has either one or even two notched 'teeth' (falcons), or a curved 'tomial' ridge (eagles and hawks), just behind it to further aid cutting.

Fig. 28: WHITE PELICAN

The huge and striking Steller's Sea Eagle of Russia and the west Pacific coast of the USA has one of the biggest beaks of all raptors, a bright orange, arching weapon capable of dispatching prey as large as seals. A female can weigh 20lb (9kg) and flies on wings of over 8ft (2.4m), so it is hardly surprising that they catch birds as large as male Capercaillie (13lb/6kg), geese, salmon or Red Foxes. South American Andean Condors are even larger, but with smaller beaks, mainly for tearing up dead animals. They might take the odd live animal, and have therefore been persecuted, but there is little evidence to support this. Their feet are weak, with only small rear toes. Large beaks usually mean that the bird has a large gape that enables it to swallow some prey or lumps of meat whole, for speed and a quick escape are also important. Other birds could be a danger for man— some authorities say that a Golden or White-tailed Eagle is perfectly capable of taking a small, human baby, as has been claimed. This was not their original condition: remember that God put a fear of humans into the animals after the Flood, and only then did they become dangerous to us (and vice-versa?).

We have already investigated the smaller feet and blunter claws of some birds, associated with scavenging, softer, easier food, or vegetarianism. The Honey Buzzard not only has smaller feet, but a smaller, less-hooked beak with tightly massed feathers on its lores to prevent wasp and bee stings. Insect-eating raptors like the Red-footed Falcon tend to have neater and shorter beaks, while the Levant Sparrowhawk that also eats reptiles has a heavier beak than the bird-eating Eurasian Sparrowhawk. Some of the most specialised beaks belong to the kites, although our own increasingly familiar Red Kite has only relatively small feet and beak for worms, young rabbits or scavenging. The Hook-billed and Everglades Kites of the Americas have very deeply hooked beaks with fine tips, with the slimmer Everglades Kite's

Fig. 29: EURASIAN KESTREL, SHOWING THE 'TOMIAL TOOTH'.

Fig. 30: GOLDEN EAGLE.

being ideal for winkling out its favourite food, Apple Snails. It is now increasingly and more appropriately called the Snail Kite (old local names like the Everglades Kite, or Dartford Warbler, are misleading in a global context, however evocative they may be to us locals. There are very few Snail Kites left in the threatened swamps of the Florida Everglades, while still fairly common in the rest of the sub-tropics of the Americas. Likewise, the Dartford Warbler is now uncommon in the UK where its favourite heaths are being destroyed, although fairly numerous around the north Mediterranean.)

Owls are also classified as raptors and take virtually all-live prey, whether mammal or insect. Their beaks are only seen to be as large as the diurnal (day flying) raptors when they are quite young and unfeathered. When adult, their unique 'ruff' or dish of feathers hides all but the tip of the beak.

The massive Eurasian Eagle Owl, now just beginning to return to the UK, can capture mammals as heavy as small deer with its huge claws, but some fossil owls would stand over 4ft (1.2m) tall! The smallest owl is the tiny Elf Owl of the southern USA at just 5in (13cm), which feeds on larger insects like crickets or moths. The nocturnal melancholy hoots and shrieks associated with this group prompted King David to lament that he was lying awake, 'like an owl of the desert' (Psalm 102:6). A Barn Owl's hisses are still sometimes blamed for 'prophesying' human deaths.

There are other birds with hooked beaks worth mentioning here that also kill a lot of their own food. The larger gulls and skuas (USA: jaegers) have longer, less-hooked bills than raptors, but can still swallow just about anything from lemmings, puffins, shelducklings, fish or octopi to crustaceans and carrion. The elegant and rapacious skuas also specialise in robbing other sea birds of fish or sand eels. Shrikes are attractive looking, pied passerines famous for their 'larders' of large insects, reptiles or birds stuck on spines or large thorns, caught with their mini-hooked bills.

Digestive systems are also special in at least two different ways. Birds have a pouch-like crop for storing food, and a gizzard for grinding it up. Crops are useful for allowing birds like finches to quickly take a lot of seeds and digest them later at leisure, or to allow some seabirds to carry food long distances to their chicks. Flamingos and pigeons also produce and feed special fluid called

Right ear

Signalling 'ears'

Left ear
behind 'ruff'

Fig. 31: EAGLE OWL, SHOWING DISHED FACE, and FALSE and REAL, HIDDEN EARS.

'milk' for their young from the crop walls. The gizzard is important for breaking down harder foods like vegetable matter, especially the seeds or grains that so many birds eat. Birds like Ostriches, partridges or domestic chickens will actually eat grit or small stones (gastroliths) to help the grinding function of the gizzard. Others, especially grebes, eat their own small feathers and even feed them to their young. They probably aid the digestion and removal of fish bones and spines. The whole digestion process is also a very rapid system, like respiration, so that flying birds do not have to carry excess weight around with them (large weight gain for migration is a special case to be investigated later). As they also need the energy from food, this means that they must eat a lot of green material frequently, as ducks and geese do, and excrete it as soon as possible. Life needs water as well as solids, and birds have a most efficient system for extracting it from the driest food, and most pass very little liquid. The liquid is converted to uric acid and is seen as white powder in the droppings, so they do not need separate urinary bladders. Water can be almost constantly recycled in the gut, so again cutting down on weight. Insect and meat-eating birds need smaller crops and gizzards (some may have none) as food is much easier to break down in their strong stomach acids.

Pellets are another form of elimination—indigestible bits like insect cases, fish scales, bones and fur, etc., are massed together and ejected from the beaks of most birds, especially raptors and crows. Owl pellets have long

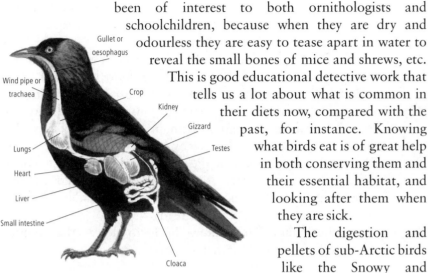

Gullet or oesophagus

Wind pipe or trachaea

Crop

Kidney

Gizzard

Testes

Lungs

Heart

Liver

Small intestine

Cloaca

Fig. 32: SIMPLIFIED DIGESTIVE SYSTEM.

been of interest to both ornithologists and schoolchildren, because when they are dry and odourless they are easy to tease apart in water to reveal the small bones of mice and shrews, etc. This is good educational detective work that tells us a lot about what is common in their diets now, compared with the past, for instance. Knowing what birds eat is of great help in both conserving them and their essential habitat, and looking after them when they are sick.

The digestion and pellets of sub-Arctic birds like the Snowy and Short-eared Owl, Rough-legged Buzzard/ Hawk, Gyr (Jer) Falcon and Long-tailed Skua/ Jaeger can tell us a lot about other creatures, for instance the lemming. These northern guinea pig-like creatures, as well as Short-tailed Voles, usually breed in about seven-year cycles. When their food source is at its maximum they breed in huge numbers, and naturally their predators' numbers also increase. That teaches us another important lesson: the numbers of prey species usually controls the numbers of predators, not vice-versa. When the lemmings and vole numbers drop, so do the raptors, sometimes not breeding at all. So when a Eurasian Magpie or Sparrowhawk kills a songbird, remember that the very fact that there are large numbers of predators usually means there are healthy numbers of prey species too. It also tells us about our fallen creation and its ecology (see chapter 7).

Sense organs

One of the most important senses for a bird is *sight*, especially for moving rapidly through the air. Though there are a few exceptions, like the nocturnal and flightless Kiwi that detects a lot of its food by touch, nothing can match the visual acuity of most birds. Peregrines can apparently see their prey from 6 miles (10km) away! It is often said that the claim of raptors having vision many times stronger than ours is over exaggerated, but some certainly have eight times more visual cells. That probably means that saying some raptor's vision is up to eight times clearer than ours is more precise. Distances must be judged extremely accurately and friends and enemies distinguished clearly. In birds like raptors the eyes could not actually be any larger than they are, as they often nearly touch in the middle of the skull. We do not see the largest part of the eye, which in an Ostrich is the size of a tennis ball. Birds' eyes can either be on the front of the skull, like ours, or on the sides. This gives a huge range to their vision, which already has a far wider field in sharper view than ours. This allows birds to detect the slightest movement without constantly moving their heads, as we need to do. Tiny warblers can adjust almost instantly between 0.5in (1cm) and infinity (microscopic to telescopic), simply by changing the shape of the lens of the eye.

Birds have three basic shapes of eyes, usually associated with light gathering and increasing clarity. The majority are flatter, with raptors' eyes more globular, and owls' fairly tubular. This generally correlates with increasing depth of field and telescopic powers. Eyes on the side of the head do have slight restrictions, meaning they only see in binocular vision at the front where the two fields of view overlap. However, it must be sufficient, for the majority of birds are designed like that. And as already noted, woodcocks can see all the way around and even above themselves, and survive perfectly well. As they mainly probe for food in the ground, their telescopic vision is not as important as a raptor's, hunting lively prey. By contrast, the few birds like owls that have flat faces and forward-facing eyes like ours, have a greater 'depth of field' to judge distances better. They often bob and weave to place their prey accurately by comparing it from two positions. And of course they have another famous ability that compensates for fixed and more tubular eyes—they can turn their heads almost completely around. They also need vision that is superior in poor light, and that is accounted for by those tubular eyes focussing maximum

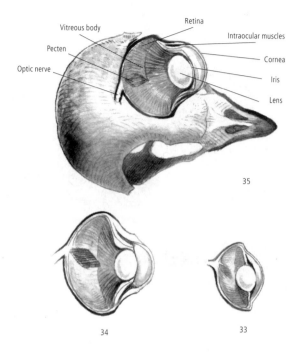

Fig. 33: 'FLAT', OR COMMONEST TYPE OF BIRD EYE.
Fig. 34: 'GLOBULAR' TYPE.
Fig. 35: 'TUBULAR' TYPE, AS IN THIS OWL'S SKULL.

light on the retina. Their night vision is 100 times superior to ours, although no bird can see in complete darkness—except by using echo location, as some other birds do. Owls also rely greatly upon sound. Once again, we must mention the superb sight of the Peregrine, which can actually see three views at once. The centre of its vision is similar to ours, but four special visual centres ('fovea') also enable it to see two extra telephoto views at either side of the main 'screen'. They have about five times more visual cells than we do, so it is not too surprising that their vision is so wonderful, but it is needed when diving headlong at nearly 200

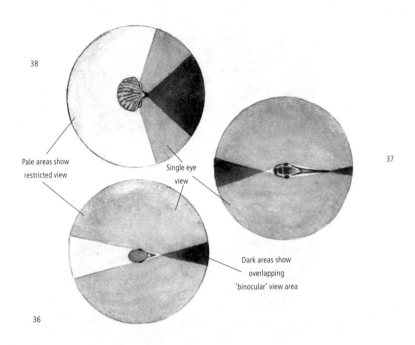

38

Pale areas show
restricted view

Single eye
view

37

Dark areas show
overlapping
'binocular' view area

36

Fig. 36: COMMONEST TYPE OF FIELD OF VIEW—PIGEON.

Fig. 37: WOODCOCK'S 360° PLUS VIEW, OVERLAPPING AT FRONT and REAR.

Fig. 38: A TYPICAL OWL'S FIELD OF VIEW.

mph (320kph). Other birds like vultures have a separate 2.5 times telephoto area in the middle of their wide-angle view.

Falcons, which hunt by day, have eyes that appear very black, as the iris is almost as dark as the pupil but many nocturnal owls also have all-dark eyes. Owls that also hunt by day, like the Little Owl or the Short-eared Owl, have a bright yellowish iris like many sparrowhawks, so it is difficult to make hard and fast rules about colour and function. Some eyes become lighter coloured as they age, like many buzzard/hawk's, or enable sexing and ageing of young Marsh or Northern Harriers. The iris can be just about any colour, with divers favouring red, cormorants green, bowerbirds blue and many raptors golden yellow. It is not known why the Northern Cormorant has the most beautiful turquoise eyes, when divers/loons and grebes that spend most of their time diving in the same coastal waters prefer ruby-red. All that is really known is that as birds get older the iris colour usually becomes paler and brighter, and probably helps in dominating others. The cormorant has superbly clear underwater vision, even though the cornea, like ours, blurs underwater. They just squeeze the lens inside and override the cornea. As all the diving or chasing activities of birds could damage their eyes, they need two more special parts: windscreen wipers and protective eyebrows. A semi-transparent third eyelid, or 'nictitating membrane' cleans, moistens and protects the eye, while raptors especially have a large projecting eyebrow called the 'supra-orbital ridge' (illustrated earlier).

It is thought that the stiff whiskers around the beaks of nightjars and flycatchers also protect the eyes, as well as guiding in flying insects. At least one of the nightjar family, the Oilbird, has the same sort of mirrored eyes that canines and felids (cats) possess, for reconcentrating light at night, as do many owls.

To see even more clearly, and for penetrating through any haze, birds have additional filters, just as we need to wear Polaroid glasses or use camera filters to do away with glare or lack of contrast, although birds' are naturally far more compact. They consist of coloured droplets of oil in the retina (at the back of the eye) and seem to enhance sharpness of vision by exaggerating the contrast between objects. They also help the bird see far more shades of colour than humans. They will probably not have anything to do with the many different iris colours, as the iris is very thick and muscular compared with ours, for adjusting the rapid opening and closing of the pupil. Most birds will probably see with similar or often superior colour vision to ours, with nocturnal owls possibly less so. Contrast is more important to them. Some birds like Budgerigars (as butterflies and bees) can also see the special fluorescence of ultra-violet light on certain areas of feathers like their cheek patches, which they fluff out in courtship display. Others probably even see infra-red light, which might further help birds like the Oilbird see in the very poor light of its cave home.

Nictitating membrane

Fig. 39: THE NICTITATING MEMBRANE OF A BELTED KINGFISHER.

Waterbirds often have differently designed eyes, for they need to be able to correct for refraction (distortion caused by water). Goldeneye ducks that always dive for their food have a clear, thickened screen in the middle of their third eyelid, which also bends the light rays thus correcting for refraction. This marvellous ability is not confined to diving birds, for herons and kingfishers must also allow for distortion when fishing, and seemingly do so without using the third eyelid.

Eyes will often be surrounded by a ring of the same sort of soft, waxy substance as the 'cere', the colourful part at the base of the beaks of raptors, and birds like parrots, turkeys or cassowaries. This can be further extended into extravagant head decorations on various birds.

There is one completely unique eye structure—the Skimmer has a vertical cat-like pupil, possibly because it hunts over water at dusk. This provision could be because most ripples and reflections are horizontal.

Hearing is also naturally important for many birds. Owls and harriers often hunt over thick grass, marsh, heath and moorland, or in thick woodland, and depend very much upon sound detection to find their prey.

To this end they have rather flat faces with forward-facing eyes and saucer-like depressions around them. This concentrates the sound as satellite or radio telescope dishes do. Their ears are large and behind these dishes, with the openings at the outside edge, one slightly higher than the other to further pinpoint sound, as illustrated earlier. A bird's hearing is believed to be much like ours, but superior in separating sounds out, especially when understanding the intricacies of bird song or detecting rustlings under vegetation or snow. This is because inside their large ears they have far more sensory hairs than we have, and these allow them to obtain far more information from song or calls. An owl's superior directional hearing is also largely due to the way its nerves process the differences between the timing and intensity of sounds. The nerve cells or neurons in its 'auditory map' multiply as well as add up, meaning each is more like a little individual processor, and computationally much more powerful. The large feathery 'ears' on the top of owl's heads are not ears at all but 'flags' used for signalling and decoration. Some birds with poor vision, like the nocturnal kiwi, rely very much upon sound as well as sensitive probing bills to find worms. Another intriguing aspect of hearing is employed by cave dwellers like Oilbirds or Cave Swiflets, which use echolocation to find their way around in the pitch-blackness. Their mammal counterparts, bats, also use this facility, sending out high-pitched clicks or squeaks to bounce off rock surfaces and thus tell the creature where they, or prey items, are. Oilbirds have flatter, rather owl-like faces to assist them.

Another 'sense' that has puzzled many people for centuries is how some creatures are able to perform well co-ordinated manoeuvres together, almost instantly, as flocks of flying birds and shoals of fish do. Some simply put it down to visual clues by leading birds, but others hold that it is far too rapid for that. Some researchers are now fairly certain that it is down to 'quantum wave resonance', or creatures 'exchanging light photons', but this is a difficult and controversial subject outside the scope of this work.[4]

Smell and taste are harder to assess, but are claimed by many authorities to be poorly developed in most birds. They are said to be able to differentiate between the same four basic tastes as humans, namely sweet, bitter, salt and sour. However, as some like ravens or Storm Petrels have a very strong and distinctive musty smell themselves, it is highly likely to be important at least to some. The petrels, for instance, nest underground but stay out at sea for most of the day. Hence when they return they must distinguish exactly which hole their chick is in, on fairly featureless island slopes and in the dark. Ravens, like vultures, often depend upon dead things so again smell is important to them. This is well brought out in 'New World' scavengers like the Turkey Vulture, which can quickly detect meat hidden under thick forest canopy and dead leaves. Other vultures soaring high over the African or Eurasian plains or mountain ranges rely more upon sight than smell, and this must be quite useful when feeding on rotting carcasses! Also when a Peregrine is stooping, it does not want the wind blowing violently into its skull, so it has little baffles to expertly slow the passage of air into the respiratory system. Gannets likewise plunge steeply and rapidly, but into the sea, so have no external nostrils at all, but do, incidentally, have inflatable 'airbags' in their necks to cushion the blow.

There is another function associated with the nostrils—desalination, or ridding seawater of its salt. Birds that spend most of their lives at sea like the Fulmar Petrel, shearwaters and albatrosses, all need to do this. The complex process involves special 'tubenoses' on the top of their beaks that excrete the salt.

Such birds also strongly rely upon smell to locate their food, which often comes from fishing industry waste. Birdwatchers can attract many of these birds to boats by using the same sort of 'rubby-dubby' as shark fishers use; a disgusting mess of rotting fish and blood. You must remember that for humans, smell and taste are very closely linked—try eating something while pinching your nostrils tight. We should be wary of making authoritative statements about what certain creatures can or cannot do, as new discoveries are being made all the time.

Fig. 40: FULMAR'S 'TUBENOSE'.

Touch depends upon a variety of senses

like contact, temperature, pressure, and vibrations. Touch receptors occur in birds in obvious places like the feet and tongue, and also in the skin at the base of certain feathers. These seem to tell the bird about the angle and movement of the feathers, which would be particularly important for flight, as well as for erecting feathers to expose bare patches of skin for temperature control. Wading birds that plunge their bills into mud, sand, grass or soil must be able to quickly work out what they are touching. They have highly sensitive receptors, especially at the tip of the beak to detect food like lugworms, cockles, or various grubs. Birds such as spoonbills that feel around in the bottom mud can detect very subtle differences, and waterfowl like ducks also have sensitive ends to their bills. The excellent sense of touch belonging to the kiwi stems from it having its nostrils uniquely in the tip of its beak: it does not seem to be able to see food right in front of its eyes, so these receptors are vital for its survival.

All of these superb features shout design—none more so than feathers and flight.

Notes

1 **Marshall et al.**, Royal Society, B, Supplement, Volume 270.
2 'Loon' is the American name for divers, stemming from their eerie wailing calls. Their Common Loon is our Great Northern Diver *(Gavia immer)*.
3 Irreducible Complexity, the fact that all biological systems have to be complete to begin with to work properly—or not at all, and therefore cannot randomly evolve, as featured in **M. Behe's** best-seller *Darwin's' Black Box*. See Bibliography.
4 See the work of **Fritz Albert Popp et al.,** and the *International Institute of Biophysics*.

Chapter 2

Feathers and flight, coloration and pattern

One particular seabird, a Manx Shearwater, flew over 4 million miles (6 million km) in its 52 long years. Now, that is rather exceptional, but it demonstrates the supreme design that lies behind flying creatures. As one scientist joked, you cannot just stick a bunch of feathers into a cold-blooded dinosaur and kick it in the tail! Little wonder then that a warm-blooded bird has such unique features engineered for that very thing—flight. Chapter 1 looked in detail at their lightweight skeletons with hollow 'breathing' bones, outstanding respiratory and digestive systems, and extremely powerful flight muscles. However, they would count for little if not properly combined—and without feathers. Flight absolutely depends upon them, yet many choose to fly as little as possible, or not at all, and some appear to have voluntarily lost the power.

Feathers are one of creation's most amazing and beautiful design features. They are often described as 'lightweight miracles of engineering design'—even by evolutionists like David Attenborough. 'What a wonderful thing is the feather,' cried fellow-Darwinian Rattray-Taylor,[1] although he could not resist adding, 'Designed? Perish the thought: let us say "which by pure chance …"'! Yet chance cannot 'do' anything. Many others have marvelled over such pre-coded design excellence and recognised the obvious: *codes need a coder*. Only birds have feathers, despite recent evolutionary claims of 'feathered dinosaurs', which will be investigated later. Feathers must do lots of jobs: they must be light, yet lift and propel, streamline, warm and cool, be waterproof, allow for diving, as well as either display or hide the wearer. That is some design challenge! To meet it, all feathers must have a strong but flexible hollow shaft, consisting of the quill or 'rachis', and many very fine *'barbs'* from the side. Together they form a flat or curved 'solid' surface area (the vanes, or web).

These are kept together by the most marvellous arrangement of hooks and grooves, which put Velcro or zips to shame. All the side barbs further branch into *barbules*, and then again into *barbicels*—tiny hooks on one side of the barbules, tiny grooves on the other. It is the ultimate and essential 'sliding joint', as for instance, a crane's or eagle's flight feather may have 1 million barbules ('evolve that!' as one Bible believer puts it). That is how the vanes can be ultra-thin yet strong and flexible enough to bond through all the great stresses of flight. *Flight feathers* especially must be flexible enough to twist and bend, yet still stay together as a 'solid' aerofoil surface and keep the bird airborne. Rapid flapping or high winds sees the flights twisting and bending in many directions, and raptors like Harris Hawks or Northern Goshawks will also crash through spiky undergrowth after their prey. However, not all feathers have these hooks, as they are not needed in the underlying fluffy 'down' feathers that both insulate and waterproof. All the feathers of flightless birds (ratites) such as the Emu, Ostrich or Rhea are like that, and some of the so-called 'feathered dinosaurs' appear to have them, so they could well be ratites. One side effect of flight is the noise that wings make, especially at speed, so the more nocturnal owls have soft fringes to their flight feathers. Unhooked tips on the flight feathers form them and provide a muffling effect. Diurnal owls do not have this feature, as they seem to rely more upon sight than hearing. Conversely, the last thing some prey may hear is the roaring from a Peregrine's wings.

The thickest and strongest parts of the feather will always be closest to the base to allow the flexibility needed, and then taper towards the tip, although certain birds have decorative enlarged ends to their tail feathers, like the Pomarine Skua, or ridiculously named Racket-tailed Drongo. There are basically five different types of feathers. Flight feathers ('remiges' or flights) are divided into primaries and secondaries, covered at their bases with smaller and smaller coverts.

Note that the primaries, especially, are 'asymmetrical', meaning that they need to have the front edge vane narrower than the rear, for maximum control. The illustrations feature the wings and flights of a Common Buzzard. However, any bird's will be just as good—pick up the flight of a bird like a swan or crow, and if the web has breaks in it, run it through your fingers and 'zip' it back together again. That is what the bird expertly does with its beak for good maintenance and quick repair, but if it is has been

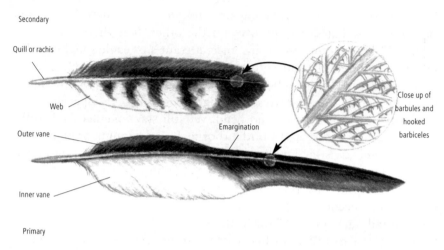

Fig. 41: BUZZARD'S FLIGHT FEATHERS.

naturally discarded it is probably worn. A good 'sliding joint' like the bird's hook and groove arrangement needs lubrication, so oil is usually provided to allow it to bend and twist without breaking the web. Most birds have an oil preen gland just above the tail, from where it is applied to the feathers by the beak, for both lubrication and waterproofing. Parrots will also rub eucalyptus oil on their feathers, and there are other interesting subsidiary effects of preening—vitamin supplementation and parasite elimination. The bird will also ingest some of the preen oil, now rich in vitamin D from irradiation by the sun. The oil also targets and destroys bacteria that damage the feathers.

Next, come the *contour* feathers that cover all of the body like overlapping tiles, forming discernible lines and patterns in many birds. Whether small or large, they are usually shaped like shields or scales, often pointed and with paler or darker edges.

If you have the chance, look closely at a Mallard and marvel at the density and changing iridescent colours of his tiny head feathers. You will probably have to be watching TV to see the exquisite head of something like a Great Northern or Black-throated Diver/Loon in close-up, but it

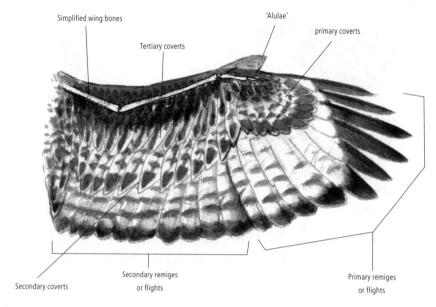

Simplified wing bones   'Alulae'

primary coverts

Tertiary coverts

Secondary remiges
or flights

Secondary coverts

Primary remiges
or flights

Fig. 42: BUZZARD'S WING.

more resembles soft, plush velvet than feathers. Whatever their size, they are only the outer layer. At the base of the contour feathers is the third type, the *down* feather, which can most effectively trap air and add extra waterproofing properties.

It is these feathers from the Common Eider's nest that make the famous eiderdowns, still superior to any man-made quilt or sleeping bag. The duck plucks the feathers from her own breast to line her nest and keep the eggs warm. Birds can easily maintain body temperature in conditions below freezing, the main danger coming from feet or feathers sticking to the ice. We only have to look at a penguin's feathers, to observe how such tiny but dense structures can protect birds from the most appalling cold. By contrast, the famous Roadrunner of Central America produces another trick to both conserve energy and survive the cold desert nights: it becomes *almost* cold-blooded! Then at dawn it rapidly warms special darkly

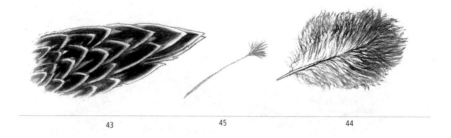

43   45   44

Fig. 43: CONTOUR FEATHERS FROM A FEMALE MALLARD'S BACK.
Fig. 44: TYPICAL DOWN FEATHER.
Fig. 45: FILOPLUME.

pigmented areas on its back to heat up and conserve some 50 per cent of its energy. Desert ravens, especially, can have a body temperature vastly lower than the extreme heat striking their shiny feathers. More supreme design!

The fourth type of feather is called a '*filoplume*', and seems to help predict wind currents when the bird is in flight.

They may look like tiny palm trees and can protrude from the contour feathers. Sometimes filoplumes may be for decoration, as well as external sensing. Some authorities separate out a fifth type—the aforementioned '*bristles*' found around some bird's beaks.

Tail feathers ('*retrices*') are most similar to flights, with the middle ones usually having the shaft centrally placed.

You can work out the feather's position in the tail by its asymmetry. Like the flights, those towards the outside of the tail will have a narrower outer edge, or vane. Most tails will have twelve feathers, although there can be only six in some tiny emu-wrens and up to thirty-two in the White-tailed Wattled Pheasant. It can even vary in one family—different snipe can have from fourteen to twenty-two. Shapes range from the commonest fan type to the most elegant curves or lyre-shapes, as in the Eurasian Black Grouse or King Bird of Paradise. They can be slender projecting spikes, coils or spoon shapes, be forked or feathery, square ended or pointed, or be so tiny as to be almost invisible (grebes or pittas), or longer than the bird itself, as in the Pin-tailed Whydah, Cape Sugarbird, widowbirds, Paradise Flycatcher, Golden or Reeves Pheasant—and of course the most famous of all, the peacock. His magnificent train rightly gave Darwin nightmares, for how could a creature with such an 'encumbrance' as that possibly be fit enough to survive? That prompted his idea of 'sexual selection', whereby such a disadvantage must balance its attraction value. While that may be true, it does not explain how such an incredible thing could randomly evolve in the first place; and some bright birds do not display until after mating.

A Mute Swan will have about 25,000 of these miraculous feathers overall, a House Sparrow some 3,500. They are usually arranged in certain feather groups like the flights, coverts or mantle, etc., whatever the size or shape of bird.

Though varying greatly in size or design they will always follow the same blueprint. A hummingbird might have only six or seven secondaries while an albatross has up to forty—but they will both have about the same number of primaries (nine or ten), whatever their shape or length, and still attached to the same bones in the same way. The flights are attached to the ulna, the secondaries to the 'hand' bones. There are also three feathers on the 'thumb' or *alulae,* vital for flight control and three or four 'tertial' feathers to smooth the transition between wing and body. Alula can also be used for swimming under water or even making strange noises to frighten predators, as Eurasian Woodcock can. Theirs are so stiff and pointed that generations of painters have used these 'pin' feathers for brushes or pens. The tertials can often be elongated for decoration, as in the Common Crane, or the elegant and slender spear shapes that curve over a Northern Pintail or Garganey's back.

Even though most are changed yearly by moulting, feathers naturally need regular care and attention, through preening, zipping, water, sun or dust bathing, oiling, powdering and combing, or even by smoke and 'ant-baths'. Water bathing is the most obvious action, usually followed by vigorous shaking and wing flapping, or resting with the feathers raised or fluffed out. Oil preening actually removes water, bringing to mind a dog or cat licking off water with a wet tongue. The feet are also important in spreading the oil and reaching most of the head, which the beak obviously

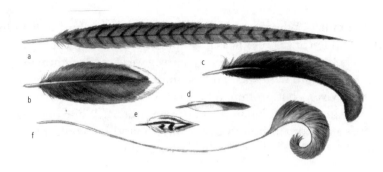

Fig. 46: A SELECTION OF RETRICES, OR TAIL FEATHERS. a: Pheasant. b: Goose. c: Blackcock. d: Goldfinch. e: Mallard. f: King Bird of Paradise.

cannot do. Once more, we can only gaze in wonder as the razor-sharp claw of raptor or parrot whizzes through its head feathers without injuring itself!

Sunbathing might produce other chemicals from preen oils, as well as vitamin D on the feathers, and be as important for light as well as warmth. It might also stimulate the movement and therefore the detection of parasites, as rigorous preening often follows sunbathing. Then the preen oil is changed twice a year. In spring, birds must both look their best and be at their fittest, ready for the rigours of migration and breeding.

The Grey Heron has a 'powder-puff' in the centre of its breast, where special feathers are designed to break down into a talc-like dust. This is applied to its feathers to absorb eel, fish or frog-slime, and then combed out with specifically designed serrated claws. Other birds produce lesser amounts of this sort of dust, and if an owl ever has the misfortune to fly into your window, it will often leave a dusty imprint. Several birds, like certain crows, enjoy smoking themselves over fires or chimneys (perhaps contributing to the 'Phoenix' legend), to deter parasites like feather mites or flatflies. Eurasian Jays like to crouch on ant heaps and allow the ants to run all over their bodies, seemingly inciting the ants to squirt their formic acid and likewise deter invaders. Some birds will even carefully rub the ants over their plumage. As for 'dust-bathing', it is probably for dislodging

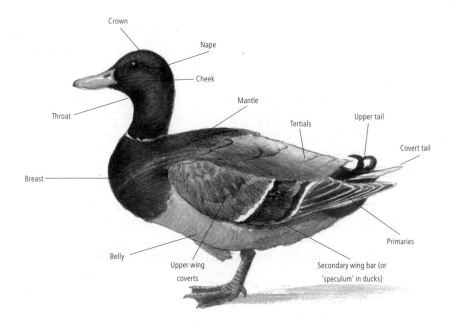

Fig. 47: GENERAL FEATHER GROUPS: MALE MALLARD.

feather mites and other parasites, and may also absorb excess moisture. This function is not properly understood, for some birds either water and/or dust bathe, while certain dry land birds like larks or game birds only ever dust bathe.

Only one bird I know of deliberately applies external make-up for its own sake. The magnificent Bearded Vulture, formerly and inaccurately known as the Lammergeier (lamb killer), is an uncommon raptor that soars on 9ft (3m) wings over some of the world's most wonderful mountain ranges, like the Pyrenees or Ethiopian Highlands. It rubs orangey clays on its breast and belly feathers, which are often a subtle peach colour to begin with and well complemented by long purpley-grey wings and diamond-shaped tail. Hornbills do not use clay, but have special coloured preen oils to enhance white plumage areas. Not to be outdone, the flamingo also enhances its pink feather hues, but from the inside by eating brine shrimps or similar crustaceans. Our Black-headed Gulls seem to do a similar thing, although all plumage when newly moulted is at its best, and can often fade thereafter. Many young falcons start off with purpley-slate plumage like a fresh, dark plum complete with frosty bloom, but soon fade to brown. This makes a 'second summer' bird easy to age in a good view, as the old, pale brown feathers are gradually replaced with darker adult ones.

Moulting new feathers can actually perform two more different tasks: concealment or display. Great-crested, and all other Northern grebes, can be seen in our coastal waters for most of the year, in inconspicuous black and white, as well as the divers/loons. They acquire these duller, winter feathers after moulting their summer finery once the breeding season is over. As spring and breeding approaches they gradually re-acquire bright new feathers, and the crest and ruff feathers ('tippets') must rapidly grow longer.

Gulls with black heads will only do a partial moult in the spring, of those black or dark brown heads. Thus their dark heads gradually appear as the ends of white head feathers are worn off to reveal the underlying colour. Colourful birds like the finches and buntings also use this clever tactic. They too will only gradually reveal their spring breeding colours, by abrasion of the duller winter feathers. Watch how our male House Sparrow slowly sports his black bib, usually largest in dominant birds, as the buff ends of the throat and breast feathers wear off.

However, moulting is not fully understood, or at least the many different ways it is done. Does a Willow Warbler shed its flights twice a year, when most birds only do it once, because of its long migratory flights from Africa? We cannot really be sure.

Even if feathers are not damaged, they will all be replaced roughly once a year, although once again there are always exceptions. Some birds may lose their feathers up to three times a year, while others may take three years to replace them all. A bird can have quite a few feathers damaged or missing before it is rendered flightless, or its life seriously threatened. Oil spills or other chemical accidents, crashing into power lines or wind turbines, have been added to traditional dangers like shooting or trapping. The small passerines mainly shed their feathers once a year and the large raptors

Fig. 48: SLAVONIAN OR HORNED GREBE, WITH NEW SPRING PLUMAGE, LEFT, and RIGHT, IN 'WORN' WINTER PLUMAGE.

slowly lose theirs over several years. They are shed in specific patterns so that they can continue flying if they need to, and usually dropped from the inside outwards. The gaps leave their wings looking rather ragged. Another good reason for only shedding gradually is the need to maintain optimum temperature during potentially cold nights. Waterfowl will often shed all their flights at once, after breeding, as the Mute Swan and many of our ducks do. Some, like the Common Shelduck, will fly to specific areas like the Wash between Norfolk and Lincolnshire, Bridgwater Bay (Somerset) or even the German coast, to gather for moulting. Not all birds moult after breeding, as already noted, with others like the Willow Grouse/Ptarmigan first going for a spring moult. This allows them to gradually acquire mottled plumage and lose their all-white winter feathers—just as the snow slowly melts to reveal the rocky and lichened mountain tops. What a nice 'coincidence', for that is exactly what the ptarmigan's plumage looks like.

As with any other biological development, the way feathers grow is marvellous to behold. They come from beneath the skin (unlike scales that are just superficial surface folds), with the flights even attached to the wing bones, and all unfold like delicate ferns from a tube that becomes the quill

Fig. 49: HOUSE SPARROW, LEFT, 'WORN' SPRING PLUMAGE, and RIGHT, IN WINTER.

and rachis. If you want to study this in detail you will need a good technical book on flight and plumage, or pick up one of a young bird's lost feathers in the spring and examine it closely.

Many carrion eaters have bare heads so that their feathers cannot become fouled with gore, with one being especially repulsive, a word to be used carefully to describe anything in God's creation. Yet there is little else to say about the bald Marabou Stork, with its great stabbing beak, and pendulous throat sac looking like some obscene diseased organ. Remember that creation is here to teach us about *all* aspects of fallen life (Romans 8:18–25).

Flight

Even evolutionary authorities note: 'the wing of a bird is constructed on sound aerodynamic principles' and others talk of the 'effortless grace' of flight, yet they believe it accidentally evolved from some dinosaur's madly flapping arm! Another thought that flight was the winner of 'the biggest evolutionary jackpot of all!'[2] That's some win, when you consider the tens of millions of folk who lose jackpots and lotteries every week—yet there are no design 'losers' in the myriad fossils. The illustration shows the perfect *aerofoil* shape of a typical wing in profile, from broader front to narrower, trailing rear.

Whether it is the short, rounded wing of a little wren or the long, pointed wing of a swallow, the same curved form, or *camber,* is there. It is

Fig. 50: PTARMIGAN IN SPRING, SHOWING WHITE WINTER PLUMAGE, CHANGING PLUMAGE, and CROUCHING FEMALE IN SUMMER DRESS.

wonderfully streamlined by overlapping feathers that gradually become longer and stiffer towards the rear. It is this special *form and angle* of a wing that overcomes gravity and produces *lift*. You can do the same by holding a sheet of paper at one end and blowing across the *top*—observe the curve and the lift. So, the faster movement of air over the arched wing produces a fall in pressure above, and the opposite happens as air slows down beneath the curved wing and increases pressure below, and these combine to effectively and effortlessly 'suck' the wing up.

The individual flight feathers of many birds are also curved and twisted towards the tip, giving an extra *'propeller twist'* to aid flying. Ducks and geese particularly use this extra power on the downstroke in their strong, direct flight. When the wing is brought upwards the feathers twist the other way and allow the air to pass easily between the narrower tips. This narrowing, or *'emargination'* of the primaries is increased on soaring birds like buzzards and storks. This produces the effect of narrow *'fingers'*, which bend upwards and provide further flight control, especially when soaring high as many other large birds do. The separated tips are almost little wings

Fig. 51: THE PERFECT AEROFOIL SHAPE OF A TYPICAL WING.

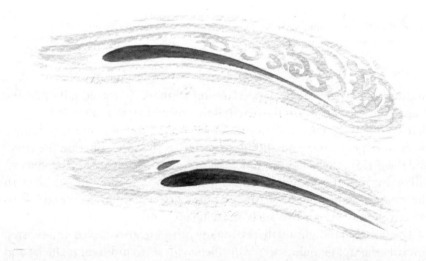

Fig. 52, 42: TURBULENCE SET UP BY SLOW FLIGHT, and BELOW, HOW IT IS SMOOTHED OUT BY THE ALULAE.

themselves, so finely do they tune flight control. This is particularly vital in large birds that fly slowly, like circling vultures or other raptors.

In game birds like Ring-necked Pheasants the narrower tips twist even

Fig. 53: CIRCLING RED TAILED HAWK, USING ITS EMARGINATED PRIMARIES FOR FLIGHT CONTROL.

more, undoubtedly connected with their rapid take-offs, and make a distinctive rattling noise. Goldeneye ducks' wings whistle, Mute Swans' make a regular sawing or whooshing noise, Griffon Vultures' actually creak, while a stooping Peregrine's passage through the air is almost a roar! Many of the larger birds produce a loud 'wafting' sound, which is what we would expect, and the passage of tiny hummingbirds is marked by a delightful trademark 'hum'—not unlike a bumblebee. Others use loud wing noises in breeding display, as the broadbills or jungle manikins do, and the American Ruffed Grouse loudly 'drums' with his.

Needless to say, a bird's *balance* must also be perfect when it is flying, with the centre of gravity beneath the wings. This is seen at its most extreme in flamingos, where the legs trail behind almost as far as the neck and head project forwards. Whatever their size or shape, all birds will fly in more or less the same way. In slow motion, certain birds like the Mallard can be seen to be almost using a 'figure of eight' wing movement, and even more so in the Ruby-throated Hummingbird which needs lift, but not propulsion, to hover on the spot.

Fig. 54: A MALLARD'S FLIGHT SHOWING THE 'PROPELLOR' EFFECT OF THE WING TIPS ON THE POWERFUL DOWNSTROKE, MIDDLE, and THE LESSER RESISTANCE ON THE UPSTROKE, RIGHT.

Hummingbirds have unique swivel 'shoulder' joints and rather rigid wings for their absolute mastery of hovering, but can nevertheless fly non-stop across the Gulf of Mexico twice yearly. They can also fly backwards, upside down or even loop the loop! So birds do not fly just by flapping their wings up and down, for this also moves their slender aerofoil shape forwards through the air, as the buzzard on page 69 is doing in normal non-soaring flight.

This causes lift and overcomes the inevitable *drag* when the wing is at the correct angle, but when the wing is tipped further back, as when a bird is landing, turbulence is set up. That causes drag and slowing down, and can be seen to induce the small back and upper wing feathers to lift and flutter, or an aeroplane to vibrate. As we would expect, our Creator has provided the perfect solution—that *alula* or wing slot.

By extending this pointed 'little wing' of three or four feathers on the 'thumb', the airflow is smoothed over the top of the wing. This allows the bird to land gracefully and safely without stalling, and is copied by the wing slots and flaps of our aeroplanes. Heavy waterbirds can plane in and apply their large webbed feet as extra brakes, while others like the diver/loons slide across the water on their broad bellies. The tail is also used in all flight manoeuvres, especially when landing or turning.

Fig. 55: HUMMINGBIRD, DEMONSTRATING RAPID 'FIGURE OF 8' WINGSTROKES, and VERY FLEXIBLE SHOULDER JOINT.

The forward movement of any body through a fluid also creates vortices (rotating zones of turbulence). The vortices are left behind as the creature moves forward, but they can hinder movement of wings or tails if the upstroke occurs too soon after the down stroke, that is, if wing or tail beats are too rapid. For most efficient flight the bird must generate enough forward thrust to leave vortices behind, but not move its wings (or flippers) so rapidly that they encounter the last vortex on the upstroke. The 'vortex trail' has been known to aeronautical engineers for many years, but the application to flapping flight has taken a great deal of intelligence, persistence and especially designed equipment to unravel.[3] Nevertheless, the majority of such scientists insist that the birds themselves needed no designer, believing, as they do, in 'natural selection' and endless, normally destructive, genetic mistakes to generate change! To create a hummingbird capable of beating its wings ninety times per second, without 'encountering the last vortex', needs very precise engineering in every department of its tiny body, especially as this action requires far more energy than any other activity. One would expect 'blind' evolution to settle for far less, mere survival in fact. However, the extravagance of the world of birds obviously speaks of joy as well as supreme design.

When a Golden Eagle seeks out warm, ascending air to spiral thousands of feet up out of our sight, it needs to be extremely well designed. Many men have leapt from high places with assorted feathers and cleverly created

Fig. 56: NORMAL FLAPPING FLIGHT, WHERE THE DOWNSTROKE USES THE MAXIMUM WING AREA, PULLING THE BIRD FORWARD and SIMULTANEOUSLY CAUSING AIR FLOW and LIFT.

wings attached to their bodies, only to crash to their deaths. It took nearly 100 years of experimentation from the invention of the aerofoil to the first successful gliding flight by the Wright brothers, in 1902. Yet everything needed to be perfect the first time if birds were to survive. Engineers know they must design 'from the top down'—it is the only way.

Birds' undoubted mastery of the air is reflected in the different ways they fly, and the many and varied wing shapes employed.

Most birds use ordinary *flapping flight* on generalised wings, as crows, parrots, buzzards or swans, etc., whereas some intersperse flaps with periods on closed wings when they appear to be bounding through the air, as do finches, woodpeckers and Little Owls. Then there are *hoverers* like kestrel or Rough-legged Buzzard/Hawk, some of whom can also *'hang'* upon the wind when it is strong enough.

In fact many unlikely birds can be *'wind hangers'*—including puffins, ravens and eagles. This involves balancing on strong updraughts, while constantly moving wings and tail to spill excess air out: the stronger the wind, the more horizontal the bird becomes and the more upright its wings and tail are tipped. It is wonderful to watch a bird like a Short-eared Owl or kestrel hanging in the strongest wind, yet with its head and beady eye absolutely motionless and fixed on the ground below. Its wings and tail will be regularly rocked by the gusts and need constant adjustment—yet the head barely wavers. Magnificent!

Tails are also very important in flight control, and can be either larger or smaller depending on factors such as how long the bird stays in the air. Hence many large raptors like Asian and African Black Eagles have quite large, fan-like tails to assist them in attaining height by presenting the largest surface area. When fully fanned, such tails almost merge with the outstretched wings to present a 'solid' surface. The beautiful Eurasian Red Kite, which is currently enjoying an increase in numbers, uses its long, forked tail constantly, as illustrated. It twists and turns beneath the angled wings as the bird searches the ground below for food, adding greatly to its manoeuvrability. The much smaller Barn Swallow likewise uses its forked tail to aid rapid turning as it dashes about the sky after flies, as the Scissor-tailed Flycatcher does from a perch. By contrast, swifts, which fly in straighter lines after smaller, less agile flies, have smaller tails. Now, large unforked tails are also used for control by other birds, such as the Sharp-shinned Hawk or Eurasian Jay, when dashing and twisting through tangled woodland. By contrast, many seabirds that also fly for long periods find their long wings are perfectly sufficient for flight control, so only have small tails. Tails usually stretch out as far to the rear as the head and neck extends forwards. To further confuse matters, many master soarers like vultures also only have quite small tails, and one of the finest fliers of all, the African Bateleur Eagle, hardly has one at all. Its second Latin name *'ecaudatus'* indicates it is 'tail-less', and its very distinctive and rocking flight is reflected in the French name of *bateleur,* or tight-rope walker. The broader wings of all these latter raptors obviously compensate for smaller tails. To once more risk generalisation, larger, longer tails are found on birds of woodland and cover, while most water and birds of the open spaces have smaller, narrower types. We shall be looking at many other, widely diverse tails as we proceed through the coming chapters, some of which are also used in the most amazing displays.

Other common tactics used in flight are *gliding* and *soaring,* specially

Fig. 57: A SELECTION OF TYPICAL WING SHAPES. A: BARN SWALLOW. B: GRIFFON VULTURE. C: MANX SHEARWATER. D: RED KITE. E: RING-NECKED PHEASANT. F: WREN. G: SCISSOR-TAILED FLYCATCHER.

Wind direction

Fig. 58: HOVERING ROUGH-LEGGED HAWK/BUZZARD.

seen in long-winged seabirds, heron types and raptors that can travel huge distances over land or sea. These techniques require minimum effort and therefore less energy. Nevertheless, many small and short-winged birds also manage long journeys from Africa to Eurasia or between the Americas, including so-called 'weak' fliers like the Corncrake, flycatchers and many warblers.

We would expect light and elegant seabirds, and birds like swallows that also have to cross the sea, to be mainly *soarers and gliders* who use the winds and rising air masses to assist them. The two are slightly different, but both are used by large birds like White Storks and Red-tailed Hawks to move between the Southern and Northern Hemispheres. They will often delay their morning departure until the bubbles of warm air currents or *'thermals'* are ascending from the heating earth, and *soar* up on wings stretched straight out. This presents the maximum surface area for lift, and the long 'fingers' are used for fine control. Then they will slightly fold their wingtips back, hiding the slots, and *glide* effortlessly down long distances to the next thermal, sometimes crossing seas in the process.

The further the wings are angled back, the smaller the wing area and faster the descent. Once again, falcons exemplify this when they plunge earthwards at speeds that would tear many aircraft apart. More reasonably, with wings angled back at some 40°, large birds like Ospreys, eagles and cranes can glide effortlessly at speeds of around 80mph (120kph). As illustrated, they will soar up as high as the thermals can take them, and then glide down on fairly gentle gradients to find the next thermal. Such large birds naturally prefer energy efficiency over constant flapping, and can come to grief when winds drop or strongly oppose them over the sea.

They are essentially land birds, yet a lightweight Herring Gull will freely head into the strongest gale over the sea with barely a movement of its wings, and is a joy to watch. Such marvellous control requires very precise 'engineering', yet even seabirds can also perish in prolonged bad weather. To further illustrate the wonders of creation, smaller seabirds like the auks (Razorbills, for example) only have short, narrow wings that must whirr rapidly across the waves, yet they all survive long winters out on the stormy Atlantic. Auks also 'fly' easily below the waves with their strong wings and webbed feet, chasing small fish and sand-eels in glittering whorls of bubbles.

Wing loadings

Wing loading is defined as the ratio of the bird's weight to its wing area. To generalise, this usually means that the longer and narrower the wings, the *lower* the wing loading. Conversely, the shorter or broader the wing shape, the *higher* the wing loading—but dependent on body weight. So larger birds like bustards with shorter, broader wings will usually have higher wing loadings—yet large albatrosses, petrels and shearwaters with long, narrow wings and fairly slender bodies, will have low loadings. Again, roughly speaking, birds that flap a lot will have shorter wings, birds that glide more, longer wings. Yet there are always exceptions and compromises, as we shall see.

Broadly speaking, there are four different wing shapes: (A) *Long, narrow* wings as on many seabirds. (B) *Broad and slotted* at the tip, as eagles, hawks and vultures. (C) *Broad and rounded* wings, as on game birds, owls or small

Fig. 59: COMMON BUZZARDS SOARING UP IN THE WARM
'BUBBLES' OF AIR KNOWN AS THERMALS.

birds like wrens or kinglets. (D) *Pointed and tapering* types, as on birds as diverse as falcons, swallows, warblers, shorebirds and divers/loons.

A. *long and narrow wings.* The Wandering Albatross has very long and narrow wings, in fact the longest of any bird, as much as 12ft (3.6m).

Hence it is no coincidence that it is one of the most tireless fliers. Its low wing loading makes it the most efficient glider of all, but without constant winds over the open seas it could not stay aloft, and even it must occasionally rest upon the waves. By using the faster wind speeds about 50ft (16m) above the water and then gliding down to just above the waves, it uses its momentum to zoom up again—over and over for days or years on end. Such long, pointed wings also generate far less drag by cutting down on the swirling 'vortices' of air that increase drag. This shape is perfect for staying aloft with little flapping, and is used by many other seabirds, although sometimes shorter or slightly broader. Thus Atlantic Fulmars, frigate birds, shearwaters, skuas/jaegers, terns and gulls will all sport long, narrow wings to some degree, and many will employ the same looping, undulating motion of the albatross, neatly echoing the peaks and troughs of the restless sea swell.

'*Dynamic soaring*' is its official name, and it can also be seen in birds crossing the windy desert dunes that so resemble waves. I recently watched

a Northern Harrier doing just that by flying along the lee side of a long, windswept bank or 'cob'.

Because most seabirds are dark above and pale below, this elegant method of flying in a sort of open spiral, or half spiral, reveals alternately flashing hues. Manx Shearwaters are famed for alternately appearing as black or white. Yet not all seabirds fly like that, and their different methods of flight are often good indicators of their identity. As previously noted, auks like Atlantic Puffins fly low and rapidly on their little

Fig. 60: THERMAL SOARING—WHITE STORKS SOARING UP ON FULLY EXTENDED WINGS, and THEN GRADUALLY DESCENDING IN A LONG GLIDE, WINGS ANGLED BACK.

wings, while cormorants tend to fly in straight lines a little higher above the sea, alternately flapping and gliding. Divers/loons and grebes also fly fast and straight above the waves but never glide. Wildfowl tend to fly in staggered, wavy lines or the varied, give-away 'V' formation of many geese. Wildfowl usually only use flapping flight and short glides, although some have been observed 'off duty' enjoying themselves by repeatedly gliding to and fro along ridges. The smaller petrels with their 'weak', fluttering flight appear totally inadequate for the rigours of the open ocean, as do those lightweight scraps of feathers, the smaller terns. Their delightful bouncing flight often makes them appear as restless puppets. As many *'pelagic'* (open sea) birds frequently pass headlands in long meandering lines on migration, they have become popular places to observe and note trademark flights.

a

b

c

Fig. 61: WING TYPE A. a: ALBATROSS. B: HERRING GULL. C: ARCTIC TERN.

The albatross, like any large flying machine, needs a long runway for take-off. As birds, or in fact any creature, cannot achieve excellence in every area this has led some scientists to accuse any Creator of 'bad design', yet they acknowledge the need for long runways for heavy aircraft, just as these heavy flying birds naturally require. It is most appropriate to mention the divers/loons here again, for they too have long, slender wings and fairly heavy bodies, and also require a long take-off. Being supreme divers with legs set very far back means they are not very good at either walking, or lifting off from the water. But their home is the water, and note that their 'primitive' form does not hamper regular flights between the Arctic and the tropics. Some Black-throated and other divers will breed in the sub-Arctic and winter in the Caribbean or Mediterranean.

B. *Broad and slotted wings.* These demonstrate a similar sort of high efficiency to the typical seabird's, but usually over land. Hence they are most commonly employed by soaring raptors that spend long hours slowly scanning the ground below for food. This type of wing often follows the form of a long rectangle, which is why some call White-tailed Eagles 'flying

Fig. 62: DYNAMIC SOARING ON SEAWINDS OVER THE WAVES, IN LONG OPEN SPIRALS and UNDULATING LINES. TOP: GANNETS, and BELOW, SHEARWATERS.

barn doors'. Larger raptors like the White-tailed, or many vultures will usually have a *higher wing loading* the broader the wings become—resulting in long hours of easy flight, but more effort for take-off. Hence the preponderance of vultures in hot climates where warm air keeps them aloft, once the morning warms up.

Along with winds directed upward by cliffs, or mountains, these invisible thermals can only be traced by circling raptors rising in them (or fortunate glider [sailplane] pilots). Israel, for instance, uses these silent and most elegant of aircraft to monitor bird migration, and keep any jets away from the circling masses of Honey Buzzards or Steppe Eagles. Vultures can fly far slower, and in far more dangerous conditions, than any man-made device ever could. In for example, narrow canyons, where gusting updrafts

Fig. 63: WING TYPE B. a: GRIFFON VULTURE. b: MARSH HARRIER. c: BARRED/TAWNY OWL.

might dash any aircraft against the sheer rock walls, but where the bird merely adjusts its twisting wingtips. The high wing loading of larger raptors also gives them very fast gliding speeds, useful and economical for Griffon Vultures converging on a carcass from far and wide. It also helps Golden Eagles carry prey as heavy as Red Foxes, or Bonelli's Eagles gliding down to the nest with large branches.

It is no coincidence that we find *lower wing loading* in the narrower-winged harriers (and kites), which have comparatively smaller bodies and a lighter, slower flight. Like the not dissimilar Short-eared Owl, they can sail low over rough ground on upraised wings, slowly searching for any mammal, insect or bird prey below. This is often called *quartering,* and is the favoured method of birds like harriers or kites. Barn Owls and Snail Kites will also methodically quarter a meadow or marsh, though their wings are different and broader, and the kite can also soar very efficiently, as can many birds whatever their wing loading.

Bee-eaters, darters, cormorants, swifts, wood-swallows or pelicans can all spread their rather different wings and soar effortlessly away when needs be. Tawny or Barred Owl's wings are shorter and broader, as we should expect from arboreal birds. Pouncing from convenient branches on to ground-dwelling mammals is more their forte, or twisting away between the trees, and they are not seen to soar freely.

The Wedge-tailed or Golden Eagle's wing falls somewhere between that of harrier and the White-tailed or Bald Eagle, still long but not as broad as theirs or a vulture's, and is clipped in towards the tail. Buzzard's wings are shorter and more rounded, yet still confuse the unwary at a distance, as both circle on V-shaped, upraised wings in a *'canted dihedral'*, like many vultures. Both stoop with them swept back, both hang on strong winds, and both live in our last wild places—yet the eagle's secondary feather is almost twice the length of the buzzard's.

Looking at a soaring raven, or even a heron, stork or crane, you will observe rather similar shaped wings to those of many eagles. They are also long and can be deeply fingered, and seemingly more so on migratory birds like Common or Sandhill Cranes, than rather more sedentary Grey Herons. Yet that is not completely true, for some northern Grey Herons travel long distances where southern birds might not need to. Neverthess, the majority of the herons/bitterns/egrets do migrate, and have fairly similar, long but broad wings, whether it is the tiny Green Heron or the massive Goliath Heron, the former being about as long as the smallest toe of the latter! Heron and stork/crane flight also differs in two other ways. Herons fly with their necks retracted, producing that distinctive bulge below, when storks/cranes always fly with their necks extended.

Secondly, herons fly on deeply bowed wings while storks/cranes fly with them rather flat or even uptilted, like raptors. I have to put in another caveat here, for some herons or egrets will fly for short distances with necks extended—though only usually associated with aggression or display, especially in egrets.

C. *Broad and rounded wings*. Several raptors like hawks and owls have wings not that dissimilar to a game bird's, though their lifestyles are very different. They have broad, rounded wings, with less fingering at the tip in the case of the gamebird.

Their flight feathers are more down-curved, stiffer and noisier. This is probably because they are used for rapid escape by ground-dwelling birds like pheasants, partridges, grouse and quail. These are heavy birds that tend to explode from cover and rocket away on whirring wings for short distances, then glide down to safety on cupped wings. Red and Willow Grouse/Ptarmigan typify that sort of low, rapid flight, whether escaping from stooping raptors or avoiding guns. Gamebirds often have extravagant tails used in display, or hardly any at all, like the tiny Common Quail that manages to cross Africa, the Mediterranean and even long tracts of Eurasia on its little whirring wings.

Moorhens/gallinules, coots, crakes and rails also share this blunter wing, mostly for local flights while others perform long-distance epics. The Corncrake journeys twice yearly between Africa and its few remaining British nesting sites in north-west Scotland or Northern Ireland. To watch it awkwardly fluttering on beautiful orange wings and dangling legs about the Hebridean meadows, one would not think it capable of crossing heaving seas at all. Such unlikely efficiency is put down to another factor: 'aspect ratio', which is defined as the ratio of the length of the wing to its breadth. A corncrake's wing has a high aspect ratio, and lacks wingtip slots. This is thought to improve sustained flight, but at the expense of a poorer take-off. By contrast, a Ring-necked Pheasant has short broad wings (low aspect ratio), and is much more efficient at taking off rapidly than a seabird. All this helps us to understand the many different shapes of birds and their wings, and their strengths and weaknesses. In this fallen world there must always be compromise, and some scientists think that air pressure in the past was much greater; hence the massive wings of many extinct birds and flying reptiles. This is a complex topic outside the scope of this book. At least when we see heavy Purple Gallinules or Swamphens crashing about the reeds, it comes as no surprise to find that they are largely sedentary and do not need sustained flight.

The 'Accipiters', or true Hawks, usually have shorter, blunter wings and longer tails. They too will be fingered at the tips for soaring but usually swept back when the bird is swooping down, or jinking between tree branches after its bird or mammal prey. Their wing and tail shape reflects a life spent much more in cover than the vultures or eagles, where both a fast turn of speed and rapid manoeuvrability are needed. Yet Crowned or Harpy Eagles of deep woodland or tropical jungle also have similar short wings and long tails. They use them for surprising and sweeping monkeys

Fig. 64: BARN OWL, SLOWLY QUARTERING A MEADOW AT DUSK.

or sloths off branches in the forest canopy. Not many of us can witness that, yet increasingly the same sort of acrobatic ambush is performed at our bird feeders by UK Sparrows and US Sharp-shinned Hawks. Hawks can loop-the-loop when following every twist and turn of their prey, zoom along hedgerows or walls, suddenly to whip over them in ambush, or even whizz under tables or through our legs! These latter incidents are not that common, but it demonstrates their single-mindedness when in pursuit of food. That is why so many come to grief by crashing into windows or other immovable objects like trees, wires and even buses, on at least one occasion. I once had the privilege of watching a Eurasian Sparrowhawk from high

above, and saw it use every bit of cover to approach distant birds feeding on the ground, flapping and gliding along every hedge and suddenly jinking over to check its line of approach. The larger Northern Goshawk has slightly longer wings, reflecting perhaps that it hunts in the open as well as deep cover, or a combination of both, as when it zooms from a soar to a ground-hugging approach on rabbits or even brown hares. The wings will be increasingly swept back as it approaches the prey, and very long legs are swung forward just before impact.

Fig. 65: FLIGHT WITH EXTENDED NECK: CRANE (and STORKS), and WITH RETRACTED NECK: HERON (and EGRETS), FOREGROUND.

The force of impact will often have both predator and prey tumbling over, and it is worth noting that many attacks by aerial hunters fail.

D. *Pointed and tapered towards a broader base.* Birds as diverse as Barn Swallows and Prairie Falcons, Carmine Bee-eaters and Red Knots have this type of wing shape. Perhaps it is no coincidence they are all very fast fliers and migratory, yet the first three can soar and glide to save energy, while the little wader must flap all the way from the Southern to the Northern Hemispheres. It is at least compensated by the fact that it is easier to fly in a flock, because the wingtip vortices of air help uplift the neighbour. Once again we can only marvel at the incredible precision of such formation flying, where many birds move as one. That is why birds like geese that fly in Vs frequently change their leader: a leader uses more energy than a follower. This method of flying in flocks serves another function: that of protection. The incredible and simultaneous precision of swirling flocks of birds (and fish) has led some evolutionists to a particularly twisted conclusion: this behaviour is only caused by selfishness! Because one bird wants to survive, it warns its neighbours so that they all stand as much chance of being taken. As usual, a prior commitment to evolutionary theory drives some to wild and unprovable speculations.

Raptors do not find it particularly easy to stoop into a swirling flock of starlings, waders or even bats, and successfully pick out just one victim. Others lunge left and right almost at random, and connect that way. Often predators will pick out the lame or weak, the inevitable stragglers in such huge congregations. The majority, or 'fittest' survive, as we would expect, but this only brings up yet another puzzle for evolutionists. Why do large flocks of waders or finches all take off when a raptor flies over, when they are safer on the ground? They should have learnt by now, after all those 'millions of years', surely? Note that raptors like Peregrines, merlins or sparrowhawks very rarely take prey off the ground, as one would expect from many raptors' hair-raising stoops.

The large, broad wings of storks and raptors are fine for slow circling and long distances with barely a flap, but the swallow's smaller wings also take it far and wide. This is yet another example of the lavishness of God's creation, where two or more 'unnecessary' modes of flight and beauty are displayed for us. Swifts have even longer, narrower wings than swallows

Fig. 66: WING TYPE C. a: CORNCRAKE. b: GREY PARTRIDGE. c: SPARROWHAWK.

Fig. 67: NORTHERN GOSHAWK AND RABBIT.

and martins, and subsequently a lower wing loading and much less drag, like the albatross. This is reflected in two ways: Barn Swallows and Sand Martins (USA: Bank Swallows) arrive before House Martins and Common Swifts because their low-flying insects come out earlier in the year. Lower flight after larger, agile insects requires more flexible and broader wings. And the swifts fly faster, higher and straighter, and take smaller, easier to catch insects that only get wafted into the heights as the year warms up.

As for bee-eaters and hobbies, they too have very similarly shaped wings and both take large insects on the wing, although speedy hobbies can also catch swallows and the like. Larger prey is more energy efficient and the term '*payload*' is used for it, especially when carrying food back to the nest. Birds have been programmed for maximum efficiency, with some even stashing food caught first thing in the morning, if they are not hungry at that time and if food is plentiful. This cuts down on payload, especially for Eurasian Kestrels that can expend a lot of energy hovering on windless mornings. Only before retiring to roost will they return for any hidden prey, and then digest it at leisure. Many vultures risk being caught unable to take off by over-stuffing themselves with carrion, and many predators have to carry heavy prey items back to the nest whole. Ospreys have perfected the art, turning fish forwards and streamlining them by carrying them torpedo-fashion. Serpent Eagles swallow long snakes in one piece with just the tail protruding for the young to pull out, and herons can swallow eels almost as long as themselves. For seabirds that spend a long time away from the nest, as penguins or albatrosses often do, the food is regurgitated almost as fresh as it went in, thanks to special chemical conditions in the stomach.

'Attackers' describes speedy predators with high wing loading, like the Eurasian Hobby or Eleanora's Falcon. This is slightly confusing, as I have just reminded you that some of the fastest and most efficient fliers have low wing loading. The difference is this: swifts and albatrosses are the 'long-distance runners', while many falcons are the 'sprinters'. A Peregrine might dive at a gravity assisted 200mph (300kph), but is no faster than a pigeon in ordinary level flight, and it rarely indulges in long chases. There are similarities in the animal world: the Grey Wolf lopes patiently after prey for long distances, while the Cheetah sprints and often soon gives up the chase.

Fig. 68: WING TYPE D. a: PEREGRINE. b: BEE-EATER. c: SWIFT. d: BARN SWALLOW.

There are exceptions, for the Arctic Gyr Falcon will often fly down a Mallard or goose by sheer persistence. The fastest flying birds over long distances in level flight are not falcons, but Eider Ducks, other wildfowl and swifts. The ducks can apparently reach speeds of 65mph (104kph) in flapping flight—not gliding or stooping. It is interesting that their wings most resemble this fourth type, pointed yet broad at the base (as shown in the first illustration).

To summarise: the Peregrine and Eider, the two fastest birds in the world, both have high wing loading and rather similarly shaped wings, but the most efficient for long distance are those with low wing loading. The lesson for us is that we should be like Paul who wrote, 'I have finished the race' (2 Timothy 4:7), speaking of his hard Christian life as a marathon; an initial sprint followed by the long haul. 'He who endures to the end will be saved' (Matthew 10:22).

Naturally, there are many birds' wings that do not completely conform to any of the four man-made stereotypes above. This almost certainly reflects their 'in-between' lives. Thus some warblers will relate most to wing shape D, if they are long-distance migrants (as the Willow Warbler that travels from Eurasia to southern Africa). Yet others will have shorter, more rounded wings, generally indicating shorter distances travelled. The Chiff-chaff is virtually identical to the Willow Warbler, yet is a shorter-winged, shorter-distance migrant from Eurasia to the Mediterranean. Other more sedentary warblers, like the Cetti's, Moustached and various American types, also have shorter, blunter wings, hence the sedentary Russet-crowned Warbler of the USA has shorter wings than the migratory Blackburnian Warbler. Although the Eurasian Sedge Warbler is very similar to the Moustached, it is more migratory, so once more we find its wings are longer. Many *corvids* (crow family) have 'compromise' wings, broad yet longish and often fingered. They are very active birds, but do not usually migrate. Their global success belies any cry of compromise. Within that family it can be seen that woodland dwellers like Eurasian Jays have the shortest and bluntest, and aerial masters like the raven, the longest and most fingered wings. But, and it is a big 'but', generalisations are always dangerous, and exceptions can always be found, for example the Northern Wheatear. This bird migrates very long distances and is still spreading

Fig. 69: TEAL SPRINGING FROM THE WATER.

world-wide (another indicator of the recent Genesis Flood), into the Americas from Russia, but not on particularly long wings.

Flycatchers represent another compromise; they have wings far shorter and blunter than aerial flycatchers like swallows, but only dart out from high perches for prey and do not spend long periods hunting on the wing. Yet they often also need to migrate, and to be able to store extra fat for the journey. So wings must always perfectly balance a bird's needs and travels. Finches and weavers/sparrows are some of the world's commonest birds, often flocking in millions and travelling around devastating crops. Such movements are not really migratory, but simply follow the planting of our crops, on wings that are generally more rounded and shorter and superbly adapted for fast turns within large flocks. Finches especially use energy saving, bounding flight, like the waxwings and crossbills that *'irrupt'* from their northern forested lands in winter. Many (Bohemian) Waxwings irrupt southwards to other countries, like the UK, to feast upon our berry crops in the winter, but sporadically and in varying numbers. It is telling that both waxwings and crossbills have more pointed wings than other finches, though the waxwings more resemble starlings, and are in a family of their own. This sporadic movement is probably caused by berries that tend to bloom best every three years or so, whereas insectivorous birds must move yearly.

Can we safely assert that birds like the Galapagos Cormorant and flightless rails have very small wings because they no longer need to fly, finding their food perfectly adequately in water or on the ground? Once more, it is frequently loss in the natural world (and fossil record), not gain.

Another aspect of flight is concerned with *attack and defence*. This is largely about protection of the nest, eggs or young from predators, or at least perceived predators. Many birds will instinctively mob raptors, flying fearlessly at them even when the predator can rapidly turn the tables. Fieldfares literally dive-bomb any intruders, disabling birds like corvids with their messy, sticky droppings. Others are content to make a lot of noise, en masse, as when Western Jackdaws or Barn Swallows mob Common Buzzards, Common Cuckoos or even raptors. Seabirds like skuas/jaegers and Arctic Terns will draw blood from unwary human heads encountered on their nesting grounds. Great Skuas are appropriately called 'Bonxies' in the far north of Scotland, and this heavy pirate can knock you almost senseless. Then some smaller birds like Asian drongos will actually ride a raptor's back, like an avian bucking bronco! Larger raptors usually shrug off such attentions as an occupational hazard, but sometimes it will mean death for the attacker, or in rare cases even disablement or death for the raptor itself. Ravens especially can be very tricky customers with their pick-axe bill and aerial mastery. One fairly reliable way of finding raptors is to look for mobbing birds—scolding tits and screeching Eurasian Jays often surround drowsy Tawny Owls, for instance. 'Ticking' European Robins and Wrens, and Blackcaps, can also give away resting raptors, or the cats in our gardens. Stooping crows are good indicators of any sort of raptor, and raptors themselves can often be found by looking above flocks of fleeing winter birds.

In extreme circumstances, birds like the Eurasian Woodcock have reliably been seen flying away with their young tucked between their feet. The Water Rail will simply walk away with its chicks in its bill, although it will also carry off and eat others' young. Many birds will abandon their young or eggs when under pressure; even temporarily abandoned nests can fall victim to egg or chick chilling, and the unwelcome attentions of corvids and cats. Human and canine disturbance is now a grave problem for many ground-nesting coastal birds, on beach, estuary or island shorelines.

Take-off and landing must also be considered: although they have already been discussed in connection with some birds. Take-off especially is usually going to involve more energy than level flight, although many small birds readily leap into the air (also during displays). Even heavier wildfowl like Mallard or Teal can jump almost vertically from the water.

It is most telling that the further back the legs or the heavier the bird, the longer the 'runway' needed. Most of us will have watched swans and geese running heavily across the water to take off, or landing by skidding splashily along the surface. They need space. One of the heaviest flying birds, the Mute Swan, races rapidly across the water thrusting its large webbed feet into the surface one after the other. Then when it wants to land it will always prefer setting down on water, so that it can use its broad belly and outstretched feet for brakes. They can land on solid ground, or grass and sand, but will need to run off the momentum—unlike lightweight gulls for instance, who set down lightly on the spot.

On take-off, cormorants use both feet together, unlike most wildfowl.

This is probably because they are heavier, with fewer hollow bones for deep diving, but divers/loons also deep dive and they use alternate feet in take-off. Mergansers and goosanders, and most other diving ducks also need to run across the water to lift off. They will often opt to fly into a headwind to assist lift and take-off, and then turn away and let the air take them down wind.

Among the land birds, some only have to open their wings into the wind to take off, or jump from branches or cliffs. Thus comparatively heavy, short-winged birds like the Atlantic Guillemot leap from high cliffs and zoom down onto the sea at roughly 45°. It is fascinating to watch the young of such birds, or even more extreme, certain Arctic geese, leap off even higher cliffs on their very first 'flight'. Most will not be able to fly properly, because their wings are not fully developed or, like young Atlantic Gannets, are still too heavy. Indeed, some juvenile birds are so well fed to survive those early days that they may be temporarily larger than their parents. Only after working that excess weight off will they be able to run across the waves and lift off. In the case of some Little Auks, Barnacle and Pink-footed Geese there will not even be water immediately below the nesting cliffs. Many will crash down hundreds of feet almost vertically on to rocks, and have to run for the sea, pursued by Arctic Foxes or avian predators like gulls. However, many young wildfowl seem to be miraculously bouncy, for fluffy Goosander or Mallard chicks also leap from trees, or even third-floor window boxes in central London!

Vultures and many other large raptors will simply open their wings and jump off high places, but only when the ground has warmed up and thermals are present in the atmosphere. Smaller raptors can leap upwards from the ground or simply let the wind waft them off higher perches. Even more control is needed when such raptors are attacking prey. Wings and tail must then be very precisely aligned to balance the need for speed and braking, with individual flight and tail feathers losing or trapping air. The wings are individually fanned or partly closed according to the need to change direction rapidly. Constant readjustments are required not only to hit the prey at enough speed to disable it, but also not to kill the predator itself.

About a hundred years ago, scientists learnt just how raptors like the

Fig. 70: MUTE SWAN TAKING OFF.

Golden Eagle could time its approach and correctly anticipate where a hare would leap next, from the paintings of the great wildlife painter, Bruno Liljefors. He pictured the full range of flight and tail feathers opening or closing and different wing angles, tipped this way or that to swerve towards or anticipate the prey's jinking course. This Swedish 'impressionist' pictured it all largely from memory in his large, life-size canvases, well before high-speed photography. He managed to distil all that fluid action of the chase into one image. Nowadays we have slow-motion video and high-speed flash to capture such fleeting moments, and consequently more understanding, but little better wildlife art. I recently watched a Peregrine Falcon stoop vertically from hundreds of feet and take and kill a small wader (Redshank) in a split second, just a foot or so above the sands outside my window. Consider the precision and God-given skill of that action. It needed first to drop rapidly enough to take the wader only after it had taken off, then slightly open its wings and fling its great feet forward and slow down only at the very last moment, then finally adjust everything to kill precisely, and throw itself speedily upwards almost simultaneously, without hitting the ground. I saw only the stoop and then the bird almost instantly flying away with a lifeless Redshank in its claws. It seemed almost effortless! It also brings up that old question—why would a good God allow such killing? I address that thorny question in the final chapters.

Many corvids seem to delight in playing at take-off and landing, holding with one foot onto branches or cliff vegetation while high winds twirl them around. It can be dangerous, as young Grey Herons, Common Ravens, or Peregrines have all been blown out of their windy eyries while practising vigorous wing flapping. Young muscles need exercise and intense practice before they can master the air, and watching young Peregrines stooping at each other is one of the best ways to watch this development, or enjoying flocks of Jackdaws whirling like black snowflakes about your rooftops or trees. One of the most delightful bird 'practices' was observed by a student here on Anglesey, among a large winter flock of Common Ravens. These clever corvids were waddling up the steepest sand dunes only to fling their wings open as they reached the windy top, which tossed them tumbling into the air. Many then landed again downwind and strutted back to do it all again. Many birds obviously delight in the wind, as when Rooks all shoot up together in spiralling clouds above the rookery, or Fulmars and many raptors hang over cliff edges, on strong updraughts.

Smaller, lighter birds rarely have any problems with take-off, and they simply scuttle or flap into protective cover, if threatened. As many young passerines or owls seem to end up on the ground below their nests and are sometimes unable to scramble back up, this is not all bad news. (Incidentally, anyone finding such young should leave them where they are, or put them back into the nest, or into cover, unless the neighbourhood cat is lurking. The bird's parents almost certainly know where it is, and it is often more damaging to take it away to a bird hospital. Many birds are extremely difficult to care for and successfully return to the wild.) Others can hop or run into take-off, or launch themselves like bullets from high perches on closed wings. This is part of both 'bounding' and stooping flight, where the wings are held closed as long as possible to aid escape and give extra speed.

Landing is not always as elegant. Larger, young birds especially are prone to tumble over, though rarely damaging little more than their dignity. Tipping or tripping up is the biggest problem, tail in the air and head in the dust, grass or water. Birds that have the greatest problems taking off will often have the most problems landing. For example, Razorbills and the like will approach the cliffs from below only to rise at the last minute, and thus plop down fairly gracefully, largely by gravity. This final stall is caused by the wings and tail tipping up and cupping and then spilling the air, with the outstretched legs also taking the force out of the landing. Wildfowl like geese, and some Eurasian Cranes and Curlews, will *'wiffle'* down, deliberately twisting and rocking as they lose the air while steeply approaching the ground. They certainly seem to enjoy that exhilarating act, often calling excitedly as they do so. (Incidentally, ravens also enjoy themselves sledging on their backs in snow.) Lapwings will likewise perform elaborate aerial manoeuvres before going to roost, though nearer the ground or water. Starlings and other passerines that gather in huge flocks outside the breeding season, also seem to delight in wonderful, swirling aerobatics that appear as animated smoke from a distance. Just what their exact purpose is we do not know, but their predators enjoy this too, for anything from Eurasian Sparrowhawks to Hobbies will gather at regular roost sights. Then there are the Red-tailed Buzzards that stoop at dusk over certain Mexican cave mouths, when literally millions of bats pour out. One particular tropical raptor, the Bat Falcon, actually makes its living doing this.

Flight is astonishing and so much more than mere feathers, bones and muscles—and even the command centre of brain, the nerves and the eyes rely on microscopic electro/bio/chemical reactions. Remember that God maintains it all 'with the word of His power' (Hebrews 1:3). 'Praise the Lord from the earth, you great sea creatures ... beasts and all cattle; creeping things and flying fowl ... let them praise the name of the Lord' (Psalm 148:7–13).

Coloration and pattern

The body forms of birds are exquisite, and beautifully designed to specifications well beyond our understanding. As with many other living things, our Creator has seen fit to endow birds with four limbs and the regular pattern of two eyes, 'nose' and mouth. Ironically, it is this 'homology', or great similarity between the design blueprints of many creatures, that led some to cry 'evolution'! It is an equally strong proof of creation, should we actually need any more.

The *colouring* of feathers is not just for beauty. Dark feathers are

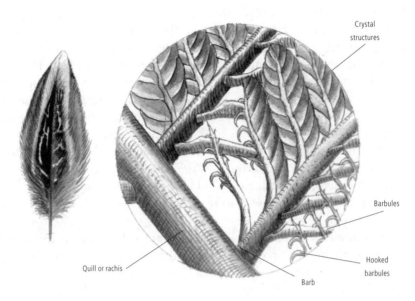

Fig. 71: FEATHER COLORATION BY 'PHOTONIC CRYSTAL STRUCTURES' ON THE TOPS OF THE BARBULES. LEFT: PHEASANT BACK FEATHER.

stronger, while dark hues can both absorb or protect the bird from different light wavelengths. As black pigments absorb light, it seems strange that we should find ravens in many deserts, but Fan-tailed and Brown-necked Ravens have shiny, iridescent plumage that reflects light and actually reduces body temperature remarkably. Also, many temperate gulls have dark wing tips that prevent excessive wear on the tips, whereas polar Glaucous Gulls and Snow Petrels have all-white primaries, probably related to the weaker amounts of yearly daylight at the poles. We have just looked at how light-coloured feather fringes wear off to reveal the splendours of breeding plumage. Colouring is extremely high-tech, as already mentioned concerning the beautiful feathers of many birds, like the hummingbird or kingfisher. They are dependent for their glittering colours upon refraction of light through minutely different sizes of *'photonic crystal structures'*.[4]

This optical effect is called 'thin film interference' and produces the iridescent colours that mark out so many birds, from magpies to manikins, glossy starlings to grenadiers, and bee-eaters to buntings. Stuart Burgess studies this subject in detail in his book *Hallmarks of Design*. He shows how just one feather, the famous eyed peacock tail feather, needs incredibly fine-tuned, microscopic films to produce all the dazzling colours and patterns. A single barb on such a feather must have almost imperceptible differences in size and height of the light-interference 'crystals' for each colour! These millions of tiny prisms scatter the light in a similar way to the sun creating rainbows through water droplets. Remember that the principal function of such barbs and barbules is to hook the feather vane together, and yet there are also these incredibly complex structures for colour on their upper surface.

Then there is the remarkable idea that such feathers are actually *colourless* themselves, relying upon the tiny 'crystals' to split white light into its constituent rainbow hues. Look how a Golden Pheasant dazzles in the light, yet shades effortlessly into the dappled woodlands. Truly, our Creator is 'the Light of the World', who then came down to further enlighten it.

There are other methods used to produce colour. Two pigments in the feather, *melanins* and *lipochromes*, produce other hues. Lipochromes produce yellows, oranges, reds, blues and greens. Melanin is the same pigment as in human skin, with darker peoples simply having more of it. So it is no coincidence that smaller, darker Peregrine Falcons are found nearer the equator, and paler, larger types near the Arctic (Tundra Falcons). This dark pigment is mainly associated with dark shades such as blacks, browns, red-browns and yellows. '*Melanism*' is used to describe dark colour forms, or 'morphs', of several creatures. The *Peppered Moth (Biston betularia)* is one famous example, even used as 'proof' of evolution (see chapter 6). Yet such colours are probably produced by the dominant 'allele' of the gene-controlling colour, and have nothing to do with evolutionary accidents. Many creatures have dark or light forms and everything in between, built in, as we see in highly variable birds like the Gyr Falcon or Red-tailed Hawk. This also applies to patterns on individual and groups of feathers, which ensures that every single bird or beast is unique. That is but one

Fig. 72: VERMICULATED PLUMAGE: THE SCOPS, OR SCREECH OWL.

reason why Jesus could say that not even a sparrow falls 'apart from your Father's will', and 'the very hairs of your head are all numbered' (Matthew 10:29–30). The principal difference between iridescent and pigmented colour is mainly light, as pigments fade in light as time passes. Some birds have either one type of pigment or refracted coloration, while others will use combinations of the two. The melanin pigment can be supplemented by others from plants or other food, which is how flamingos and canaries produce their beautiful pink and yellow hues, using vitamin A *carotenoids*, as are found in brine shrimps and carrots. But where does the seed-eating canary find them? They can be transformed from yellow to orange by deliberately feeding them paprika!

Next down the scale comes *'erythrism'*, or a preponderance of reddish hues in the plumage, then *'flavism'*, where yellowish hues are dominant, all the way down to *'albinism'*—or a complete lack of pigment. This usually weakens a creature, though some survive and others are only partial albinos. Bright green African touracos, or louries, have their own exclusive pigments, *turacoverdin*, and a rich purpley-red *turacin*, for their splendid scarlet wings.

Yet it is not just colour that defines beauty in birds, for some of the most stunning are dressed in rather drab greys, browns, creams and whites. It is the way they are combined that counts. Scops and Screech Owls, nightjars, potoos and frogmouths all rely upon the most astonishing

Fig. 73: BLACK-THROATED DIVER, OR PACIFIC LOON.

'vermiculations': extremely subtle and fine wavy barring, scribbling, and dappling marks to camouflage them.

They just happen to look exactly like the bark of trees, or dry leaf covered woodland floors. Similarly, certain insects could not possibly 'accidentally' evolve precise markings that exactly mimic vegetation, even dying leaves, so such patterns must be in-built, yet with enough variation to make each creature's unique minute differences recognisable amid the general theme. We are all individuals, even sparrows and sheep, and such individuality comes from almost infinite recombination of our genetic inheritance. This is nothing short of miraculous, especially when it is most probable that such variety (and speciation) comes from *lessening* amounts of genetic information. The original genetic base, and other hereditary factors must have been incredibly rich and is only gradually being diluted (see chapter 6).

It is almost impossible to single out just one group of birds for special commendation, for their beauty comes in many different ways.

Divers/loons are one of the most resplendently dressed of any bird, striped and speckled with silvery dots, squares and streaks on black or grey grounds.

Their kind of beauty is rather subtle and sophisticated alongside, for instance, the Green-headed Tanager with its dazzling lapis-blue, turquoise and green plumage. An American Painted Bunting puts together the most unlikely and brilliant colours, while Golden Orioles often look like the sun's rays flashing through the bright, young leaves of spring. Parrots and hummingbirds, kingfishers and finches: the list is endless. Our Creator has truly blessed us. Even the plainest bird like a Meadow Pipit or young Palm Warbler reveals considerable beauty when viewed in detail; one of the advantages of binoculars and telescopes. Apart from tropical fish and some beetles, birds undoubtedly have the most glorious colours and combinations of hues of any creature. We shall always be touching on the splendid variety of birds in the world, as we look further at what they do and how they do it.

Sexual Dimorphism. This describes variety in colour, as well as size, among birds like waterfowl, pheasants and raptors. Usually it will be the female who is far less striking in pattern and colour, partly for camouflage purposes when sitting tight on ground nests. Many such females have discreet, brown and cream chevron-patterned plumage, especially designed for merging with dry grasses. They are also often slightly smaller, as among swans, geese and ducks, yet the first two of these groups share the same plumage as the male. However, they make up for any loss of face by being the warmongers, as many females do the 'quacking' and point out rival ducks for seeing off. They can be very vicious too, with both male and female Common Shelducks even occasionally drowning a rival's chicks.

As for much larger size differences, some of the most notable are among the raptors. Most male falcons or *'Accipiter'* style hawks, for example the Eurasian Sparrowhawk or USA Sharp-shinned Hawk, are at least a third smaller than the females. This has led to male Peregrine Falcons being labelled 'tiercels', from the French for 'one third'. These size differences point to an effective use of food resources, with nippy male sparrowhawks taking smaller birds in thicker cover, and larger females tackling bigger birds in more open ground. This difference has reached its greatest height in the Australian Variable Goshawk, its very name a masterpiece of understatement. Not only can these birds be anything from all white to all dark, and all shades and patterns in between, but the males can be as little as one fifth of the size of the largest females, though presumably not within any individual pair. This size difference also indicates what could be a common problem for fossil classification—how many creatures have been labelled as different species, or even families, merely because of size variation?

Notes

1 **Gordon Rattray-Taylor,** *The Great Evolution Mystery* (Abacus, 1984).
2 **Steve Leonard,** *Journey of Life* (BBC TV, Spring 2005).
3 'Moving creatures tuned for efficient cruising', *Nature,* vol. 425, p. 707, and *Nature Science Update,* 16:10.
4 **Jian Zi, Xindi Yu, Yizhou Li, Xinhua Hu, Chun Xu, Xingjun Wang, Xiaohan Liu and Rongtang Fu,** 'Coloration strategies in peacock feathers' in *Proceedings,* National Academy of Sciences of the United States of America, 28 October 2003, Vol. 100, no. 22, pp. 12576–12578 (viewable on-line at http://www.pnas.org/cgi/content/full/100/22/12576) and *New Scientist,* 18/10/2003.

Migration

The list of long-distance and gruelling journeys accomplished by birds is quite astonishing. We have already mentioned some of the most remarkable, and shall do so again in later chapters. As usual, we are forced to see deliberate design in some of the feats, like the Blackpoll Warbler that initially flies the wrong way before it hits the right southward winds. Then there is the Lesser Golden Plover that flies out from Alaska and must hit the tiny dot of Hawaii, 2,000 miles (3,000km) out in the Pacific Ocean. Too much stored body fat, and it wouldn't make it—too little and it couldn't make it. Body weight must be right first time for the exact distance, with no way for a thrush-sized, land bird like the plover to adapt it once over the lonely seas. There are no other islands en route, and drowning birds are of no use to the survival of the species. It takes just 2 oz (56gm) of fat to accomplish this, yet some birds like the Eurasian Garden Warbler must almost double their weight to reach Africa. Many species will feed frantically for about three weeks before leaving, storing the fat almost dry around the lower body. Some must double their weight in only ten days, and actually change the shape of some internal organs. These facts utterly refute the myth about 'genetic mistakes' being able to improve anything. Such changes obviously require highly sophisticated, built-in instructions, with no room for error. Others, like some geese or Arctic Terns, will even store enough fat to produce eggs and survive for some time after arrival. Indeed their wing muscles will also increase in size to carry this fat, the most energy-efficient biochemical fuel known. So as the bird approaches its destination with gradually lessening amounts of fat on wings and body, it gets lighter and can fly more easily. This must be very welcome to Arctic Terns that can almost circle the globe each year, with one covering over 14,000miles (22,500km) in just ten months.

Various peoples, as in the Bible and classical Greek writings have long noted migration. Aristotle observed the various comings and goings of birds in the autumn, yet thought that departing Redstarts had 'transmuted' into arriving Robins! The famous English nature diarist, Gilbert White (1720–93), was one of the first to *ring* or *band* birds in the autumn, and watch for their return in the spring. After the middle of the last century it became a science, and has greatly aided our knowledge of migrations and essential resting places en route. Rarely is any damage caused to the birds by the lightweight, aluminium bands, or coloured plastic rings on waterfowl or crane/stork legs, although birds can be killed by 'cannon-netting' which traps small flocks for weighing and ringing. The net is furled, laid out in a straight line and weighted at the ends, and later fired over roosting flocks of waterbirds. As this is often carried out at the high tide mark, birds can be drowned in the short time taken to free them from the net. Land birds are usually captured in very fine curtain nets (mist-nets), or funnelled into disguised 'Heligoland' traps for ringing. Similar narrow enclosures are also sighted over waterways to corral waterfowl. Captured birds are usually placed into dark bags to quieten them, then weighed, measured, ringed and quickly released. This is how much of the information about migration routes, weight gain and bodily changes have been collected. The system depends on the fairly random recovery of the rings from dead birds in foreign lands, and collation of the distances, times and weights, etc. Although some living birds are caught more than once, others are marked with bright dye that means recapture is unnecessary. White birds are especially liable to have their plumage marred by bright orange or scarlet dyes, though they naturally wear off or grow out. Observations and recoveries continue to come in from all points of the globe, as the rings are marked with the appropriate country's natural history museum address (post free), or similar institution. One particular Great Cormorant, a bird not particularly associated with long distance travel, managed to get from Anglesey to Italy. Many others also regularly travel huge distances: there was even a report that a flightless Kiwi somehow reached Anglesey in 1853!

All this has been greatly aided by the growing popularity of bird watching in the last half of the twentieth century, with many individuals happy to spend their leisure hours helping the few professionals. Across the world, varying but increasing degrees of interest in and knowledge of wildlife and conservation have aided birds, especially in saving their vital habitats. Breeding and wintering 'Atlas' bird surveys are now fairly common, at least in the UK, USA and parts of Europe. Seasonal movements are fairly predictable, as are the special places that birds regularly drop into, so this further pinpoints birds' needs. Now, satellite tracking has added to the information gleaned from ringing, by fixing extremely small 'sending' units to birds such as wildfowl. This has allowed scientists to track birds on particularly long journeys, but it is expensive, and it is only really appropriate for larger birds at present. Whooper Swans wintering on wetland and wildfowl reserves in the UK have been fitted out for their return to northern Russia, and eagerly followed on TV as they undertake these tremendous travels. So technology is helping map the vital stopover points for our birds, just as Sir Peter Scott first painted the singular bill pattern of every winter swan visitor to his first reserve, and accurately logged their yearly returns. Whooper and Tundra Swans have varying amounts of black and yellow on their beaks, unique to every individual. By contrast our native Mute Swans differ far, far less, the smaller black bump on the female's bill usually the most difference detectable by us (though she is generally smaller).

I can think of no better way to watch migration than from a glider (sailplane), or hang-glider. Flying with birds has become a fairly common event for some fortunate scientists, gliding with eagles and pelicans across Israel, or even leading rare cranes down through the USA. Avoiding crashes with birds prompted the first, while last-ditch avoidance of extinction accounts for the second. White Whooping Cranes are now very rare in North America, so a few have been captive reared, fostered by much commoner Sandhill Cranes, and led down to their Texas wintering grounds by a small aeroplane. It was biologists like Konrad Lorenz who gave us the idea of birds 'imprinting' themselves upon the first creature to come along, especially man. Waterfowl, especially, will follow us if they have lost their parents, and even learn to fly by chasing us as we travel in boats, vehicles and aeroplanes. But these are comparatively rare events, and around the world, the situation is fairly grim for both birds and their habitats. There are very few places that have not been mapped for their value to birds—and hence to all creation. The world is criss-crossed with their routes and 'service areas', often defined by water and space, whether in mountains, coastlands, woods or on plains or fields. Human encroachment on these areas usually continues apace.

Fig. 74: SIMPLIFIED GLOBAL MIGRATION ROUTES. a: ARCTIC TERN. b: BARN SWALLOW. c: NORTHERN WHEATEAR.

The distances birds travel vary greatly, but whether they do or not is mainly due to climate, breeding grounds and food availability. We shall look at just how these migrations probably came about in chapter 6, and the significance of future planning on both birds and lands. Certainly since the Ice Age distances have been getting longer between the continents, with either side of the equatorial belt getting drier, forcing birds to traverse greater and more difficult distances. That partly explains why many Eurasian or Winter Wrens that live all around the Northern Hemisphere, vary so greatly in their travels. Some may move just down the road, or fly 2500miles (3700km) from Scandinavia to Spain, or from Canada to Mexico. Others 'leapfrog' each other, so Whimbrel will cover much longer distances than the similar Eurasian Curlew, because Whimbrel breed further north and winter further south, in Southern Africa. It all seems to be a question of increasing adaptations to certain foods and habitats.

One of the most telling cases is the Blackcap, which shows that same variation within its own species. Because of milder winters, they have very recently become partial migrants in some areas of the UK, so already have shorter wings that must also have been genetically 'built-in' to cope with rapid environmental changes. There are still many Blackcaps with longer wings that migrate to Africa, and when the types are deliberately and intensively bred together, they immediately show parental preferences. This is a rather good proof that migration is also genetically pre-programmed, but does not address the question of how the birds could pre- or re-program themselves. The logical answer is that our Creator allowed for inheritance to be adaptable to His *foreseen* contingencies.

There are many recognised 'flyways' used by migrating birds, usually but not always north to south. They naturally follow shorelines, rivers and mountain ranges, and most land birds prefer those shortest sea crossings. Wetlands and estuaries are natural magnets for many species. They offer food and shelter, and will gleam like beacons from above. Some water birds will land on wet, shiny roads by mistake, especially at night. Weather also affects their movements, and many will wait for optimal conditions, like following winds. Height and night are also important for many birds, with the reduced air pressure at height conducive to easier flight, and even the colder air probably preventing overheating. Darkness is also good cover for large, vulnerable flocks of birds like songbirds, often seen as dense masses on radar. Yet birds are very adaptable, with some wildfowl staying north for a while if the winter is mild. Conversely some others, like the Common Cuckoo were called 'calendar birds' because they arrive back on virtually the same day each year. Only now with widening deserts and seeming climate change, they can be early or not arrive at all. Others may now never leave, like the Blackcaps, or the Barn Swallows I have seen here even on New Year's Eve. Male Chaffinches voluntarily stay on their Scandinavian breeding grounds while the females and young head south. Other slight mysteries involve Eurasian Swifts and Reed Warblers, who head off south well before any major seasonal changes are apparent to us. Birds are also often very choosy about where they go, with UK Barn Swallows wintering in one southern African country, but rarely mixing with the German or Russian swallows in neighbouring states. Doubtless this applies to many different species, which will also often exhibit variations in colour, or bill length, as in Dunlins, which breed in many different parts of the sub-arctic north.

How do they do it?

As to just *how* birds manage to migrate so accurately and consistently, that is another question. Experts are divided upon the mechanisms used, so here are some of their ideas. Almost certainly birds will need to use more than one method, as for instance when the sun, moon or stars are obscured by thick cloud.

(a) *Seasonal changes*, including lengthening or shortening days, and changing temperatures. Much of this must be built in. Even when marine creatures like shellfish are deliberately carried far from the sea, they instinctively respond by opening and closing their shells to the tidal patterns they have left far behind. Similar tests with young European warblers demonstrate similar seasonal urges, even in darkened laboratories.

(b) *Sun, moon and stars*. Birds like the young Manx Shearwater sit outside their burrows for a few nights before take-off, seemingly memorising the star map, or rather, strengthening their in-built guidance/map system, and the map will change in the southern hemisphere they unerringly head for. Their parents can safely leave them at home to follow, as do some swallows and other migrants. The shearwater chick will have no food for about two weeks before it leaves, so that should help it to make a start, but it must have enough fat reserves for the non-stop journey to South America, once again showing great precision and foresight. The amazing travels of one particular Manx Shearwater are now legendary. It was taken from its nest in Wales and flown to America, released, and found back at the nest just twelve days later. The poor bird then had to set off for South America! Adult Barn Swallows also leave well before the young, but they will usually make it, unless bad weather or other factors prevent them. Then they will return to the very same nesting site by the next northern spring. And birds have been shown to quickly learn to use their 'sun compass', even probably seeing its ultra-violet light through thick clouds. Hummingbirds and homing pigeons are known to see into that 'far light' range.

(c) *Magnetism*: every living thing has a weak electromagnetic field in and around it, and pigeons and other birds have been found to have small amounts of magnetic crystals in their heads. Blanking out their heads in experiments has the effect of disorientating them to the earth's own magnetic field. Other birds studied in especially deceptive or moving chambers usually manage to orient themselves the right way. However, it has been suggested that pigeons function better when *light* is allowed to supplement the 'magnetic receptors', which are probably just behind the eyes. The very latest experiments seem to confirm this. Blanking out one particular eye of a Eurasian Robin does not affect its ability to orientate. However, when the other is the only one covered, all is lost. Birds can also tell which hemisphere they are in, simply by the angle of inclination of the magnetic field towards the poles.

(d) *Polarised light* from the sun also affects parts of the sky even after it has set, so many birds can seemingly work out the sun's position even when it is hidden.

(e) *Visual clues, infrasound and even smells:* coastlines and large rivers, estuaries and headlands, mountain ranges and similar features could all be familiar to returning birds. Landscape also has its own distinctive 'infrasounds' associated with prominent features. Some now seem to use motorways as visual clues, and in fact, the warm updraught from such busy highways probably assists them.

It has been suggested that birds tend to rely upon built-in magnetic stimuli to begin with, and then improve at using others as they get older. However, they can probably use them all, whichever is most appropriate at the time. Homing pigeons are known to be able to work out their way home by mentally 'following' the twists and turns of their transport—usually only circling once when released, and then heading straight home. From the earliest times we have used such birds, and even swallows and shearwaters, to reliably carry our own messages. But route memory cannot possibly explain the travels of many other birds.

There are many outstanding examples of migration. In the fall (autumn) of the north-eastern USA, millions of small songbirds and waders/shorebirds head out over the Atlantic for South America. This is the longest sea crossing of any songbird, taking about 80 hours for the 3000mile (4500km) flight, for they know that they will find seasonal tailwinds to aid their flapping flight. Also there will be hardly any predators, unlike on the longer land route via Central America. That narrow strip of land is the favoured routes for millions of raptors, for these birds know that there are no thermals over the sea. They simply spiral up on warm morning winds to soar and glide down to reach the same areas of Central America. World-wide, such birds always prefer the shortest sea crossings, such as Sweden to Denmark, Gibraltar to Morocco, Greece to Turkey, the narrow Red Sea, or south-east Asian islands. Using these routes, raptors, storks and similar birds will funnel down into the Southern Hemisphere by the million each season. It is said that some 3.5 billion birds will be channelled through the Middle East alone at migration time. That is why Israeli jets are so careful to avoid them, for collisions are lethal to both sides. Their careful studies have shown that there are peak times and heights for certain birds, like White Pelicans or Levant Sparrowhawks, even to the time of day. Yet though spring and autumn are predictable peak times, migration actually starts as early as January in such places, and only trickles out in December. No doubt modern climate changes will further affect our birds' movements, which have long fluctuated anyway. Nile Crocodiles still survive in the heart of the vast Sahara Desert, relics of very recent wet times. There are huge river beds clearly visible from space, and in similar deserts world-wide—features resulting from the global flood recorded in Genesis 6:1–8:22 (see final chapters).

Finally, think of the world population of Spectacled Eiders. They choose to travel *north* from their sub-Arctic breeding grounds each autumn! They actually winter out in the ice, keeping large areas of water unfrozen by their sheer presence and movement alone. We shall look further at other individuals and how they use their wings in various inventive ways in the coming chapters.

Courtship and breeding behaviour

Inevitably, many aspects of the wonderful breeding cycle of birds have already been covered. Their very names often declare marvellous nest building abilities: weavers, ovenbirds, tailorbirds, mud-nest builders and woodpeckers, etc. Travels are often for breeding purposes, as are special plumages and songs. As soon as the breeding season is over, birds must start anew, in one way or another. After only a brief time for rest and for shedding worn-out feathers, they must often move on before beginning the whole cycle again. Reproduction is one of the most important and dangerous functions of a bird, as with many other creatures, for it often means exposure and extremely hard work and consumption of energy. This is just one of the many objections to any kind of reproduction actually 'evolving' by random processes. Many huge problems are involved, since any 'mutations' must survive the supposed 'laws' of natural selection (let alone how any 'first' accidental life could chance upon reproduction, anyway!).

Firstly, many birds must display openly or advertise their presence with song to both potential predators and rivals. Secondly, the males will often have to use lots of energy seeing off such rivals or predators by engaging in lengthy songs or flights. The female also requires large energy reserves to produce her eggs. Thirdly, the female (mainly) must sit tight on the nest for long periods, often out in the open, sometimes in large, noticeable colonies. Fourthly, the act of sitting will often mean enforced absence from food gathering and dependence on a mate to provide. Fifthly, both birds might have to forage far and wide for extra food. Finally, having to tend possibly hordes of conspicuous, noisy and rather helpless young birds is very hard work in itself. All these activities open birds up to unwanted prominence and risk of predation. Hence many will be inconspicuous or camouflaged, but others are the exact opposite in dress and behaviour. There will always be many exceptions to our 'rules'.

Chapter 4

Food supply

Food supply is of paramount importance in raising young. As we have seen, birds whose food supplies are cyclical will have fewer young, or sometimes not breed at all. Others, like crossbills that rely upon conifer seeds, will breed more successfully in 'good cone years'. Golden Eagles once more figure in this work for sound biological and biblical reasons: the *'Cain and Abel'* syndrome. As with many large birds, some eagles will often only raise one chick, but lay two eggs (which is not the case for all large birds). The younger or weaker chick will usually be killed by the stronger or older, often because of food shortages, but not always so. Younger and older offspring in the Bible also have great significance. God is continually teaching us something: remember the cries of Job, Solomon and Paul to look to creation for our instruction. Golden Eagles often live in bleak, wild lands where there is less prey, and hunting is frequently 'closed down' by foul weather. By contrast, the Imperial or Booted Eagles of warmer Mediterranean lands often raise two chicks. Climate and food availability are frequently tied together. Yet once again, we see paradoxes: well oxygenated cold waters have more marine life than tropical, contrary to our superficial reasoning. And warm climates have more insects than cold. It seems that the best way is to winter in the warmth and only head into the comparatively colder zones for breeding, and that is what so many migrant birds do. The brief summers of northern lands are also rich in massive insect hatches and plant foods, as needed by the incomers.

That breeding is definitely tied to food supply can be seen most clearly by contrasting birds of cold and warm climates. Many birds of the tropics, where differences between summer and winter are negligible, can breed at any time of the year. Foods are available throughout, although still subject to some seasonal variation. Fruits and seeds, insects or marine life like krill or sardines appear mainly at specific times. This affects the breeding of many birds, not just tropical species. Many birds become cyclical nomads, following the hatches of insects or ripening of seeds and fruits. Weaverbird 'cities' can spring up rapidly in direct response to such crops—or our grain crops.

The most famous examples are the migratory birds that specifically come north, then return south, to bask in a continual insect-rich summer.

We have already mentioned many of them, and how their annual return is eagerly awaited by us in the colder north. Even if it only spends about four or five months with us, where a bird breeds is regarded as its home. Barn Swallows are important 'harbingers of spring' as well as being extremely beautiful blue and cream creations flickering through the skies and exciting our hearts, which is why their falling numbers doubly concerns us. Undoubtedly the widening Sahara and Sahel deserts and dwindling oases are badly affecting them, resulting in fewer nests each year in north-west Europe. Old farm buildings are being demolished or 'over-tidied', and new European Union legislation demands the destruction of their nests in animal barns. Their future does not look good, but they will survive and gradually adapt their routes around the desert, probably. Declining numbers of flying insects are also being blamed for their comparative scarcity.

Territory

Space is the first requirement for breeding, although many migratory birds will display, and even mate, well before they arrive in the north. That is almost certainly because such lands are locked in snow and ice until as late as June, and darkness starts to descend again by September. Females also need to feed en route, to be able to form their energy-draining eggs as soon as possible. Speed is essential for all involved, because the young birds, though not yet born, must be ready to fly south by the end of the brief summer of 'the midnight sun'. Almost twenty-four hours of daylight means life in the fast lane, indeed. Territories allow birds to breed in comparative peace, marshal a suitable feeding area, and probably reduce predation. However, personal space is not always governed by food sources, for sometimes birds will feed outside it. Welsh Manx Shearwaters may defend their nest hole, yet cannot possibly protect fishing grounds all the way to Portugal. Certainly nesting or feeding areas are energetically defended by many birds, whether they are small or large, and from both friend and foe. The odd thing is that some males will defend a display area but not go near the nest area, although this is predictably confined to just a few birds, like Capercaillie and Ruff. Gannets nest so close to each other that almost continuous bickering ensues, and even fights to the death can sometimes occur. One hundred thousand are packed on to one small south-east African island alone. This sort of concentration of birds has even spawned an industry: the harvesting of 'guano', or bird droppings from several southern oceanic islands. Many seabird islands are literally white with a thick carpet of recycled fish waste, rich in nutrient and thus good for fertiliser. Properly managed for both birds and us, it is a sustainable industry.

In their turn, the gannets are reliant upon the annual surge of billions of sardines coming up from the cold southern oceans to breed off Africa. Fur Seals rely upon the young birds for food, dolphins and sharks rely upon the sardines too, as do some whales, and so on. This unbroken, circular chain stretches from sun-enlivened waters rich in microscopic plankton, through sardines, birds, seals, fish and cetaceans to whales, which die and rot, and it all starts again. But the very fact that this complex and obviously designed chain is breaking down means much more than 'evolutionary' extinctions. Remember that evolutionary theory insists death is natural and essential for slow, 'survival of the fittest' development. On the other hand, the fossil record is actually one of rapid, mass deaths resulting from global catastrophes.

Such close breeding both helps and hinders, for it is bound to attract predators. On the plus side, many eyes ensure that attackers are spotted well in advance, and close proximity means safety in numbers. Maturity and seniority ensure the most favoured are settled in the middle of the colony, with the newcomers forced to the dangerous edges. That is where skuas, Arctic Foxes and raptors are most likely to take their prey. It is the same with flocks in flight, and the safety of individuals in large and tight throngs, as discussed in chapter 2. Most seabirds' tiny territories contrast well with the aforementioned Golden Eagles, which each need some 200 sq. m. (500 sq. km.) of Scotland's more barren areas, for example Wester Ross. Once again, food supply is the main criterion, and Peale's Peregrines in north-west America, for instance, can breed relatively close together, perhaps 300ft (90m) apart (Gibraltar's Peregrines are also running out of breeding space, probably because of the excellent food supply: thousands of gulls [2005]). Many birds will tolerate greater concentrations of nests when food is abundant, and sociable birds like weavers can weave massive colonial apartments as well as cities.

Man's protection of birds also results in higher nesting density, provided food is available—our gardens are good examples. Some songbirds may emulate the gannets by defending only the area around their nests, but usually breed alone. Black-necked Grebes deliberately nest among noisy Black-headed Gull colonies, using them for general protection, or at least diversion. Roughly speaking, the further apart birds nest, the safer they will be. The usual caveat is needed here though, for Lapwings seem to need others of their kind around to stimulate breeding. That is one of the reasons their breeding population has plummeted on our UK farmlands, where changed farming practices are the main cause: formerly they bred in good numbers (see chapter 7). The Lapwings were successful as loose colonial nesters, and still vigorously and corporately defend their piece of pasture in some places. Other waders/shorebirds will also threaten even large beasts like cattle that are in danger of trampling their ground nests. Many other birds will at least protect a surrounding area of pasture, wetland, woodland or garden from most comers, especially if they are of the same species, and sometimes viciously. Both European Robins and Kingfishers are far from the friendly little chaps of greeting card fame: they sometimes fight to the death over territory. They will even defend areas outside the breeding season, though the Robin will often be near its breeding patch, and the Kingfisher sometimes away from his, sometimes down by the sea (this depends upon local circumstances). Territories are even defended far away from non-breeding areas, as for instance by some waders on winter estuaries. The Lapwing protects its patch by dive-bombing and the most wonderful skirling calls, which give it one of its other names, the Pee-wit. Not content with that, one particular individual drops in here every winter to spend an inordinate amount of energy chasing others away from his little stretch of estuary mud about 30ft (10m) long. By contrast, as darkness falls it will happily join the rest of the flock of around 2,000–3,000 birds for the security of the roost.

The riverine territories of birds like the common Kingfisher are often defined by a length of waterway alone, as one would expect of fish-eaters. Dippers likewise are easy to log, as they will always fly ahead until they reach the end of their territory, before turning and whizzing back down stream. This is how many birds are surveyed in the spring, by mapping their

Fig. 75: ATLANTIC GANNET COLONY.

breeding areas. Many raptors will display above their fiefdoms in ritualised flights, usually going to the edges to 'fly the boundaries'. Golden Eagles and Northern Harriers are among many that do just that, engaging in exhilarating, rolling and stooping displays designed to impress both neighbours and mate.

Thus the woods and hills are fairly evenly divided up, each territory with its proud 'sky dancing' standard above, in heraldic display. Short-eared Owls applaud themselves by wing-clapping before they have even finished their fine performances above the few remaining heather moors or quiet hills. Woodcocks are even stranger, alternately burping and squeaking as they fly around their favoured woods at dusk, tightly and accurately turning at angled corners as if on an invisible leash.

Display

For most birds, display is a vital part of courtship and protection of territory, as has already been mentioned. Usually, it is the male that has the most colourful dress and leads the way, with either dress or song, though good singers are often the dullest birds that use their colours for camouflage—that master singer, the Eurasian Skylark, otherwise blends in well with the grasses. There are exceptions to dominant males too; the brighter female phalaropes, for example, supervise the whole business as soon as arriving in the north. This leaves the (slightly) duller males to do the entire job of sitting and rearing, while she goes off to entice other males, and makes the most noise. Such females are described as *polyandrous*, like the jacanas that also mate with several males. There are rather complicated degrees of polygamy, polyandry and promiscuity within the minority of birds, with different proportions of display, mating and nest building by both sexes involved. Up to eight 'harem' Rheas lay in the same male's nest, one after the other, and then go off and leave all brooding and rearing to the male. Pheasants, and some other gamebirds, are different again, with the females doing everything alone except for briefly meeting and mating with a male. Polygamy is only practised by a minority of male birds, such as the Pied Flycatcher who establishes his first nest and female on eggs, and then goes off to mate with one, or even two other females, all of whom need constantly feeding, including the chicks. He can overdo things, sadly resulting in some nests failing, or at least some of the chicks. Then again, nest failure can also be attributed to several other factors like food scarcity, adverse weather, predation or disturbance.

The vast majority of birds, some 95 per cent, are in normal pair bonds, and even mate for life, like Mute Swans, Brent Geese or many large raptors. Generally such birds will divide breeding duties between male and female fairly evenly. The male will often sing or display vigorously, continue to chase off rivals and help build the nest. He will often also take over sitting duties when required. The female has equally hard work to do, energy-wise, producing eggs and constructing, or helping to build, the nest, then sitting tight for long periods on the eggs and young. Once again, these duties vary from bird to bird. Females seem to do most of the sitting, males most of the flash and fighting. In some birds, the sexes separate after breeding, sometimes then arguing over feeding areas. The young of birds like our Kingfisher and Grey Heron soon become rivals for fishing space themselves, and will be driven off into marginal territories at the summer's

Fig. 76: GOLDEN EAGLE 'GOLDEN HEART' DISPLAY, OR STOOP.

end. Others are much more dependent, like the young Golden Eagles, Peregrine Falcons and wildfowl that stay with their parents almost until next season. Then woe betide any who hang around, for they risk a severe beating! The first year is a crucial time for many birds out to make their way in the wide world, and causalities are high, roughly speaking between 33 per cent for large, and 60 per cent for smaller broods.

Migration and territory

Migratory males especially, will often arrive at the nesting areas, explore them and be singing by the time the females turn up. Resident birds might have defended their territories all winter, even from the previous August in the case of the Eurasian Robin. It is usually the male who chooses the nest area, even if a female has defended an adjacent patch or garden. So 'your' garden Robin might well be a composite bird. Birds will just not take the first mate that comes along either, as we saw with the Sedge Warblers that choose the best and most distant genes by an individual male's song. Males will often advertise from their choice nest site, or half-built nest, by song or ritualised display to many passing females. Several males can band together to form mutual display grounds, or '*leks*', already mentioned in reference to birds as varied as jungle manikins to Sage Grouse of the wide-open American plains. These last perform the most extraordinary, upright 'drumming' or whirring of their wings that can be heard over considerable distances.

Fig. 77: RUFFED GROUSE 'DRUMMING' DISLAY.

Seniority is often paramount, and even colour in certain birds—Reeves prefer darker black and orange males to paler-collared Ruffs (Ruffs and Reeves are the males and females of the same Eurasian wader species, *Philomachus pugnax*). *Lekking* is male display at its most exotic and manic—prancing, dancing and flashing gorgeously coloured feathers, fans, crests and lyre tails, plus booming, drumming, huffing, puffing, bubbling, popping, gurgling, whirring and rattling wings and tails—you name it, they do it. The quietly coloured females of many do not even bother to be present sometimes, and will often turn up later and usually go for the most obvious, centrally placed and experienced player. Males of some jungle species may never manage to mate: all that exertion for nothing. Some birds of paradise, along with other forest dwellers, are the commonest lekkers, flaunting their amazing plumes in a dazzling variety of ways and calling excitedly.

Song is not important to them but, as with many other forest birds, calls must be loud and penetrating.

This is reflected in one of the North's most famed songsters, the Nightingale, who usually pours forth his liquid cadences from deep cover. He too shivers his wings, but in no way approaches the acrobatic antics of the paradise bird, nor its glittering hues. He does have warm brown plumage and a smart, reddish tail, but really stands and falls on that song, as do the Blackcap's or Garden Warbler's rather similar songs, from respectively higher and lower in the trees. Other birds will sing loudly from very prominent perches, exemplified by the 'Stormcock' or Mistle Thrush who delights in the tops of the tallest trees, even in gales, hence its old English name. Mockingbirds and Blackbirds also advertise their presence clearly, while the complete opposite is provided by birds like the Corncrake. This bird is the finest of stealthy movers and a considerable ventriloquist. I remember stalking one by its call until I was directly above it, only to see it from the corner of my eye some way to the left, and sometimes it can sound like more than one bird. The interesting thing is that birds know exactly who is singing and whether they are regular neighbours or new rivals: energy is not wasted checking out every songster.

Birds that live and nest in the open have other strategies, such as song flights or energetic displays. Many *Sylvia* (scrub) warblers like the Whitethroat launch themselves from the tops of low bushes or gorse in swooping song flights, pouring out their scratchy songs before plummeting back to earth. This is a popular form of display, also used by larks and pipits in many countries, often ending in 'parachuting' down with wings and tail cocked upwards.

African Whydah Birds take this form of flag waving to extraordinary degrees, using their long, black fluttering tails as they jerk and hover above the long grasses. Perhaps the strangest is the Little Bustard, which jumps up and down vertically while puffing out its black

Fig. 78: RAGGIANA BIRD OF PARADISE DISPLAY.

throat like some blustering little sergeant-major. This will be one of the few chances we have to see this rather uncommon denizen of the few remaining Spanish and other European steppes, which is not the case with his larger cousin. Great Bustards are large, turkey-sized birds, especially when turned 'inside out'. Males do this to attract the smaller females, by fluffing out most of their feathers at the most extraordinary angles, and retracting their head back into them.

Song is also important in separating very similar species. Chiff-Chaff and Willow Warbler are notoriously difficult to distinguish in the field—until they begin to sing. Perhaps 'call' would be more appropriate, for only the Willow Warbler really sings, while the Chiff-Chaff merely repeats its name over and over. Arctic and Common Terns are likewise very close 'kissing-cousins', with only subtle plumage differences to our eye. Their voices sometimes are alike, too. I think the clearest difference is in the Common Tern's more drawn out, low 'kreeerrrrrrrrrrrrr' call. It is also typical of birds that use presents of food during display to strengthen pair bonds and demonstrate hunting abilities.

Fig. 79: MEADOW PIPIT 'PARACHUTE' DISPLAY; and below, AFRICAN WHYDAH BIRD FLUTTERING DISPLAY (NOT TO SCALE).

Food presentation, or bowing and offering fish headfirst, is just the thing for many terns and other seabirds, as it is for kingfishers. Bee-eaters and

Fig. 80: GREAT BUSTARD, TURNING ITSELF 'INSIDE OUT' IN DISPLAY.

other insectivores offer large, crunchy dragonflies and the like to their loved ones. Raptors go for mammals and birds, while a female Barn Owl likes nothing better than a nice, juicy rat. This sort of behaviour does not necessarily cease at egg laying, as many birds have to supply their mates and young with food until well after the juveniles leave the nest. In fact, male Eurasian Sparrowhawks are often considerably smaller than both their mate and young, and are in actual danger from them. Often they must whip in and out very rapidly with the grub, or not even approach the nest tree at all, but arrange a nearby pick-up point with the female. Other raptors indulge in tricky '*food-passes*' while in the air. A male Marsh Harrier will approach with prey dangling from his talons, call the female off the nest and then drop the food to her. She will often be upside down at this point, so perfect timing is needed. That sort of food pass is also seen in display, even at great speed. I have watched Peregrines expertly exchange a

Fig. 81: ARCTIC TERNS IN TYPICAL 'FOOD BEGGING' DISPLAY DURING COURTSHIP.

Fig. 82: MARSH HARRIERS FOOD PASS, MALE ABOVE.

dead Redshank in very rapid, low level flight with barely a pause by either bird.

We might not have many brightly coloured birds with dazzling advertisements here in the North, but we can still watch some impressive displays. Three of the four divers/loons might occasionally perform while still wintering just offshore of the English mainland, but for the full wonder we must go to the central and northern Scottish lochs, or the Hebrides and Shetland Isles. North Americans are more fortunate, with Common Loons still to be found on many lakes, dancing, wailing and singing out those wonderful tremolo cries. Male and female Red-throated Divers are also typical, darting and diving about the loch

Fig. 83: RED-THROATED DIVERS/LOONS, 'PORPOISING' DISPLAY.

Fig. 84: PART OF THE WESTERN GREBE'S DISPLAY.

surface, 'porpoising' or rearing up with open wings, regularly giving vent to one of the bird world's most beautiful skirling cries. They often sound like a natural part of the keening Scottish winds. Golden Eagles might only perform their wonderful 'golden heart' display in those same lonely glens, but many can watch Red-tailed Buzzards and other raptors do similar displays in various habitats. This distinctive rising and falling flight is typical raptor display, stooping on closed wings only to pitch up again, and is also used for warning rivals. Undoubtedly it proclaims both their mastery of the air and potential hunting prowess.

The eye-catching display of the Great-crested Grebe is another delightful reminder that spring is here, though not quite as mad as the upright race across the water of its American cousin, the Western Grebe.

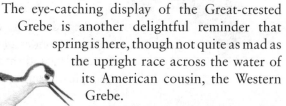

Great-crested Grebes are more sedate and elegant in their ritualised movements, bowing, crouching with head plumes spread, head turning, until finally rearing up together and presenting gifts of waterweed to each other to be used for the nest.

Copulation usually follows any display, and is very brief compared to the length or frequency of many displays. I

Fig. 85: BLACK WINGED STILTS MATING.

suppose that is a good thing for Eurasian Swifts, who often do it on the wing at great speed! Or for flamingos on stilts perched precariously atop

Fig. 86: GREATER FLAMINGOS 'FLAMENCO' DISPLAY.

each other, all legs, necks and wavering wings. Black-winged Stilts and Greater Flamingos do manage to retain their dignity though, by preceding the balancing act with elegant *'flamenco'* gestures (the Spanish dance was actually inspired and named after the flamingo display).

Mating may take place several times in many species and consist of little more than quick joining of the male 'cloaca' and female vagina together to pass the sperm, tails twisted aside. Most males will stand or sit astride the female and grasp her neck or head feathers in their bill during the act, whether on land or water. Many then perform ritualised preening of their back feathers, almost like modestly looking away. This is included under *'displacement activity'*, where birds take out their 'emotion' or aggression by various actions. Looking away and thus avoiding eye contact is the commonest, often accompanied by preening of the back or rear feathers. The edge of territories is a good place to observe this, where rival birds like coots or cranes might meet and posture to each other. It might also involve tossing up bits of earth or sods, as some creatures paw the earth and threaten, and often that is all that is needed. Strangely enough, Secretary Birds have been observed dancing like cranes and tossing up sods most acrobatically—but with no other birds visible on the open African plains: could they actually be enjoying themselves!?

The dancing of cranes is a global phenomenon of great wonder, especially celebrated in Oriental art. The black and white Manchurian Crane's ballet, performed against snowy Japanese landscapes, is an especially beautiful example. Cranes are tall, elegant birds widespread in the world, but often threatened, needing wide-open, marshy spaces to survive.

Fig. 87a: MANCHURIAN CRANES 'DANCING' DISPLAY.

Palm Cockatoos cleverly drum with sticks on resonant logs to get their mates' attention, but display in some birds is not always recognised by us, as it is so minimal. It can also be spread over a long period, and therefore be much more gradual, among resident pairs. Again, migratory birds need speed. Some will appease their mates by '*food-begging*' like young birds, crouching, shivering their wings and calling softly. There is often a fine line between attraction and aggression, as we saw with some sparrowhawks. This is probably

Fig. 87b: COMMON SNIPE DIVING DISPLAY WITH OUTER TAIL FEATHERS EXTENDED.

tied to the need for constant *'pair bonding'* among birds that do not stay together outside the nesting season. Gannets continue to 'sky point' together throughout nesting, while many heron-types will often rustle their bustles when they return to the nest. Many herons and egrets have long back feathers to shake and fan like delicate lacy capes, a fact that almost led to their downfall and the rise of the modern conservation movement (see chapter 7). White Storks certainly like to advertise their bonds by noisily clattering their beaks together and bending backwards, for all to see. Similar methods are used by all manner of gulls, or wildfowl like Eider and Long-tailed Ducks (USA: 'Old Squaws'). Throwing back their handsome heads, they cry out an ascending 'whoo-whoo-whoo-whoooo', while the smaller Goldeneye also flicks water by kicking out his yellow feet behind him. Boobies slowly dance and waggle their brightly coloured feet, albatrosses likewise comically bob and posture—all very different to the Common Snipe and his vibrating tail. He extends his two, specially twisted

Fig. 88: BOWERBIRDS' NESTS. a: SATIN BOWERBIRD WITH HIS COLLECTION OF BLUE OBJECTS. b: VOGELKOP GARDENER'S TENT-LIKE NEST, and COLLECTION OF REDDISH ARTICLES.

outer tail feathers while dropping earthwards at great speed, and produces a wonderful 'bleating' sound, so typical of our remaining wet pastures and hills.

Finally, there are other birds that not only build perhaps the most amazing nests of all, but also deliberately adorn them with all manner of gewgaws: the amazing Australasian Bowerbirds. Just look at some of their nests, which are actual thatched buildings with supports, arching tunnels or weird tower sculptures as well made as many human dwellings. Not content with that, all manner of decorations—coloured berries, beetle cases, leaves, fungi, twigs, shells, even glass, bottle caps and plastic bits—are gathered by the males after they have constructed their 'bowers', to further entice the female in for mating. He will frequently rearrange his colourful treasures into more aesthetic or light-catching arrangements, adding or taking away blooming flowers and the like with considerable artistic flair. And if he needed anything else, he can then paint and plaster the interior using a twig brush and coloured vegetable or charcoal pastes! Such designs are constantly developing and rapidly changing: obviously not the outcome of slow, blind, 'evolutionary' processes.

Nests and eggs

D isplay can also consist of presenting nest material to the mate, or perching atop half-finished nests, as some male weavers do. Raptors and various corvids bring in *branches* for their large homes, often, like the Osprey, deliberately breaking off dead limbs in flight. Now, that's also rather dangerous. This could well be for an old, traditional nest, some eventually becoming so large as to cause the tree to collapse. One Bald Eagle nest in Ohio weighed two tons!

Africa's Hammerkop stork also builds a huge domed stick nest in trees, strengthening it with mud or dung. Other birds can move into its lower reaches, a not uncommon feature of such large nests. Birds might even use someone else's old nest, as Peregrines use Ravens' which nest earlier in the year, or a Wood Sandpiper in an old thrush's nest. Long-eared Owls have a sometimes fatal tendency to use an old Carrion Crow's—for gamekeepers will often mistakenly shoot them out. Almost anything that can be used for a nest will be used, whatever its colour or consistency, although mainly local and natural components are preferred by most. Of course, the easiest way is not to bother building at all and simply parasitise others, as the cuckoos and cowbirds do. The very simplest are often just *scrapes* in the ground, natural rock *ledges and caves*, or *tree or ground holes*. Many seabirds like terns and gulls employ the first, cliff-nesting auks and some raptors the second, while holes are favourite for many birds from Bank Swallows/Sand Martins to bee-eaters. If holes are not available, the birds will dig them, sometimes deep underground. Our Kingfisher's nest tunnel might well be 3ft (1m) deep into a soft riverbank, and this offers constant temperatures and safety from most predators.

Snakes are not a problem for Eurasian Kingfishers, but may be for other tunnelling birds such as Africa's Carmine Bee-eaters, and the like. The New Zealand Kiwi's burrows can penetrate as deeply as 12ft (3.5m).

When there is material handy, birds like divers/loons will use it, but a Ringed Plover's best defence is its beautiful eggs, speckled and splashed like seashore sand and pebbles. Little more than a few stones will be arranged around the scrape.

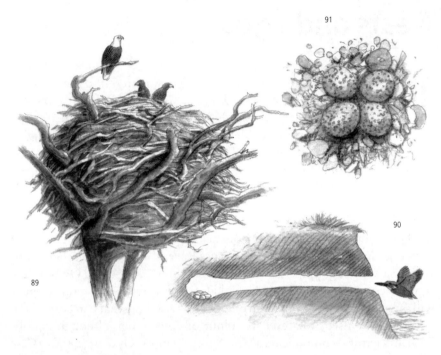

Fig. 89: LARGE BALD EAGLE NEST.
Fig. 90: KINGFISHER BURROW.
Fig. 90: RINGED PLOVER 'SCRAPE'.

Camouflage is the norm for many birds that nest out in the open, or they simply cover their eggs when they leave the nest. This is also useful for maintaining temperature. We have already lauded that absolute master of *burying* eggs, the Mallee-fowl of Australia. He uses his strong feet to constantly adjust the huge mounds of earth or sand covering the eggs, then a thermometer bill to check the exact temperature. This does not mean that they or most of their cousins can then go off gallivanting, in fact the very opposite, for constant attendance is needed to ensure the eggs hatch. Because the female regularly lays eggs, the male might have to nest-sit for up to eleven months per year! Brush Turkeys are close relatives who use vegetation piles instead of earth, while others successfully gauge the ambient temperature of rock crevices or volcanic soils and can then abandon the process completely. Now, there are sometimes fatalities in the little chicks digging their way out of such mounds, but hole-nesting birds generally have a significantly higher fledging rate than conventional nesters. Some tropical shorebirds bury their eggs for short periods, especially in searing midday sun.

Many waterbirds, globally, simply reach out and gradually build up a pile of *water plants*, as grebes, swans and coots do. This often has the advantage of floating and thereby adjusting to fluctuating water levels, though it will usually be attached to some vegetation. Surrounding reeds and rushes are another very useful living base for a nest. Some are strong enough for bitterns and the like to both perch on and break off, or down, and weave together. Colonies of heron-types are commonly found in reed beds or trees growing among them, or nearby. The nests naturally need to become more complex and stronger as they are placed higher up in the reeds or trees. Rails too, use waterside vegetation for their fairly simple cup nests, as do many ground nesters from Reed Buntings to Cetti's Warblers. Cormorants too, like both reeds and trees, or are equally at home on piles of old seaweed on rocky seaside slopes, or islands. Other waterbirds like penguins and pelicans might use little more than a scrape in the ground, or add anything from a few stones to a large pile of vegetation, the method used by the Dalmatian Pelican. King Penguins have also been commended, for their snug, portable, heated *'foot-nests'*, absolutely essential for the harshest environment on earth.

Flamingos must build little *mud cups* in their shallow salty lagoons to raise the nest level and to keep their wonderfully ridiculous legs and pink plumes unclogged and clean. Sadly, the high alkalinity of the African lakes in which Lesser Flamingos live will sometimes cause the build-up of heavy soda 'anklets' on the legs of the smallest chicks, and they will be doomed to die. Such birds also require fresh water nearby, for drinking.

Grasses must be one of the commonest and best materials available, dry or living, for they already grow in the most widespread manner and are easy to pluck and mould. As already mentioned, weavers are master builders, and the illustration below shows one of the finest of their gourd, bottle and tubular, *hanging nests*.

Fig. 92: EMPEROR PENGUIN'S 'FOOT NEST'.

Fig. 93: CASSINS WEAVER NEST

Fig. 94: AFRICAN PENDULINE TIT'S NEST, WITH ARROWED CAPTIONS. A: FALSE NEST. B: REAL NEST AND ENTRANCE.

Fig. 95: BLACKBIRD'S NEST.

Fig. 96: 'BAKED' MUD NEST OF THE RUFOUS OVENBIRD, OR HORNERO, WITH SIDE REMOVED.

Fig. 97: TAILOR BIRD and SEWN LEAF NEST.

What makes them even more spectacular is the knowledge that they must each learn this remarkable grass-weaving craft with their bill, and quickly, or they would die out—again, no time for blind evolution and endless mistakes. A weaver colony may consist of thousands of nests swinging from a grove of trees, or be a massive 'thatched' tree structure. Some thornbills also build such communal 'flatlet' nests, but from twigs, and never on the huge scale of the sociable Weaver. Their nests have superb warmth retention in desert areas where temperatures may plunge below freezing at night. Oropendolas of South America do not have that problem, and their hanging nests are nothing like as neatly woven as a weaver's, but their form also raises a question. These long, bag-like structures just happen to perfectly imitate the aggressive wasps' nests in their midst, yet protect the birds from them. How could random and blind genetic mistakes possibly programme a bird to persist with such a foolhardy task, until they were tolerated? There just has to be strong elements of deliberate planning in there from the beginning.

Pipits and larks often use little more than grass, and simply burrow into the base of tufts and make a snug cave, which is then lined with finer materials. Warblers' nests are not that dissimilar, growing in complexity as they ascend higher in the undergrowth. Other birds add dry leaves, lichens, mosses and then bind them together with *spiders' webs*—like Eurasian Chaffinches, goldfinches, Goldcrest/Kinglets and Winter Wrens. Birds living deeper in the forest typically use lesser amounts of grasses, because they are not often available. Their nests can be either beautifully shaped cups, or domes with a side entrance. Hummingbirds and orioles make some of the daintiest, little more than purses of tiny lichens and mosses strung together with spiders' webs and slung in forks. That sort of nest is often artfully disguised with lichens. The Long-tailed Tit produces one of the finest, although its long tail will have to be bent to fit in, so it is easy to spot one that has recently left the nest. Many of these birds will use their natural body form to shape the internal cup or dome of the nest, slowly twirling round and round in it as they add feathers, hairs, fur, downy seed heads and the like. The interior will often be as dense as man-made felt, and even as strong. The nests of the Eurasian Penduline Tit are tough enough to end up as children's slippers! Their African cousins build a similar gourd-like nest, but add a false door and a shallow cup to deceive exploring snakes. The false door even has a welcoming porch above it—but the real door is actually in the porch lid, and carefully closed and flattened to disguise it each time the bird leaves.

The real nest cup is deep inside the beautifully woven bag: it is absolutely impossible to explain such ingenuity away as 'fortuitous evolutionary accidents'! The aforementioned and incredible constructions of Bowerbirds come into the same category. Lyrebirds, dippers and coucals are among others with much simpler domed nests and side entrances, yet still discreet, safe and snug. Dippers, and some swifts, will also nest behind waterfalls for additional security.

Mud is another common and natural substance used, from the waterproof lining of a Song Thrush or Blackbird's twig nest to the amazing Ovenbirds of South America. This is one of the most complex structures of any bird, and can take up to nine months to build. The Ovenbird was so named because the nest resembled an old Dutch Oven, and is often constructed from mud pellets alone left to harden in the sun. It even has a curving internal passage and separate nest chamber.

Some, like the Mudnest Builders of Australasia will also use mud alone, or add varying amounts of other plant materials with it. They build high cups or bowls balanced upon horizontal branches, like the striking black and white Magpie-larks. Even more remarkable are the mud structures stuck to rock walls, buildings, caves or under bridges by several swifts, swallows and martins. Here, mud is mixed with differing proportions of saliva and old plant debris to form lasting 'concrete' structures. They range from the 'simple' half cups of House Martins, through 'mud and debris' nests of Barn Swallows, upside-down bottle-shaped chambers of Red-rumped Swallows, the 'saliva and debris' cups of the Little Swift, and climax in the pure *saliva hammocks* of the Edible Swiftlet (of 'bird's nest soup' fame). One cave swift takes invention and protection one step further, by nesting in sea cliff caves whose entrances might be submerged during storms: yet they survive.

Such nests are quite a long way from the thin, minimal *platforms* of twigs used by many of the pigeon family, sometimes with the eggs clearly visible from below. Eurasian Magpies build very distinctive domed and spiky nests of thin branches, as if sensing their unpopularity. Several birds utilise spiders' webs to bind all these varied materials together, as it is so incredibly strong and common. Some turn to discarded string. They cannot, though, match the tailorbirds or cisticolas of southern Asia and Australia, which expertly *sew* their nests together from living leaves. Adjacent leaves will firstly have neat holes punched along matching sides, then be expertly sewn together with plant fibres. The nest is then built inside this 'cone', and naturally begs the question: how could this possibly 'evolve' without pre-coded instructions?

Scrambled eggs beneath failed nests will certainly appeal to predators, but hardly add to the bird's chances of survival.

Corvids, as well as bowerbirds, are noted for an eye for bright, shiny things, and various silver items and valuables have turned up in European Jackdaws' nests. Most are quite happy with silver paper and the like, but one Bombay crow's nest contained many gold spectacle frames, stolen from a jeweller's open window! Golf balls, plastic bags, fishing net, wire and bottles all find their way into bird's homes, and doubtless other strange items, too.

Hole nesters are also fairly common in the bird world, using everything from already existing burrows to custom-made or customised chambers and tunnels. They must be very welcome to birds often nesting away from any concealing vegetation. Rabbit burrows are popular with many northern seabirds from shearwaters to puffins, and Eurasian Shelducks and Little Owls will also use them. This sometimes leads to disaster for seabirds like Atlantic Puffins, when Brown Rats move in. Certain Welsh islands have had to be cleared of rats, which have escaped from shipwrecks, by conservation bodies, in order to ensure the return of Puffins. (Ironically, the Black Rat is now also rare, so is itself conserved on a nearby island.) Smaller birds also, like the Northern and other Wheatears, will use rodents' burrows or even dig their own. In the Americas, that Little Owl look-alike, the Burrowing Owl, will dig in desert, spare lot or the middle of a highway roundabout, alike. Long legs, lots of loose earth and flying insects make this a successful bird. The last two conditions also go for *Coraciiformes* like kingfishers, bee-eaters, todys and motmots. Others of the order such as rollers, hoopoes, and hornbills prefer tree holes, while some can also dig into termite mounds. Hornbills are not the only birds to customise the size of a tree hole with mud to fit, even if the male is the only one that cements his mate in for the duration! Eurasian Nuthatches often customise theirs, while Rock Nuthatches stick neat, bottleneck mud 'porches' onto the rock clefts they nest in. Unadorned tree holes are favoured by many woodpeckers, whether or not they have hammered them out themselves. Many species of birds as diverse as ducks, falcons, owls, parrots, bluebirds, tits, flycatchers and redstarts can all use tree holes, with or without linings. With the advent of our tree-felling and over-tidy society, many of these birds have readily taken to our nest boxes. New conifer plantations are also supplied with boxes (also for bats and Red Squirrels), because young, thin and resinous trees are not usually suitable for burrowing into.

Of the many birds that *ground nest*, either with or without materials, nightjars and woodcocks are special because of absolutely superb camouflage. Their plumage seems woven of dead bracken fronds and old, dry leaves and grasses like some miraculous fairy robe, thus rendering them nearly invisible. Many female ducks, gamebirds and waders also blend into their dried vegetation nests very well, with their subtle buffs, creams, chevrons and streaks. Purple Sandpipers are quite uniformly dark birds in the winter when they hop about our rocks, but shift to a more dappled, rusty and pale-edged plumage in summer. Sanderling and Dunlin likewise change, and when crouched upon their nests blend well into the masses of mosses, lichens and dwarf plants and flowers of those sub-Arctic spaces on the tundra.

Finally, surely the strangest nest of all belongs to the lovely, snow-white White or Fairy Tern (*Gygis alba*) of many tropical coasts and isles. She lays her single egg on *bare branches* with only the slightest hollow, or in the forks of branches, the pinnacles of rocks or even on the narrow tops of bird reserve signs!

How they survive at all is miraculous, but then the chick must also sit out, or should I say balance out, its time there, yet they too are successful and widespread. Several tree-nesting swifts at least *glue* their eggs to the often-vertical palm fronds.

Nests are also useful out of season when they can be used for *roosting*. Winter Wrens do that, often communally—up to fifty-six have been found in one UK nest alone! Once again we lag behind in invention, this time of strong, warm, stretchy materials woven only from mosses and the like.

The nest must both protect and keep the chicks warm enough, especially in our cold north. The opposite problem is overheating, and many tropical birds protect their eggs by burying them or bringing in water on their dense breast feathers, or in their crops, to provide cooling. Brooding sub-Arctic birds can be covered in snow, or drenched with rain. Disturbing birds at the nest should always be avoided, because bad weather can be fatal for many eggs and chicks. Most females have special bare areas of bright pink skin beneath the breast feathers, called *brood patches,* to warm the eggs. Otherwise identical pairs of birds can often be sexed using these patches: the males do not usually have them. (This might be where the medieval idea of the 'pious pelican' feeding young its own blood came from. It also speaks of the age-old biblical understanding of Christ's blood shed for our sins.) Another wonderful nest temperature regulatory system is used by birds like the Mourning Wheatear of Middle-Eastern deserts. He places specially selected flat stones at the nest entrance, which function as solar panels to store the sun's heat during the day, and then slowly release it during cold nights. This can only be another of God's wonderful design features.

Birds must greatly increase the size of their reproductive organs before breeding, especially females, as they shrink considerably for the rest of the year. Weight saving is always important for flying creatures, especially when travelling long distances with extra fuel in the form of fat. Hence the eggs are produced individually and laid before the next one begins to form in the ovary. In some rarer cases (petrels and turkeys), fertile eggs can be produced up to two months after mating, though most are produced quickly, if infertility is to be avoided. Further mechanisms allow the eggs to remain in some sort of stasis until all are laid, when brooding can commence. Birds that lay many eggs, like Ostriches or partridges, utilise this, but the chicks of Barn Owls or Northern Harriers are staggered in age. This does not seem to affect their chances of survival, although the smallest will often be the one to miss out, should food become scarce. Most birds conscientiously feed all their chicks in succession; while with others it is 'first come, first served'.

Eggs

The *shelled egg* is yet another superb piece of design, a marvellous, very complex and self-sufficient bio-system for protected development. Some reptiles, like crocodiles, snakes (and dinosaurs), also lay them, though they are usually leathery and not as sophisticated, and the vast majority of

Fig. 98: FAIRY, OR WHITE TERN 'NEST'!

reptiles do not tend their young at all. As with the development of any life-form, the process is absolutely miraculous, from the tiniest egg and sperm to the young and adult. Everything needed is either microscopically pre-programmed into the fertilised ovum, or provided by the adults and assembled into that most perfect nursery, the egg. Its clever contents and shape assure nutrition, water, temperature control, and allow for limited movement and shock protection. The outer shell is a complex structure of three parts: external *cuticle*, chalky *testa*, and inner *membranes,* which are respectively attached to either the testa, or the albumen inside. This allows a vital air space at one end, which also seemingly condenses and saves water. The porous shell allows two-way exchanges of gases, or breathing, yet prevents excessive absorption of water. Most of the egg consists of *albumen,* a viscous, watery, white protein that surrounds the *yolk* and prevents drying out.

It also has bactericidal properties and provides further nutrition. Most

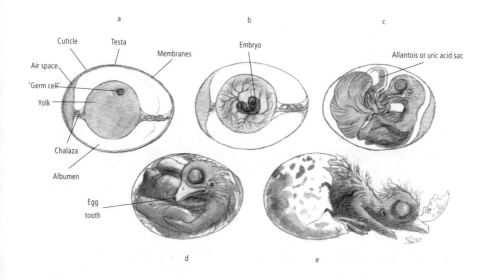

Fig. 99: DEVELOPMENT OF A TYPICAL SONGBIRD'S EGG. A: NEW LAID, SHOWING 'GERM CELL'. B: ABOUT SIX DAYS, SHOWING EMBRYO. C: ABOUT TWELVE DAYS, ABSORBING YOLK. D AND E: FULLY DEVELOPED, THEN HATCHING, ABOUT FOURTEEN DAYS.

of us are familiar with the *yolk*, a yellow ball of fat globules in an incredibly thin yet strong membrane, attached at both ends to the shell by thin, twisted ligaments *(chalazae)*. They ensure that the main part of the yolk, the early embryo, remains uppermost when the bird regularly turns the egg. Progress is rapid after laying, with a white spot of *blastoderm or 'germ cells'* appearing within a few hours. This early embryo consist of three layers that will form all the necessary organs and limbs, and progress will then temporarily cease in those birds where brooding does not commence until all the eggs are laid. Within seventy-two hours a large headed embryo with four limb buds is in place, well supplied with blood vessels from the yoke and beyond. Spine, head and eyes develop first and by seven days the head will be approximately half of the body size. A ten-day embryo will be very well developed and recognisable, with the first feathers appearing. All this time the yolk is rapidly shrinking and a special waste sac of solid uric acid is forming (the *'allantois'*).

Precocial and altricial

From now on, maturation depends upon whether the chick is *'precocial'* or *'altricial'*. *Precocial* chicks develop within the egg longer because they are almost completely independent at birth. Many, but not all, water and gamebirds are precocial, and hatch as beautifully camouflaged fluffy chicks able to run, swim and feed themselves as soon as the down dries.

Altricial young are nearly always hatched as blind and helpless (as illustrated) and need to stay in their well-made nests for weeks—like the majority of birds, the songbirds. There are the usual exceptions, as various seabirds or herons are semi-precocial or semi-altricial. Water and carbon dioxide are steadily lost through the shell, and the bird becomes so large that it must change position and curl up lengthways, as illustrated. Its increasingly high metabolism rate makes carbon dioxide loss more difficult, so it must break into the air space and commence air breathing. 'Pipping' of the egg is the next and final act, where the egg-tooth, or *'caruncle'*, on the end of the beak starts to hammer upwards at the shell. A pheasant chick will take about thirty-three minutes to escape, from its first pipping. This growth and escape has been described as one of *'the most impressive of biological phenomena'*, especially as the chick is, by now, so cramped and tightly curled up, with its head bent backwards. In addition to absorbing the yoke, the chick has been taking calcium from the shell for its bones, thus weakening it and assisting its exit. This is clearly a beautifully balanced and well-designed system, with no room for error. We only have to look at the disastrous mutations that produced egg-shell thinning in poisoned raptors during our 'Silent Spring', to realise that.[1] Other genetic faults result in twisted beaks and limbs, or complete wingless-

Fig. 100: 'PRECOCIAL' YOUNG: LAPWING CHICK.

ness: there is never improvement as evolutionists must imagine. The young bird has already been making 'cheeping' sounds to communicate with the outside world, and also a mysterious clicking. This is probably connected with respiration, and continues for some short time after hatching. Yet it is not found in altricial birds that do not hatch out of their eggs synchronously, so is possibly also related to communication.

Incubation varies from only eleven days in some passerines, to eighty days in kiwis and the Royal Albatross. Additionally, fledging and flight might take 115 days for large raptors like the Griffon Vulture, and up to nine months for the biggest albatross. Such giant birds might only breed once every two years. Larger birds also usually lay larger eggs to match their longer brooding periods. Precocial eggs will usually be larger, too, but incubating times are also dependent upon whether or not birds nest out in the open, and they tend to have shorter brooding times for safety. Hole or cavity nesters tend to have longer nest development for the same reason, since it is then easier to guard from predators. Some brood parasites must partially incubate the egg within their own bodies before laying, so that their own egg hatches first and is best developed. This is important for the European Cuckoo, whose single chick then must drive out the legitimate youngsters, even though it is blind. Honeyguide chicks have a vicious pincer-type bill to begin with, used for killing the host's chicks. Strangely enough, many other brood parasites' chicks, like the Great-spotted Cuckoo, happily grow up with their host's young without any discernible problem, and removal of such brood parasites' eggs does not increase the host's breeding success. Matching the egg of the host does not matter for parasites like American cowbirds, but it does matter to the Common Cuckoo, for any bad copies are liable to be ejected by the host. Sadly, such Reed Warbler or Meadow Pipit hosts will not question when that similar egg develops into a single voracious monster, looking nothing like themselves: some will even have to stand on top of the huge young cuckoo to feed it. African widowbird young not only imitate their host finch's chicks, but also have the precise throat spots that stimulate the host adult to feed it!

Many species, like the White-rumped Swiftlet of Australasia, will use its first brood youngsters to help incubate the second brood. The total number of broods will depend upon food and climate. Even in our northern summer, many smaller songbirds like Barn Swallows can often have two or even three broods. UK Stock Doves are exceptional in having up to five sets per year in the few areas where a long seasonal availability of seeds and grain still remains.

Our largest bird group, the passerines, tends both to lay the smallest eggs and require the longest time in the nest. Some large raptors lay large eggs and yet also need to spend more time in the nest. They also differ in needing far fewer food items brought to the nest each day, because they are larger items, for example Bald Eagles or Ospreys bring in large fish, while small birds like Great Tits with large broods might have to bring in food some 1,000 times per day. Many such altricial young will increase their weight by ten times in as many days—a phenomenal growth rate. Laying many more eggs is obviously an additional inducement to regular food visits. Precocial young have done much of their developing in the egg, so grow more slowly once hatched. They are also mobile and able to feed themselves, although the parents often also feed them for some time. Partridge or Common Gallinule chicks will typically follow their parents around in small, loose groups, both food-begging from them and taking their own food. It is no coincidence that so many birds produce young during periods of plentiful insect supply, as our Blue Tits time their breeding to certain caterpillar hatches.

Eggs vary from the huge, 3.5lb (1.6kg) of the Ostrich down to that of the tiny hummingbird, that may weigh 4,500 times less. (The extinct Elephant Bird's egg was even larger, some 12in (30cm long.) Colour and pattern can vary hugely, too, and eggs are not all necessarily 'egg-shaped'. Guillemots produce pointed ones to prevent them rolling off narrow cliff ledges, while some owls will lay almost round eggs.

They may be shiny or chalky, rough or smooth, with shells thinner or thicker depending upon individual needs. The shape usually depends upon the bird's form: small, slender aerial hunters like swallows and hummingbirds lay small, slender, elongated eggs. Many ground-nesting plovers produce pear-shaped eggs that fit together neatly into clutches of four, pointing inwards, as we saw. As for colour, that varies hugely from the most brilliantly 'enamelled' turquoise of the tinamous', through many vermiculated buffs to cream and white. Some, like the Guillemot's, must be

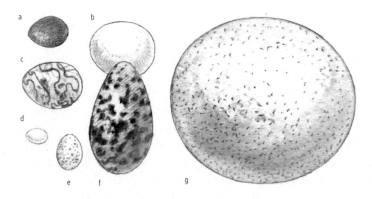

Fig. 101: A SELECTION OF EGGS. A: DUNNOCK. B: LITTLE OWL. C: BALTIMORE ORIOLE. D: HUMMINGBIRD. E: TIT OR CHICKADEE. F: GUILLEMOT. G: OSTRICH.

beautifully and individually 'scribbled' for easy detection among hundreds of others on similar ledges. This sort of patterning and colour is unique to each egg, and produced by pigments in the uterus just before laying. They can fade or change colour with wear and exposure. An African courser's egg is not only black, but *exactly* matches the patchily scorched earth after a bush fire—quite astonishing! Many other species have superbly patterned eggs and have been threatened by egg collectors. It is almost beyond belief that some willingly drive birds to extinction, just to hide eggs away in secret, illegal collections. Recently, the last Red-backed Shrikes to nest in Britain had collectors queuing up to steal their eggs, knowing full well the result. Only biblical wisdom explains such disgraceful behaviour, and only deliberate denial of the love and morals clearly 'engraved upon our hearts' by God, encourages it.

We have already seen how many hole-nesters like kingfishers and owls have white eggs, and open nesters, well-camouflaged ones, but cliff nesting Eurasian Shags, for one, have gone their own way without suffering any noticeable increase in predation—their exposed eggs are white. However, most are beautifully matched to their backgrounds, with beach nesters like terns being a sandy buff and speckled. Woodland floor or low vegetation

Chapter 5

nesters like nightjars have appropriately blended and cryptically patterned eggs, and tree or soil nesters are heavily blotched to match patchy shadows. Baltimore Orioles and Guira Cuckoos have two particularly striking 'modern art' egg patterns, with black exquisitely scribbled and scrolled across pale grounds.

Eggs are not always sized according to the body, for the little Kiwi's egg is as large as the giant extinct Moa's, and will almost completely fill its body cavity. Obviously that sort of production is very costly in terms of time and energy. The compensation is in the large yoke sac that sustains the chick throughout the long brooding period, largely undertaken by the male Kiwi. This highly nutritious egg yoke will further sustain the chick for about a week, before it leaves the burrow to fend largely for itself. Such a huge egg is half the size of the adult bird and a quarter of its weight, whereas an Emu's or Ostrich's egg is only about a hundredth. Great Tits, for example, will eventually lay more than their own body weight in eggs, while each egg is only 0.15oz (1.7gm).

Strangely enough, discarded eggshells are not usually eaten even when the female might shortly be laying again, though Peregrines have been seen eating the yolk remains. This is probably because enough calcium for egg development cannot always be stored, and mainly comes from snail shells or bones eaten only just before the egg starts. The bright white inside of eggshells exposes birds to nest predation, and this is a good reason for getting rid of them. Incidentally, Egyptian Vultures have come up with a great way of cracking the very tough shells of Ostrich eggs; using their beak to drop or throw large stones at them.

After hatching, many young altricial birds have special functions for dealing with irregular food supplies and wandering parents. Bad weather or prey movements might force prolonged absences for aerial insectivores or seabirds, so the young have thick down or rapidly build up fat supplies in good times. Some can even enter a torpor-like, hibernatory state for the duration, like some young swifts. Young Emperor Penguins huddle together in large swarms, all facing inwards from the freezing winds as they gradually shed their grey down. A bird's first coat of feathers will gradually grow through the fluffy down, which will usually be preened out by the chick's feet and beak.

Vigorous wing flapping exercises are employed by many birds at this time, especially aerial predators and seabirds, as they gradually 'grow into' their huge feet and bills. Leaving the nest is the next big problem. Some gradually move away from the nest in exploration of shore, tree or cliff, others launch fearlessly off on their first flights. Adult Peregrines will tempt the young off the nest by mild starvation, and releasing live prey to teach them to hunt for themselves. Practice makes perfect for raptors, but many warblers, wildfowl or wrynecks must rapidly get it right to cross the seas to distant continents, and they will not usually have parents around to pester for food.

The bright yellow or red mouths of many chicks stimulate such *'food begging'* even after leaving the nest. Those special coloured 'gape spots' of birds like finches are also designed to attract attention while in the nest.

These markings on the tongue or palate can even be luminous blue in the case of young parrot-finches, presumably for their darker nests. Conversely the young will peck at the adult's bill for food, with gulls like the Herring Gull having a special red spot as a target. Others just grab the food and pull! Pelicans and cormorants go even farther and actually allow the young's head right inside their throats to guddle[2] about for fish. We have already seen how pigeons and flamingos produce nutritious 'crop milk' for their young, dribbling it out while the chick has its beak inside hers. Many seabirds and herons will effortlessly vomit up their fishy catches already pre-digested, while kingfishers and terns will present their young with whole fish, headfirst. Some parents are overoptimistic in this aspect of feeding, and finally swallow big fish themselves, unlike most raptors that carefully tear up most prey items. Prey or food that is too small is first gathered together before presentation by songbirds, and often stored as a 'bolus' or ball in the huge gape (swifts). If prey is abundant, then the ingenious Atlantic Puffin can simultaneously catch and

Fig. 102: 'ALTRICIAL' YOUNG: KESTREL.

Fig. 103: A: BEARDED (TIT) REEDLING'S GAPE SPOTS; and below, B: Blue-faced Parrot Finch. C: HERRING GULL CHICK STIMULATED BY THE ADULT'S RED BILL SPOT.

store up to sixty-two small fish (though eight is about average) in its colourful beak. It holds them between the tongue and upper mandible, alternately stacked head or tail first.

Most young will follow their parents around for some months after *fledging* as the bond is slowly broken. Mallee Fowl chicks literally have no time for that, and scoot off immediately on hatching. Delightful as the sight is, young Great-crested Grebes or Mute Swans will not be allowed to ride on the adult's back for very long, or beg for their fish in the case of the grebe. Learning to gather food is one of their most important priorities, along with keeping an eye open for predators.

Nest sanitation is also an important consideration for altricial young that spend a long time there. Different types of birds use various methods, with the majority, the songbirds, favouring 'bagging'. This is a wonderful trick whereby the chicks regularly produce white, pre-packed *'faecal sacs'* for the parents to carry away and dump; far more biodegradable than our 'disposable nappies'! Not surprisingly, this ingenious method is also characteristic of hole nesters, and some parents can eat the sacs. By contrast, many raptors' nests can become littered with bits of rotting food, and even dead chicks can be trampled underfoot. Some do at least continue to bring in green, leafy branches that deter bacteria and parasites. Interestingly, one American cowbird chick itself somehow deters botflies (larvae of farm animal-bothering gadflies) from its host family's nest. Asian House Sparrows soon learned to eat, and line, nests with quinine-containing leaves when malaria struck their area. More Intelligent Design! Raptor young always go to the nest edge to squirt the white 'mutes' well away from the nest, sometimes resulting in large white streaks, then bright green patches of fertility—a sure give-away of raptor nests on some cliffs. Precocial birds naturally do not have a problem with their droppings, scattering them far and wide. Various blood-sucking fleas, ticks, bugs, flat-flies and other insect ectoparasites live on the birds and in their nests, as they tend to live on every other living thing. Rarely do they seriously bother healthy birds, though some hirundine (swallows) and swift chicks occasionally bear weakening loads. Not surprisingly, communal nesters are host to the largest numbers. Birds are also subject to endoparasites, such as varied gut worms. This is the rule, for 'the whole creation groans and labors ... together' (Romans 8:22) at the moment: for help is 'on the way' (Revelation 22:20).

Birds have obviously always been very successful, even when we take into account the relatively high mortality rate in their first year. Half to two-thirds of many raptors will die during their first winter, and out of an average ten Eurasian Shelduck or Blue Tit families, only two or three might endure. Only two shelducklings have survived the first few months of life on 'my' large estuary this year (2004), while twenty-three have flown from just two families elsewhere on Anglesey. The difference may be their much smaller and more sheltered estuary, nearby houses and fewer natural predators. It is very telling that some birds now are largely successful only when they breed in our gardens and neighbourhoods—or conversely, in the last wild places. The middle ground of over-managed countryside often spells their doom.

Nevertheless, an astonishing array of birds has long flourished worldwide, despite local and global fluctuations. In the next two chapters we shall look at how they came to be so successful in the first place. Finally, we shall look at what they have meant and still do mean to us, and whether or not they will continue to survive while sharing the world with the most destructive creature of all—Homo sapiens, and why we are so destructive.

Notes

1 *Silent Spring* by **Rachel Carson** was the book that awoke many to the huge problems of chemical pollution in the 1950s and 1960s. (See my final chapter.)
2 A Scottish colloquialism meaning to grope in the water for fish.

Origins: creation or evolution?

As I remarked in the Introduction, the natural grace, elegance and incredible design of birds is indisputable, even to the many evolutionists who are always talking about their 'design'. Yet we still often hear the claim that they needed nothing more than different environments to accidentally 'evolve' this intricate design from cold-blooded dinosaurs—even when the latest information about the unique, real life of warm-blooded birds is known to so many. Television regularly brings us many superb wildlife series, naturally reliant upon an incredibly high standard of close-up photography and technical expertise. The man-made equipment that is used cries out 'design and designer', yet even when filming the most precisely engineered marvels like birds, the narrator will tell us that it only needed blind accident and climate to shape them. Sadly, most viewers or readers are not that discerning, and tend to take as fact anything thrown at them, especially by people assumed to be 'authorities'. Throw it often enough, and it clearly sticks. As with all great deceptions, there is some truth in there, as climate and environment can cause *rapid built-in* adaptations in some creatures, as we noted concerning the wings of the Blackcap. However, those relatively tiny changes within strict genetic boundaries are light years away from the idea that slime could accidentally evolve into conscious beings!

As ardent evolutionist Steve Jones admits, evolution was 'force-fed' to him and many others from the cradle. He had little choice, yet many like him now ensure that the real facts of life are kept from mainstream science and the media, thus perpetuating the myths. All the media exposure and endless programmes, books and articles assume evolution has happened—because we are here, it must have happened! Is that what passes for 'natural' science nowadays? Thirty-three other leading mainstream scientists have just remarked about so-called 'Big Bang' theories, that the sort of lack of evidence and large amount of fudging in cosmology would not be allowed in any other branch of science.[1] Vital funding and prestige absolutely depend upon conforming to the 'establishment line': that is evolutionary, and it will not allow any challenge, even from within. For instance, the cosmologist Halton Arp's work on Redshifts and Quasars thoroughly upset the idea that their age and distance were related. Because he so upset the ideas of great age for the cosmos, he was subsequently ridiculed and marginalized by the international, thoroughly evolutionary scientific establishment; his damning evidence was almost completely suppressed, but not properly refuted—only now is he allowed his say as others awake.[1] Personal abuse is often the preferred action, diverting us away from the many scientific problems. We see this repeatedly nowadays, when even admitting there just might be a few problems with the theory of evolution elicits hysteria. *Intelligent Design (ID)* is at last being taught in some American schools—alongside neo-Darwinism—without any reference to God at all. British Christian schools like Emmanuel College, Gateshead, also teach both theories, and have thereby annoyed prominent UK evolutionists like Richard Dawkins, despite attaining the highest academic standards and top examination results from the authorities! This is simply the result of teaching *deductive reasoning, or how to think—not what to think*. It was reported recently that some American teachers refuse even to read a legal disclaimer before science lessons, namely, that evolution is only a theory with many scientific objections to it. The false claim that creation = faith, while evolution = science, persists.

Evolutionists also disagree strongly among themselves about *how* evolution happened, yet it is always untruthfully claimed to be proven to *have* happened. They have many wild theories and claims about the origin of birds from reptiles. Dinosaurs did not die out, they cry, but are still living in your garden, and when you eat fried chicken you are eating Dino-McNuggets! Well, that sort of claim must be tested under the rules of real science. When science follows its own strict rules of observation, hypotheses and testing, it is reliable, but it is woefully inadequate when it comes to speculating on unobserved and supposedly distant phenomena like 'evolution'. Remember that 'evolution' is applied to everything nowadays, and random 'Big Bangs' and endless blind, genetic mistakes *can* be tested, and result in chaos, destruction or degradation.

The connection between dinosaurs and birds can also be tested by investigating their many differences: dinosaurs are dinosaurs and birds are birds. So evolutionists always whistle up 'very special conditions' and 'endless, random chance', yet when we talk of special creation, they cry 'foul'. We have actually reached a time when arrogant, atheistic mankind, so thoroughly brainwashed with wild evolutionary theory and random 'Big Bangs', can deceive themselves into believing that *'Nothing made everything out of nothing'*, is more logical than believing that *'God made everything out of nothing!'* However, the mass of evidence for Intelligent Design and an infinitely wise Creator is accumulating continually.

Remember that flight is incredibly expensive in terms of energy requirements, but evolutionists claim that it has supposedly, accidentally, 'evolved' at least four times and in very different forms. Once would be remarkable enough! However, as usual, the first creations were complete from the beginning, yet obviously with built-in variety to adapt within strict genetic confines. All the so-called 'living fossils' tell us that the most important component, DNA information, must have been there from the beginning, virtually unchanged—so where is the evolution? Variety alone is not evolution, and we have in fact lost much variety, as in those wondrous, early Cambrian or 'Ediacarian' sea creatures, armoured fish or massive Ice Age mammals. Thus 'ancient' insects and pterosaurs always had perfect flight, and are still among the most sophisticated fliers known to science. It is beyond belief that our beautiful, complex and widely variable birds, insects, bats and extinct flying reptiles could all be explained away as genetic 'accidents'. (Note: some say the flying reptiles were not reptiles, but just the giant bats they so resemble. We cannot go into the ins and outs of that argument here. I have also illustrated a 'gliding' phalanger, though they are not true fliers.)

Not all evolutionists go for Richard Dawkins' far-fetched idea that the incredible pageant of life is merely the 'inevitable' side effect of some 'selfish gene's' inexplicable urge to reproduce itself, yet many media and academics uncritically lap up that sort of fantasy, and ceaselessly pass it on. The immense number of contingent genetic accidents required to fuel this travesty of 'science' belies belief. Evolutionist Gould actually dared to put a figure on it, and guessed it would require *'60 trillion contingent events'* to

Fig. 104: DIFFERENT FLIGHT MODES (NOT TO SCALE). A: INSECT: SWALLOWTAIL BUTTERFLY. B: BAT: LONG-EARED. C: PTEROSAUR: PTERODACTYLUS ELEGANS. D: BIRD: ATLANTIC GANNET. E: GLIDING MAMMAL: PHALANGER.

accidentally evolve us. *That's 60 trillion random, blind cosmic and genetic accidents, all miraculously not eliminated and somehow saved up for the unseen and future 'glorious accident' of life!*[2] Well, believe if you must, but please don't call it science.

To sum up briefly, evolutionary theory assumes that birds have evolved from reptiles, probably small theropod dinosaurs, or from Coelurosaur (gliding lizard) types (illustration ahead), or even crocodilians, by natural selection working on blind genetic mutations. Yet these are copying mistakes in DNA—and usually lead to *less* genetic information, not more. Mutations are usually over 99 per cent destructive, or at the very best neutral, and the only mutation that could possibly aid evolutionary theory is the virtually unknown *'beneficial, inheritable genetic mutation'*. Trillions of such 'beneficial' mutations would be needed to produce just one 'new' or 'linking' creature! Yet our millions of different life forms would need millions of transitional links between them, slowly, blindly groping through endless trials and errors. They do not exist—yet many objections do; and from evolutionists themselves.

See the 'Revised Quote Book' (RQB, details in bibliography) for many prominent evolutionists' own exposés of evolution, 'missing links', and the folly of relying upon damaging mutations, etc. Here are just a handful of quotes about mutations from prominent evolutionists:

- 'Mutations … are the basis of evolution'. *World Book Encyclopaedia,* vol. 13, 1982, p. 809.
- Yet 'Most of them are harmful and lethal', Carl Sagan. *Cosmos* (1980), p. 27.
- Yet they 'are necessary for evolutionary progress', but also 'The greatest proportion are deleterious', Peo Koller, *Chromosomes and Genes,* 1971, p. 127.
- 'No matter how numerous … mutations do not produce any kind of evolution', Pierre Grasse, *Evolution of Living Organisms* (Academic Press, 1977), p. 88. (RQB quote 72, p. 17).
- Because 'random genetic mutation is inadequate in scope and theoretical grounding', J. S. Wicken, *Journal of Theoretical Biology,* 4:1997, pp. 351–352. (RQB quote 32, p. 17).
- Arthur Koestler confirmed that 'random genetic mutations turned out

to be irrelevant', *Janus—A Summing Up* (Random House, 1978), pp. 184–185. (RQB quote 76, p. 18.)

• And this accidental genetic change is their only mechanism—bearing in mind that DNA is especially engineered not to change!

Evolutionists must also speculate on no real fossil evidence at all, ignoring their 'first bird' Archaeopteryx for the moment, that cold-blooded, hissing reptiles have somehow overcome massive differences in morphology, and changed into warm-blooded, singing birds. We have already looked at many of the differences, in unique lungs, cardiovascular system, limbs, pelvis and hips, sternum and skulls: all highly specialised and often confined only to birds. Then the problems of a massive change from scales to feathers are ignored and all objections, as usual, glossed over.

What is not generally known is that there are no suitable theropod, dinosaurian ancestors before Archaeopteryx, or that the so-called 'bird-hipped' (*Ornithischian*) dinosaurs are not theropod dinosaurs either, for they are *'Saurischians'* with a normal pelvis. The skeletons of these upright theropod dinosaurs otherwise do bear a superficial resemblance to bird skeletons; but then many lifeforms are 'naturally' built upon similar lines. It is also painful to see, as in various television 'documentaries', ludicrous simulations of supposed reptile/bird evolutionary intermediaries, paraded as fact. It should be obvious that a dinosaur with increasingly feathery arms, like the hypothetical *'Proavis',* could neither fly nor catch its food. Such a series of freaks would be certain to be eliminated by 'natural selection'—just about evolution's sole fact—yet unable to tolerate unfit accidents. Evolutionists continue to repeat the same tautological reasoning: 'the fittest survive because they are the fittest, and they are the fittest because they survive'—although it does not explain how they became the fittest, nor can it explain the biggest mystery of all—how life 'evolved' from non-life to begin with! It is postulated that feathers accidentally evolved from frayed scales on some dinosaur's arms by endless genetic mistakes, and were used to catch insects before they were efficient enough for flight. Yet feathers have to be in top condition to fly, and useless for anything when broken and bashed about as some crazy sort of insect-catching net, which would not work anyway: they would waft insects away!

Another great objection comes from studying flight itself. As we have

Fig. 105: 'PROAVIS', BASED ON OSTROM'S IDEA THAT EVOLVING FEATHERS COULD BE USED AS AN INSECT CATCHING NET!

seen, the most difficult part of flight is maintaining any form of stability at *low speeds*, which takes large amounts of energy, and demands highly specialised anatomy to overcome all the drag. Yet this is how flight supposedly evolved, as some sort of reptile increasingly bounded along, getting higher and higher! You only have to look at kangaroos, rather similar in build to some dinosaurs, to see that they do not use their little forelimbs in any way when jumping, and gradually adding feathers to fingers would only *slow* down all the reptile's functions, including catching its food.

Another myth is that reptiles suddenly had to develop feathers for warmth before they were used for flight, but hair is far simpler and more effective for that. Also, down feathers are not waterproof, and chicks can quickly cool and even die. The incredible complexity of feathers would require so much energy and chance to develop, and anyway, where are the reptiles with hair or feathers in today's cooler world, after 'millions' more years of constant mutations? Of course, we see none.

Don't be misled by those authoritative-looking charts in books and magazines.[3] They often deliberately show *'Archaeopteryx lithographica'* at the *end* of the dinosaur-into-bird process, when it *preceded* most of the other candidates in the fossil record. It is also hard to witness such authorities as David Attenborough saying that it is 'easy' to imagine a frayed scale turning into a feather.[4] He of all people should know better. Anybody who has even casually looked at a feather, and marvelled at its aerodynamic design and complicated system of interlocking filaments and barbs, could never mistake it for something as superficial as a scale. Scales are just folds in the skin, and are all shed in one piece. Feathers are more like hairs, growing from deep within the skin and sometimes even attached to the bones, and they are also from different DNA sites than scales. We have seen how every feather is an individual and beautifully designed lightweight miracle of engineering, and how each is uniquely marked, and we are seriously being asked to imagine that a scale could somehow fray into thousands of fine equidistant strands. Then, as it would be useless for flight or protection, rapidly and accidentally evolve millions of essential barbs and barbules to effectively zip it back together, and all by blind, random genetic mutations! Remember that a single peacock-sized secondary flight feather has about one *million* barbs, and the barbs would then have to accidentally evolve trillions of those 'photonic crystal prisms' for the dazzling array of colours and patterns of such birds.

If all that was not difficult enough, the poor creature would then have had to rapidly evolve the essential oil preen gland. This is needed to keep the feathers in shape, especially that unique 'sliding joint' of hooks and barbs. And the gland is in a place inaccessible to reptiles, the upper tail base. As if it didn't have enough problems already, changing most other organs and functions without somehow dying! Even some reputable evolutionary scientists call evolution (a) a 'modern myth'; (b) just 'a fairy tale for adults'; (c) taught by '… great con men …' and 'may be the greatest hoax ever'.[5]

What does the fossil record actually say?
Unfortunately for evolutionism, the real fossil record reveals a rather different pattern than the popular notion of development of reptiles into birds, and it must be stressed that there are many problems also with the geological column (see later in this chapter). Avian evolutionary authorities like Alan Feduccia acknowledge that the fossil record for birds

is actually very good. The relevant fossil layers are spread over what evolutionists regard as the past '220 million years'. The earliest known bird fossils are so-called *'Protoavis'* (not the imaginary 'Proavis'). Their finder, Sankar Chatterjee of the University of Texas, describes the two skeletons as 'modern, crow like birds' from a Texan quarry 'full of bird bones'. Unfortunately for supporters of Archaeopteryx, Protoavis is claimed to be more 'evolved', though sharing its tailbones, and the skeletons are dated 'Triassic'—about '220 mya' (million years ago).[6]

Dating 'Protoavis' to '70 my' before Archaeopteryx, and '100 my' before the so-called 'feathered dinosaurs', means they were contemporary with some of the very earliest dinosaurs. It must be said that 'Protoavis' and its discoverer are very controversial, although mainly to the advocates of the 'theropod to bird' theory it supplants. Chatterjee has published photos of the fossils; but many bones were crushed (although so are many other fossils). Other 'true birds' have also been claimed, in 'earlier' Jurassic rocks than Archaeopteryx.[7] Also, there are millions of varied bird tracks found fossilised alongside dinosaur footprints throughout the world, from the 'Jurassic' onwards,[8] even well before dinosaurs, supposedly way back in the 'Carboniferous'.[9] Again, it must be stressed that many of these evidences are open to interpretation and bias. The Bible merely says that birds were created on day five, *before* many other land and sea animals, including dinosaurs. Of course, the fossil record does not reflect any sort of order in creation, but rapid destruction and fossilisation by massive watery inundation and Ice Age catastrophes. This also means that anything but a very general 'order' of destruction is also often very difficult to assess.

Archaeopteryx—bird or beast?

Most international experts have long recognised that *Archaeopteryx* is a bird, with a 'modern' bird's skull and fully formed, asymmetrical flight feathers. There have been questions about its pelvis, but (Feduccia, pp. 72–75, 1999) has no doubt of its bird-like character, which later birds also share. Further research now confirms that the complex inner-ear and skull bones all show Archaeopteryx to be a very advanced flier. Furthermore, only one of its claimed twenty-one 'unique' reptilian features—*tail bones*—remains as unique. Tailbones are still present in modern flightless

Fig. 106: COMPARISONS OF A FLIGHTLESS BIRD (NOT TO SCALE) A: OSTRICH, WITH B: ORNITHISCIAN DINOSAUR (HADROSAUR); C: GLIDING REPTILE (COELUROSAURUS); D: 'PROTOAVIS'; E: ARCHAEOPTERYX. (NOTE—B TO E ARE MAINLY GUESSWORK, BASED UPON VARIOUS RECONSTRUCTIONS.)

bird embryos, and not all reptiles have tails or teeth. Archaeopteryx apparently has hollowish bones like the majority of birds. Because it has no *developing transitional features* between reptiles and birds, top evolutionists like Stephen Jay Gould saw Archaeopteryx as 'curious mosaic' which 'do not count'.[10] The recent find of a '70 my'-old fossilised parrot bill from the late dinosaur age further upsets evolutionists, and what of the 'young' radiocarbon (^{14}C) dating of many 'old' fossils? We will look at the various radioactive-dating methods and all their many problems soon.

The information about Archaeopteryx's bird skull was first published in the *Journal of Vertebrate Palaeontology*, in 3:1996: 'The avian features of the skull demonstrate that Archaeopteryx is a bird, rather than a feathered, non-avian archaeosaur.' Along with S. Rietschel's diagram from evolutionist Pat Shipman's book *Taking Wing*,[11] we can try to picture it

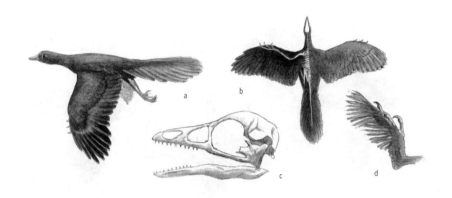

Fig. 107a: ARCHAEOPTERYX LITHOGRAPHICA. A: MY OWN IDEA OF HOW IT MIGHT HAVE LOOKED. B: RECONSTRUCTION AFTER REITSCHEL, 1998. C: SKULL RECONSTRUCTION, AFTER MARTIN, L. and BUHLER, P., FROM FEDUCCIA, 1999. D: MODERN HOATZIN CHICK'S WINGCLAWS.

more as it might have been. I see it as perhaps similar to the Hoatzin, the living South American bird that also happens, like many others today, to have wing claws (although only when young). Modern evolutionary experts like Feduccia also picture Archaeopteryx with a feathered, bird's head.[12]

As there are now seven fossils of Archaeopteryx, other bird features have become clearer, such as the unique sternum, or breastbone, essential for carrying flight muscles. The asymmetrical flight feathers are only found on flying birds, and *wing claws* are also still found on many adult birds like the Ostrich, Emu, Spur-winged Plover, ibis, swan, rail, gamebirds, touraco, and young Hoatzin. As with many other features of life, the wing claws on modern birds are reduced—another example of '*devolution*'. As for Archaeopteryx's *teeth*, they are different from reptile teeth and similar to slightly 'later' birds, like Hesperornis. Fish-eating birds like Smew, mergansers and goosanders also have teeth-like serrations today, as shown in chapter 1. Archaeopteryx's general form resembles long-tailed, short-winged, arboreal and wetland species as diverse as our sparrowhawks,

Fig. 107b: COMPARING ARCHAEOPTERYX'S GENERAL FORM WITH LIVING BIRDS. A: COMMON MAGPIE; B: HOATZIN; C: PHEASANT COUCAL.

coucals, pheasants, cuckoos, magpies, cormorants and darters. It also had very sharp and deeply curved claws, found only on tree-dwelling birds—not ground-dwelling birds, thus further weakening that 'ground-up' (*'cursorial'*) hypothesis of the development of flight by madly flapping dinosaurs.

'Feathered dinosaurs'?

The recent claims of so-called *'feathered dinosaurs'*, a mere '120' and '70 million years ago' (mya), are rather irrelevant anyway, for should the predecessors of birds still be developing over '90 million years' after 'modern birds'? Should not ape-like creatures also still be 'evolving' too, and all the other millions of 'missing links' and freakish accidents still be around? We also need to consider the oft-overlooked fact that at the very least; *two* freaks are presumably needed to perpetuate these mythical evolutionary 'links'? It would be difficult enough to produce one fully functioning freak that would not be automatically wiped out by 'natural selection' but for two freaks that just happen to have the same compatible, accidental additions to be alive at the same time, for procreation to occur, is once again stretching credibility to breaking point.

Meanwhile, back in the real world, it has now been recognised that the so-called feathered dinosaurs like '*Sinosauropteryx*' were not feathered at all. Some authorities think that the 'feathers' are just frayed reptilian *collagen* (cell strengthening) fibres, or decorative frills along their backs.[13] 'Hairy Frogs' and other creatures have very hair-like fleshy tassels, and frayed collagen is thought to be the 'fur' on certain extinct flying reptiles, like pterosaurs. Apparently, such 'fuzz' is not at all uncommon on dinosaur fossils.[14] (Note: this is one of the controversial 'bat-like' features claimed for these reptiles, already alluded to.) '*Sinosauropteryx*' had a tremendously long tail, and most importantly of all, compartmentalised, theropod-type dinosaur lungs—not bird's lungs.

Many lung function experts pronounced that a theropod dinosaur's 'bellow-like lungs could not have evolved into the high performance lungs of modern birds.'[15] As we have seen, bird's lungs are totally unique, and the dinosaur-type lung, like ours, would be utterly useless for the high-energy requirements of birds. In the bird the air is almost totally exchanged every breath, as explained earlier. This superbly designed system is essential to exchange the maximum amounts of oxygen and carbon dioxide at incredible speed, and birds can fly at heights that would destroy dinosaurs. Any 'accidental' evolutionary change from a dinosaur to a bird lung system would need to rupture the diaphragm! As Denton says: 'The fact that the design of the avian respiratory system is essentially invariant in ALL birds merely increases one's suspicion that no fundamental variation of the system is compatible with the preservation of respiratory function.'[16] Simply put, bird's lungs are perfect and unique, and essential for their unique, highly active lifestyle. Thus birds also differ from other life in having very high levels of antioxidants, to combat destructive free radicals.

The whole '*feathered dinosaur*' debate hinges on one very important and extremely difficult requirement for the promoters of dinosaur—into—bird evolution: the change from cold blood to warm blood! The newly evolved '*dinobirds*' are claimed to have needed 'proto-feathers' to keep warm, but the evidence again is back to front, because the feathers were doing the opposite—they were 'devolving'. As flightless ratites like the Rhea possibly have done so by 'unzipping' their feathers, and become fluffier. The aforementioned 'dino-fuzz' could account for the 'feathers' on *'Sinosauropteryx'* shown in several close-up pictures, and we do not know if the photos have been 'enhanced'.[17] Later, true bird fossils also seem to show a similar sort of dark, feathery halo effect around the bones. Could chemical reactions, or bacterial action in fossilisation, form these radiating fur/feather halos?

The same applies to more recent finds like the Chinese *Dromaeosaur* *'NGMC 91-A'*, found in 2001 (Dromaeosaurs are small, theropod dinosaurs—upright, bipedal carnivores). Leading 'theropod into bird' experts claim them as the most likely feathered ancestor, yet many again question the evidence of feathers. Nor could they qualify because of their comparatively massive size, averaging sixty-six times larger than Archaeopteryx, or their specialised anatomy. As for other 'feathered dinosaurs', like *'Caudipteryx'* and *'Protoarchaeopteryx'*, experts like Feduccia think that they are just flightless birds, like the Emu. (I must point out, in fairness to Alan Feduccia, that although he believes that birds evolved from some sort of reptile, he thinks real science cannot be used to maintain current popular theories of 'dinobirds'.)

At least one of the latest Chinese 'dino-birds' to fool the experts was a deliberate fraud: *'Archaeoraptor*

Figs. 108, also 106, 118: COMPARING A MODERN EMU, WITH A: 'PROTOAVIS', AFTER CHATTERJEE. B: CAUDIPTERYX ZOUI, AFTER *NATIONAL GEOGRAPHIC*, VOL. 194, NO. 1.

liaoningensis' (see below). Yet there are many 'unconscious' frauds as well. Looking again at the various 'feathered dinosaurs' in the *National Geographic*,[2] many points jar. They show the massive *'Unenlagia'* with wings, when there is not even the slightest evidence of feathers! *'Velociraptor'* is at least shown at its correct, small size, not as in Spielberg's evolutionary 'Jurassic Park' fantasy. No sign of any feathers here either, just a bird-like sternum and flexible wrists. That just leaves bird-beaked *'Caudipteryx'* and *'Protoarchaeopteryx'* in the fray—although they appeared long after old Archaeopteryx, but they are deceptively shown coming after it. Fossil reconstructions are often imaginative guesswork— and vary widely. 'Apeman 1470' was pictured as everything from black ape to white man. Remember that all life forms share various structural designs (see pp. 166–169 on homology).

'Confuciusornis' was first shown incorrectly as an upright, rather cartoonish 'dinobird'—simply because one was needed by evolutionist Kevin Padian, one of the strongest proponents of dinosaur-into-bird evolution.

It was not in the *National Geographic* chart, possibly because it was 'too close' to old Archaeopteryx in dating. It was also undoubtedly a bird, with a 'modern' toothless, keratinous beak, and no tailbones, yet it also had clawed, flight-feathered wings like Archaeopteryx. Others have teeth, some have 'more modern' wings—interpretation is very subjective and relies mainly upon blinkered evolutionary preconceptions, not always common sense. The cover of Feduccia's book[12] simply shows Confuciusornis as a modern bird, yet with wing claws, from an excellent fossil of two with very differing tails—probably male and female.

Others claimed as 'dino-birds' or 'transitionals' include *'Mononychus'*, even though again there is no evidence of any feathers. *'Bambiraptor'* has none either, yet is still another modern contender. Now *'Mononychus'* is thought to be a burrowing 'Maniraptor' (theropod 'hand-predator' with large claws).[18] This dethroning of evolutionary icons is very common, yet unfortunately unaccompanied by the exaggerated media fanfares that greeted their first appearance.

Another candidate is the beautifully bizarre, possibly gliding reptile, *'Longisquama'*. This appears to have very long overlapping scales

a   b

Fig. 109: CONFUCIUSORNIS SANCTUS. A: AFTER PRATT, H.D. IN FEDUCCIA, 1999. B: AS A 'DINOBIRD', AFTER FEDUCCIA, 1999, BASED UPON PADIAN, 1989.

extending out from its back, in 'wings'.[19] Some reconstructions show them swept back in damselfly position, at rest. It is claimed as a first stage in the evolution of feathers, yet they look like scales. And several gliding reptiles use flaps of skin for escape and transport between trees, without being in any way birdlike. The huge differences between reptile and bird, scales and feathers are virtually always ignored.

At the end of January 2000, evolution faced another appalling upset: the aforementioned 'Archaeoraptor liaoningensis' was exposed as probably the 'worst fossil fraud scandal since Piltdown'. The prominently exhibited, *National Geographic* 'dinosaur-to-bird transitional' fossil was shown to be some sort of bird/dinosaur's upper half, glued to what is probably a dinosaur's tail. It was illegally imported, but even after being discredited it was claimed as being *two separate* transitional forms! Once again, there was no real evidence for this claim, but there was a very strong motive for face-saving.

Also, when it comes to 'dinobirds', most never consider that the so-called 'proto'-down feathers, claimed to be on some specimens, might merely be juvenile down feathers as on the many modern flightless birds, like Emus or Ostriches, they so resemble. One of the latest claimants for 'dinobirds' came in 2003, in the even more bizarre form of a *four-winged* beast![20] Not content with the huge problems inherent in accidentally evolving a two-winged bird from some form of reptile, *'Microraptor gui'* was also paraded as a 'dinobird'. So is it an over-feathered freak or another Chinese fraud? It looks suspiciously like the hypothetical 'Proto-bird' or 'Proavis' imagined by Heilmann et al,[21] and not to be confused with Chatterjee's 'Protoavis'. There is obviously a lot we do not know about these strange fossils, and one only has to look at the immense variety and ingenuity in various real creation 'kinds' to be wary of being too dogmatic. We look forward to more accurate facts and less fantasy.

Yet another strong objection to dinosaur-to-bird development also comes from evolutionists themselves, including Feduccia.[22] Birds could not have evolved from dinosaurs because they use completely different 'finger' sequences in the development of their limbs, they claim. Assuming the same original five-fingered *('pentadactyl')* limb, as evolutionists must, dinosaurs use digits 1, 2 and 3, while birds use digits 2, 3 and 4, as in Archaeopteryx's wing claws, and with the frequent, opposable, rear claw of birds at number 1. Such development comes from different genetic sites, which should make it impossible to 'evolve', because of the built-in guards against change. And only tree-perching birds usually need that back claw.

Darwin's finches—and other built-in changes

Of course, the classic explanation for evolution in birds, or any other life form, is extrapolated from the comparatively minor changes found in Darwin's favourite, *Galapagos Island Finches.*

These birds display similar beak variety to our own Eurasian finches, from thick Hawfinch-type down to slenderer Goldfinch (though the slender billed Galapagos 'Warbler-finch' is by no means proven to be a finch, but might be a warbler). As the island finches had also possibly adapted their beak shapes from one common finch-type bill, to suit differing food sources, Darwin posited that given huge aeons of time,

Fig. 110: A SELECTION OF GALAPAGOS FINCHES SHOWING VARIATION IN BEAK SHAPE. (SKETCHED FROM 'ORIGINS' VIDEO). LOWER RIGHT, USING TWIG TO PROBE FOR GRUBS. TOP-RIGHT, SO-CALLED 'WARBLER FINCH'.

anything could turn into anything else. It was no coincidence that people like Charles Lyell were then increasingly forcing lots of time into the geological record, and Darwin did not know those volcanic isles were young, anyway. He also knew absolutely nothing of the incredible complexity of the cell or of genetics—to his generation, cells were just a vague blob of 'protoplasm'. To visualise molecules eventually turning into man, or *macro-evolution*, is a very far cry from the sort of *micro-evolution* that the finches display, which is just built-in variety within a biblical 'kind'. Remember that evolutionists have not found a single convincing transitional fossil in the voluminous record—when trillions are needed for

Darwin's 'finely graduated organic chain' of development. He himself acknowledged this (and the difficulty in forming complex organs by 'numerous, successive, slight modifications') to be very strong objections to his theory.[23]

Our own Great Tits can effortlessly change their beak shapes twice a year (thicker for nuts in winter, thinner for insects in summer). Several Cameroon finches are born with optional beak shapes, and Oystercatchers shape theirs to a personal food preference (sharp or blunt, as either hammerers or stabbers of shellfish). Then the Laysan Isle finches have recently demonstrated just how superficial and rapid such a change actually is. Like the Hawaiian Honeycreepers, which rapidly adapt their bill shapes to differing flowers—'adaptive radiation' as it is officially called. And tits remain tits, and finches remain finches. Evolutionists have to believe the risible idea that painfully slow, blind and goal-less, random genetic mutations, then 'guided' only by natural selection, have eventually changed the bird's beak shapes in response to the different food sources, even though mutations usually remove information. The Laysan Isle finches were deliberately introduced to different isolated islands in the 1960s specifically to study this, and quickly showed the falsity of the theory by rapidly adapting their bill and body shapes. Note also that lizards introduced to other islands rapidly changed their leg length to adapt to tree climbing. The much studied Galapagos finches have also demonstrated rapid bill adaptation, back and forth, as food sources varied, showing only built-in variety at the genetic level.[24] It is now thought to be governed by a protein called BMP4, which has a key role in determining whether a bird has a thick stout beak or a narrow pointed beak. BMP4 is the signalling molecule that controls the formation of bone. Embryos of the different species of Galapagos finches were examined, finding that the distinctive shape of each species' beak was determined by when and where the protein was active during development. Equally damaging to evolutionary theory, it turns out that the changes are not the result of genetic mutation, and *no new information is added.*

Like the incredibly complex 'simple cell', all the information for variation had to be there at the beginning: *'irreducible complexity'*, to quote best-selling microbiologist Michael Behe.[25] This book has often been challenged, but never refuted. Most engineers know good design must be 'top-down', which also ironically settles the 'cursorial' theory of bird flight. This is the already mentioned and discredited 'ground-up' idea that furiously flapping, increasingly feathery, dinosaurs could eventually take to the air. Once again, we see how easy it is to destroy evolution's bleak vision of incredible complexity and variety arising accidentally out of so-called 'simple' beginnings. There is no such thing as a simple cell, or a primitive life form: all life forms have always had virtually the same incredible DNA as we have, right from the very beginning. It is either all there together at the beginning, or it cannot work—or as one truthful biochemist said, we have to imagine all the sophisticated components of a cell already there, with the functions they would have in living things—*before there were living things!*[26]

This is just one of the many obvious objections to the idea that genetics provides proof of evolution. DNA is information, not at all material, and naturally requires an intelligent coder—first. Everything leads back naturally and eventually to a divine Coder. The fact that the universe is still here shows it had a beginning, and therefore also required a First Cause, as Genesis says. If it has always been here, as some claim, yet was also running down, then it would already be long dead.

Entropy: the breakdown of order

Ironically, the 'ruling paradigm of the universe', *entropy,* enshrined in the Second Law of Thermodynamics, confirms that everything is breaking down. Everything is becoming more disorderly, going from a higher to a lower energy state or temperature, in any system, universal or biological. Although controlled, some sort of oxidisation is even at work in every life form from the moment of conception: part of the Fall. Entropy naturally increases with time, evolution's imagined ally, and the only real changes we see are mainly of a loss of information, for example flightless birds, loss of sight or a decrease in size, among many life forms. A 'big' point well worth repeating: many things, including humans, have simply become smaller, and this is not evolution, whether trees, ferns, dragonflies, mammals, fish, crocodiles or cockroaches. Some penguins used to be as big as people! Wild pigeons, dogs, cats, crops, etc., all have a far richer genome than their

Fig. 111: GALAPAGOS FLIGHTLESS CORMORANT.

overbred, domesticated cousins, hence the need for preservation of genetic biodiversity. Changes for increasing specialisation, and inbreeding, are expensive and often irreversible. This usually leads to problems like immune system failure, weakness and infertility. A popular TV programme on isolated creatures like the African Ngorongoro Crater lions easily demonstrated this, as did relict Welsh Red Kites of the early twentieth century, or my poor, overbred, 'genetically challenged' Red Setters.

So the idea that the *loss of flight*, like the Galapagos Cormorant's, demonstrates evolution is simply wrong. The cormorants are apparently 'willingly' losing the use of their wings, as they are no longer needed by a bird living on a virtually predator-free island surrounded by fish-rich waters.

Yet this idea is part of the tragic evolutionary notion that we have nearly 200 redundant 'vestigial' organs in our bodies. Tell that to the American teenagers accidentally killed by having their 'useless' endocrine glands irradiated by an evolutionised medical profession! In this case, man's ignorance of many of the functions of living creatures, distorted by false science, produced disaster. These things tell you much more about most evolutionists' blind determination to eradicate a Divine Designer than about reality, and do real science a massive disservice.

Homology and microbiology

Evolutionists have long pointed to the concept of *homology*, or the similarity of body plans of many creatures, as proof of evolution from common ancestors. For instance, the great similarities between structures like limbs, throughout the vertebrate kingdom, are claimed to point to a shared ancestor. But, and it is a big but, these superficially similar arms and legs do not arise from the same parts of the genetic code in the different creatures. Evolutionists cannot explain the fact that many have randomly evolved the same pattern for both front and hind legs at the embryonic level, by blind, chance mutation, when they do not remotely resemble each other at maturity, and there are no transitional, half-limbed freaks in the fossil record. The very different and perfect pentadactyl limbs of bison, bat or baboon, or very different pheasant and penguin wings point only to a common Creator and blueprint, as we would expect from any good designer.

I must point out that some proponents now say that evolution is *not* blind or random, but that only the genetic mistakes are, but this does not address the main problems. How did complex Information precede life, without God? How were all the fortuitous accidents somehow 'saved up'

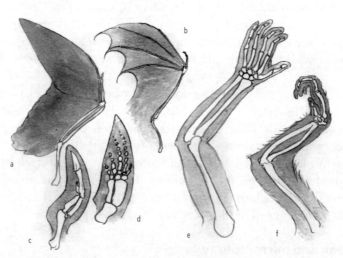

Fig. 112: 'HOMOLOGY'—SHOWING SIMILARITY and DIFFERENCES IN THE PENTADACTYL LIMB OF A: BIRD; B: BAT; C: PENGUIN; D: PORPOISE; E: HUMAN; F: CHIMPANZEE. (NOT TO SCALE).

until needed? Would not 'natural selection' as a matter of course eradicate any useless passengers? The truth is, to quote the late, leading evolutionist S. J. Gould, 'The extreme rarity of transitional forms in the fossil record persists as the trade secret of palaeontology'![27] Or to paraphrase evolutionist Francis Hitching: 'there is a consistency in the missing links—they are all missing!'[28] Remember Darwin's, now Dawkins', crumbling 'faith' that all those missing links will someday, somehow, show up.

Hopes that the world of genetics, or microbiology, would provide the links have often made their case worse. It turns out, when certain parts of the genetic code of different life forms are compared, we see huge discontinuities; for instance, fruit flies have 4 chromosomes, we have 23, apes 24, snails 27, goldfish 47, and roses, anything from 14 to 56.[29] Quality, not quantity, as the latest downgrading of our own number of genes to 'only' about 25,000 ably demonstrates.

We can compare other cellular components, like the amino acid sequences that constitute proteins like insulins, cytochrome C or haemoglobin. And evolutionary biochemists like Dr Michael Denton found huge and completely un-evolutionary discontinuities in many life forms.[25] For instance, the cytochrome Cs differ markedly even in two so-called primitive bacteria. Anyway, there is no such thing as a 'primitive' life form, as the recent media attention on the micro Nematode worm's 40 per cent parity with our DNA shows. Then the insulins of Sperm and Fin Whale are identical to those of dog and pig—but are completely different to the Sei Whale's.

Many life forms are often even more isolated at the genetic than at the tangible level, with the Embden Goose's egg white protein, lysozyme, having little of its amino acid sequence in common with domestic hen's egg lysozyme. We are more closely 'related' to a carp, than a carp is to a lamprey (a 'primitive' fish), if we compare the amino acids in human haemoglobin with those of the carp. Although chimps were once wrongly claimed to have only about a 2 per cent difference in their DNA from ours, their DNA had not been counted and investigated. So we are more closely 'related' to hens and fish than to chimps, according to our amino acid sequences. Colin Patterson, once senior palaeontologist at London's Natural History Museum, evolutionism's high temple, was unable to find a convincing fossil transitional form for his book *Evolution*.[30] He, and others, wrote that the latest classification technique, *'transformed cladistics'*, was transformed *away* from evolutionary theory, and returning to Linnaean classification. Broadly speaking, that is the idea of 'discrete boxes' of life forms in a kind of hierarchy—but unconnected by any links, and that is effectively creationist classification based on biblical 'kinds'.

Peppered moths and peppered falcons

Looking closely at another of evolution's sacred cows, the *Peppered Moth (Biston betularia)* again only reveals built-in variation reproducing 'after its kind', to quote Genesis. Dark forms of the moth were once claimed to be the result of *'industrial melanism'*, or newly emerging mutations to match the darkening tree trunks of the industrial revolution.

Thus they were 'evolving' camouflage so as not to be picked off by birds, but there have long been dark and light forms, and Kettlewell's famous moth research is now admitted to be seriously flawed.[31] Many researchers have only ever found the odd one on tree trunks, anyway—for they are nocturnal, and hide away in the treetops when all their famous bird predators were supposed to be eating them. Virtually only dazed, laboratory bred moths land on tree trunks in daytime when deliberately released for study. That is both highly unnatural and very unscientific. Once again, evolutionary preconceptions rule. The moth's migration patterns show both light and dark forms in many areas, often independent of trunk colour, and moths remain moths, showing only wide colour variation, and no new genetic information. The only Peppered Moths likely to be seen on tree trunks are the ones on the famous, deceptive photographs, and mainly dead, and glued on!

There is a theory that states, generally, that larger, lighter life forms will dominate in more northerly regions, and smaller, darker ones towards the equator. It certainly seems to apply to many birds, if not British *Peppered Moths*. The magnificent, sub-polar *Gyr Falcon (Falco rusticolus)* is one of the pinnacles of creation, long considered only fit for kings to fly, and it too displays very diverse plumage patterns. From the all-dark form of Labrador, it segues effortlessly through grey Scandinavian-Russian forms, all the way to the sparingly speckled and most spectacular white morph,

Fig. 113: BUILT-IN VARIATION—A: GREENLAND AND LABRADOR GYR FALCONS. B: LIGHT AND DARK
PEPPERED MOTHS (NOT TO SCALE).

formerly known as the *Greenland Falcon*. Just like the Peppered Moths,
they display endless variation in colour and pattern. Yet Gyrs remain
falcons, even when bred by us with Sakers or Peregrines. Left to itself,
everything we meddle with by selective breeding will breed rapidly back to
normal, unless we have gone too far, and hindered its survival 'outside'.
Dingoes and American wild dogs have bred 'back' from domestic dogs into
healthier, uniform 'mongrels'. That provides no succour for evolution,
which as an improbable accident in the first place is even more unlikely to
be able to *reverse* itself—especially by mythical 'improving' mutations.

Dark and light Arctic Skuas, Eleanora's Falcons, Common Buzzards,
Great Blue/White Herons or Fulmar Petrels—and many other creations
with light or dark forms, like pumas, jacks, violets or people—remain dark
or light birds, cats, fish, flowers or people. Change is strictly limited, for
stretching the genetic code only usually weakens it, as our breeding
experiments frequently show: many pets and stock animals perish of
inherited abnormalities caused by over-breeding—which only dilutes the

genetic code. Labrador retrievers and Alsatians often suffer from hip displacia, flat-faced dogs have breathing difficulties, Dachshunds have weaker backbones, and so on. The Bible states that 'there is one kind of flesh of men, another flesh of animals, another of fish', and another of birds' (1 Corinthians 15:39) This anticipates the horrific problems already arising from mixing the genes or organs of different flora and fauna, let alone deliberate 'therapeutic' slaughter of many human embryos in much 'stem-cell cloning'. Truly, men 'call evil good', especially now (Isaiah 5:20).

The final chapter will look at an old charge against creationists, concerning biblical 'fixity of species', although no longer valid. It is true that some used to think that the biblical word *min* (translated 'kind') alluded to 'species', but it obviously does not. If creatures can still interbreed they are not, strictly speaking, separate 'species'. 'Kind' must refer to a grouping similar to 'Family' or 'Genus', for some speciation is not only possible but also rapid and even built-in, as we can still see today, or in hybrids. However, change beyond the level of 'Order' would appear to be impossible, so crabs will always produce crabs, however varied, and horses will always be horses. Certainly, dinosaurs could never breed Dabchicks! The assumption of rapid speciation by built-in variety explains how the creatures preserved by God in the recent Flood have become the vast number of species we see in today's world.[32] Modern science would have us believe that there is a gene for this and a gene for that but this is a gross over-simplification, as complex combinations of the same genes appear to code for several traits. The recognition that we do not have as many genes as once thought means combination is vitally important. Then there are other factors, like *'methylation'*, which controls the switching on and off of genes. This involves *'imprinting recognition proteins'*, which is 'nature's' way of ensuring that every baby has two parents. It also ensures strict genetic boundaries, by failure to read the imprinting marks of even some other close species! Remember all those giant creatures that used to live here—it is suggested that information-losing mutations, in genes coding for such imprinting recognition proteins, might actually be a good mechanism to explain rapid post-Flood speciation in all life.

The empty, drying earth would have been an excellent place for rapid spread and adaptation of individual Kinds of life, with huge blooms of plant and water life, and their millions of seeds, fruits and eggs. This availability of lots of food would stimulate the very high birth rate of many 'lesser' creatures, yet with initial low numbers of larger predators. All this should have resulted in speedy recolonisation of the earth. It is possible that there was a 'division' of the earth in the days of Peleg (Genesis 10:25), perhaps around 2250 BC. 'Continental Drift' of 'tectonic plates' appears to be a well-attested phenomenon not just by secular science, but also by some theologians who cite the biblical references to Peleg. This is hotly disputed by others, who see it as just the dividing of peoples in the Table of Nations, yet admit continental break-up at that time would explain much.

One example of *'speciation'* occurred when Herring Gulls *(Larus argentatus)* became Lesser Black-back Gulls *(Larus fuscus),* and now do not *usually* interbreed: though they can, as all the 'intermediates' obviously can. As they spread around the glaciated regions, the backs of Herring Gulls gradually became darker and their legs yellowed (as in the Mediterranean Yellow-legged Gull). By the time they had ringed the globe, at least two new species of Lesser Black-back Gulls had been formed.

This is termed 'ring speciation', and is probably how most speciation happens. As the subjects vary slightly from their parents and gradually cease to breed with them they can take on local 'accents' and characteristics: the Lesser Black-back has a deeper call and different migratory behaviour, probably caused by different glacial ebb and flow in Eurasia and the Americas. Its darker back could be explained by wintering near the Tropics. However, it is due only to recombinations of existing DNA and environmental circumstances, and does not involve any *new* genetic information, but less, and the gene pool is gradually weakened. Again, varying combinations of the same genes and even different number of chromosomes are thought to produce a lot of variation of certain characteristics—but not evolution. Polar, Eurasian Brown and Grizzly Bears, for instance, are virtually all the same 'species', as are the various river dolphins, also found in Asia and the Americas. Yet all are still gulls, bears and dolphins—again demonstrating what must have been recent isolation of populations. Some offspring seem *programmed* to actually distance themselves from their parents, perhaps by habitat differences as well as slight genetic losses, until they can no longer breed with them. We have seen this sort of thing, for instance, in the loss of long hair in certain dog or cat breeds—and the multitudes of weakened freaks that have been produced by 'selective (that is, over) breeding'. Inheritance is not just confined to genes, as 'cortical', or cell-wall, inheritance also contributes information; another important reason to doubt wild evolutionary speculation about changes, or the current and very dangerous pop-science of 'a gene for this, or a gene for that'.[33] This is more about trying to evade our moral responsibilities, than it is 'science'.

Songbirds other than Galapagos Finches can also provide us with snap-shots of speciation. Eurasian Bullfinches, Goldfinches and Canaries especially, are all interbred by breeders and produce various colour combinations, though they cannot always necessarily breed any further. They sometimes become 'Mules', as sterile offspring of horse and donkey were called, for that reason. 'Hybridisation' is fairly common, and both divisive and functional, for it usually only occurs between similar 'species', and when

Fig. 114: 'RING SPECIES'—A: HERRING GULL (LARUS ARGENTATUS); B: LESSER BLACK-BACKED GULL (LARUS FUSCUS GRAELISII); and C: LESSER BLACK-BACKED GULL (LARUS FUSCUS).

needed. More often than not it will result in sterile offspring, but does seem to work when males are scarce, as when male birds of paradise were being hunted out. Also, when Capercaillie were reintroduced to Scotland, the females would often attend Black Grouse display leks to procure mates, and fertile young resulted (called, I think, the 'Racklehen' in Germany).

Generally speaking the results are often weaker—colours tend to run to the dullest form, and even behaviour is affected. Most hybrids will breed back to the norm over time, while others, like certain ducks, go on to breed further and more complex crosses. Once again this raises the problem of 'species' within classification, where many creatures should be reclassified as sub-species, at least. Eurasian Greenfinches and Chinese Greenfinches can still happily interbreed, probably and simply showing how they were 'split' by glaciation in the Ice Age, some 3,500 to 4,250 years ago. Siberian Tits and Boreal Chickadees also still demonstrate this overlapping, or 'ring' or 'sympatric speciation', among many other birds. It would be interesting to see African Longclaws try to breed with American Meadowlarks, for they were probably, very recently, the same 'species'. I first noticed their great similarity when sketching the two in situ, for both are upright, bright yellow-fronted lark-like birds of open country, with distinctive black chest Vees.

Endemics

'*Endemics*' are one-off, isolated, birds that have developed local characteristics, or split into similar species, usually on recent volcanic islands. The famed Galapagos Finches are good examples, but even Winter Wrens become slightly larger and darker on remote Hebridean islands, like St Kilda. This all vindicates the biblical record that life can only reproduce '*after its Kind*', and that very rapid 'speciation' was deliberately built in to repopulate the earth after the Flood. The Ice Age quickly followed, causing large fluctuations in sea levels and eventually isolating continental landmasses, and thus their flora and fauna. Continental Drift could also have contributed to those isolations during the glaciation. Many rapid mountain and island-building episodes seem to have punctuated these troubled times, and further isolated or mixed different populations of lifeforms. There are so many fossil assemblages resulting from the Flood and its tumultuous aftermath, when the earth was still settling down, with the inevitable catastrophic effects of volcanic activity. Floodwaters also came from underground 'fountains of the great deep' (Genesis 7:11) breaking out, indicating massive crustal movements, followed by 'rebound' of the land as the glaciers later melted. This was probably when the Grand

Canyon and similar features *suddenly* appeared, as truthful secular scientists are now realising. 'Raised beaches' are but one result of all this activity. The fossil record certainly points to tropical creatures once living in temperate lands, like hummingbirds, giant hippopotamuses and palms in Northern Europe, to name but one—and mammoths. Tropical tree fossils are found near the North Pole. Fairly accurate maps of Antarctica *before* it was frozen have also been found, clearly pointing to both drastic, short-term changes as well as the thoroughness of man's early knowledge and travels. Global famines and huge earth movements are described in many global literary sources including, of course, the Bible (authors like Bill Cooper collect such records. See bibliography).

Fig. 115: AMERICAN EASTERN MEADOWLARK (STURNELLA MAGNA); B: AFRICAN YELLOW-THROATED LONGCLAW (MACRONYX CROCEUS).

There were large famines in Abraham and Joseph's time, seemingly corresponding to Neanderthal's hard life in glacial Europe.

The recent nature of all this is still being witnessed. In the thirteenth century, Marco Polo recorded the wet nature of areas of central Asia that are now far drier, and large inland salt lakes and seas are still disappearing today, although also assisted by us. It is not just the Sahara that is still spreading and revealing huge under-sand riverbeds visible from space, but also northern Indian deserts, and doubtless on other continents, too. It is now known that the Aborigines actually created much of the central Australian deserts themselves, comparatively recently, by over-burning the bush, as did North American Indians. Massive Australian lakes have since disappeared as a direct consequence. Man has also recently created small deserts in a mere ten years or so, by felling areas of shallow-rooted, rain forest trees in Central America. This allows the soil to be rapidly washed away, which then no longer attracts rain, and so on. Land falls into the sea even today at an alarming rate, just as isles appear and erode and age in months! The effect upon wildlife must have been equally fast. Hawaiian honeycreepers are pretty little birds noted for their variability, like many island dwellers, and the beak of the Iiwi is presently shortening almost as speedily as its favourite deep flowers are disappearing.

Most telling, the peoples of the Pacific have recorded in their history when many of their famous volcanic isles, like Samoa and Hawaii, first appeared from the depths.[34] Likewise, the Maoris of New Zealand some 600 years ago witnessed the rapid volcanic emergence of Rangitoto Island in the Tamaki Strait just off what is now Auckland. It is now completely forested. Remember also the speed with which mankind is claimed to have slaughtered huge numbers of giant Ice Age mammals in many lands, when 'natural' catastrophe was not also doing the same thing.

Cattle Egrets only crossed the Atlantic to the Americas in the nineteenth century, and now Little Egrets have just followed them. That raises a very interesting question: will they interbreed 'back' with the similar American Snowy Egret with whom they undoubtedly share a recent, common ancestor? Little Egrets were rare UK birds about 20 years ago, yet flocks of over 100 now grace many southern estuaries. Even here in North Wales, single records in 1998 have changed to a flock of 60-plus by 2004. In mainland Britain, Fulmar Petrels, Collared Doves and Hen Harriers have also fully 'arrived'. There were none here about 50 years ago, but now they are in every suitable habitat, unless persecuted, like the harrier, for daring to take 'our' Red Grouse chicks on keepered moors. The world is full of similar stories of rapid spread from few pioneers—exactly as the Bible indicates in Genesis 10. It is probably speeding up today, because of environmental change. All this is frequently the exact opposite of evolution's theories: speed and youth reign, not gradualism and age.

Evolution's time is running out
The glib and standard answer given by evolutionists to the many objections raised by creationists is usually something like, 'given millions of years just about anything can happen'. But can these millions of years truly be found

Fig. 116: HAWAIIAN HONEYCREEPERS : A: IIWI. B: AKIAPOLAAU AKIALOA (HEMIGNATHUS WILSONI). C: KAUAI AKIALOA (H. PROCERUS). D: CRESTED HONEYCREEPER (PALMERIA DOLEI).

in the *geological record?* If not, then evolution's unlikely case simply founders yet again. They desperately need these great ages, of course, for the sort of painfully slow, blind chance processes that an accumulation of trillions of genetic mistakes demands. Trial and error—but where are the errors in the fossil record? According to some evolutionists, the earth has had hundreds of millions of unique, fully developed life forms living upon it, only to be destroyed by massive catastrophes: hardly natural selection! Just where are the absolutely necessary trillions of linking, transitional fossils in our voluminous fossil record? There is not even one showing developing, transitional features—just a few 'fully formed mosaics', like Archaeopteryx or Lungfish.

That just about sums up the fossil record: it is virtually always a record of loss, rapid catastrophe and death; not gain, slow *'Uniformitarianism'* and life. There is often a reduction in size, for example in birds like the massive 'Argentavus' (a 'teratorn', or vulture/eagle), which had a huge wingspan of 25ft (8m). These large raptors are conventionally dated to around '5–8 mya' ('Miocene', 'early' Ice Age times), along with other similar, but smaller teratorns. Now, when we condense these times more reasonably, it can be seen that many of these fossils are actually from about the same times; rapidly preserved together in volcanic ash or tar pits. 400,000 bird remains alone come from the American La Brea tar pits, disregarding the many giant mammals also found.[35] Times were tough, and this is reflected in the large number of disaster stories from most of the world's peoples, when fire and flood, meteorite bombardment and Exodus-type 'ten plagues' scenarios seemingly affected the whole earth. We shall be looking briefly at this historical scenario in the final chapter, where giant birds are just one of the many common links.

The earlier fossil record (Jurassic onwards) has some extinct flying reptiles that were even larger, having up to 40ft (14m) wingspans. These pterosaurs were seemingly post-Flood, yet their existence supposedly calls for very different atmospheric conditions than today. Strangely enough, the huge, extinct 30lb (14kg) Haast's Eagle in New Zealand was supposedly related to one of the world's smallest eagles, the Australasian Little Eagle, which typically weighs less than 2lb (1kg) (and not unsurprisingly to creationists, looks just like our Eurasian Booted Eagle). Yet the Haast's Eagle was between 30 per cent and 40 per cent heavier than the largest living bird of prey alive today, the Harpy Eagle of Latin America, and was approaching the upper weight limit for powered flight. Evolution's main problem is once again the extremely rapid rate of 'mutated' change required between the Haast's and Little Eagle, even within their time frame of '1–2 my'.

It is claimed that none of these huge creatures could fly in today's changed air pressure, theorised by some creationists to be a consequence of losing the possible 'swaddling band' of pure water vapour from around the earth (Genesis 1:9, 7:11; Job 25:8, 38:9). If these waters indeed fell as part of the drowning of the earth, that could have opened life up to ageing cosmic rays and a different climate, also reflected in our own reducing human life-spans since those times. Wonderful corroboration comes from standard dental tests on Neanderthal Man's teeth—some lived for up to 300 years! (They were often bigger, stronger and brainier than us—not the deformed brutes of evolutionary preconceptions, warped by the first rickety and arthritic skeletons found.)[36]

This whole subject is fraught with difficulty as we attempt to reconstruct

The design and origin of birds **179**

Fig. 117: A: PTEROSAUR (ORTHINOCHEIRUS). B: ARGENTAVUS. C: HAAST'S EAGLE. D: BOOTED EAGLE. (TO SCALE.)

the pre-Flood and post-Flood world. Disasters abound, as creationists should expect from both biblical and geological records, yet sketching out a clear scenario is often impossible. Huge fossil assemblages have been laid, rocks rapidly hardened and then frequently upended, planed off, relaid and so on! These great fossil beds have prompted popular notions for the sudden extinction at various periods: like the dinosaurs 'about 64 mya', by massive volcanic or asteroid action. But this does not explain why the birds or small mammals did not also disappear, or all other saurians like crocodiles, etc. Neither can evolution properly explain the apparent huge global increase in both bird and mammal species around this time. From the upper 'Cretaceous' down into the 'Eocene' was a time of major mountain building, and massive fossilised fish deposits, denoting large-scale, watery catastrophe again. The so-called iridium layer at the 'Cretaceous/Tertiary' boundary *seems* to support the idea of massive meteorites causing chaos here on earth, but there are many problems with interpreting what actually happened. These 'explosions' of all sorts of giant and other bird fossils: ducks, waders, seabirds, owls, raptors, cuckoos, swifts and kingfishers, etc., were all laid down by disaster and simply show what was around in localised areas. Many birds, like the so-called 'primitive', flightless wildfowl *(Patagopteryx)*, grebes *(Baptornis)*, terns *(Ichthyornis)*, tropicbirds *(Prophaeton)*, storks *(Propelargus)*, secretary birds *(Amphiserpentarius)*, New World vultures *(Neocathartes)*, rollers *(Geranopterus)*, swifts *(Aegialornis)*, flamingos *(Palaeolodus)*, flightless auks *(Mancalla)* all suddenly appear, fully formed, in the '70my+' of late Cretaceous/Tertiary, and on into the recent Pleistocene. Yet these and other fossils are so relatively common they have not been properly assessed, and were all victims of rapid, localised fossilisations, spanning probably no more than a few hundred years in reality. More damning evidence from 'Cretaceous' fossil beds *(Discovery.com* 4:4:2005), revealed *unfossilised* bird bones, and some Moas are so 'recent' as to be mummified not fossilised.

There were many giant creatures around in post-Flood and Ice Age times, including other huge birds dated to 'Tertiary' times, '50 mya'. *Reconstructions* of the flightless 8ft (2.6m) *Diatryma* and the similar but later, and larger, *Phororachus,* show Emu-type birds, but with thicker necks and massive carnivore's beaks, larger than a human head.

As large as these 'terror-birds' were, the 'later' Moas towered over them (only exterminated about 400 years ago), and they could have resembled the much smaller Caudipteryx, as well. Lots of variety, just as today, once we collapse the unreasonable time frame—and bearing in mind that island birds can tend to gigantism. Teeth were also still around on 'Tertiary' birds like *Osteodontornis,* although they fall somewhere between Archaeopteryx's 'bird teeth' and our merganser's 'serrations'. It seems that many life forms were generally becoming smaller and less armoured, or strong. This fits in rather well with the biblical scenario of loss and catastrophe, plus rapid adaptation in various areas of life: as the patriarchs' drastically falling lifespans also demonstrates. Evolutionists, of course,

Fig. 118: COMPARISON OF VARIOUS FLIGHTLESS EXTINCT BIRDS, WITH A: MODERN OSTRICH. B: CAUDIPTERYX. C: GIANT MOA. D: PHORORHACUS. E: DIATRYMA. (TO SCALE, THOUGH AS USUAL THE EXTINCT BIRDS ARE OFTEN BASED UPON GUESSWORK and OTHERS' RECONSTRUCTIONS, AS IN FEDUCCIA, 1999.)

disagree about the timescale, even if many are now rediscovering the truth of '*Catastrophism*'.

Such changes much more resemble creation than evolution. Like the 'Cambrian explosion' that supposedly started it all, we seem to see huge varieties of life suddenly appearing, fully formed. Of course, this is where interpretation of the fossil record becomes vital. Both creationists and evolutionists are using exactly the same material data—rocks and fossils—but coming to very different conclusions. It is also important to point out that many fossil assemblages are *ecological*, not necessarily *evolutionary*: that is, many of the same life forms might occur in the same sedimentary type, as well as being *contemporary* with other deposits of different life forms.

Evolution's fancies and forgeries

When it comes to fossil reconstructions, we must also bear in mind evolution's sad history of many fossil forgeries and errors. Right from its modern inception when proof was quickly needed, there have been many frauds, mistakes and denials, both conscious and unconscious:

• *Ernst Haeckel's* nineteenth century human and animal embryo forgeries, supposedly showing us 'recapitulating' (reliving) our evolutionary history, were exposed long ago. However, they have only just been widely admitted as such in our press, and are still used by university textbooks, during supposedly authoritarian debates and on the media, both press and television.

• The dangerous and sometimes fatal notion of 90-plus *'vestigial'*, or evolutionary 'left-over' organs in the human body, is still sometimes taken seriously. It also remains in many textbooks, and pop science.

• The reinventing of what appears to be a small *Rock Hyrax*, as *'Dawn Horse/Eohippus'*, at the bottom of the famous 'Horse series'. Yet all can be found jumbled together, or in rapid succession—and are just large and small horses, as today, with even some 'primitive' horses with three toes still existing. Also, loss of side toes is just that: loss, not gain.

• The false claims, based on only two little bits of skull, that *'Pakicetus'* was the aquatic missing link between land animals and whales: when it actually is some kind of wolf! Any claim that land animals could gradually became cetaceans is ridiculous; for whales breathe through the tops of their heads through a totally separate windpipe to their mouth and digestive system—unlike land animals, which would simply drown.

• Dawson, de Chardin and others' deliberately forged 'Piltdown man' ape/human skull, with filed down and even filled teeth, somehow 'fooled' the British Museum experts for over 40 years.

• 'Colorado' man was built from a horse bone (as other *'Ape-men'* from dolphin bones, etc.) and

• Brutish *'Nebraska man'* was reconstructed from a single *pig's* tooth!

• *'Java' and 'Peking'* 'ape-men' were invented from various bits of ape and human bone, found apart in space and time—and both near 'modern' human skeletons.

• *'Australopithecines'* are just small apes, probably like Bonobo Chimps, but often dishonestly shown with human feet and hands (its supposed human knee bone was found far away and much lower in the strata). This is only so they can be 'forced' into the modern human footprints at Laetoli, which are supposed to be far 'too old' for man.

• Other *'ape-men'*, like *'Laetoli'*, *'Kanapoi'*, *'Boxgrove'*, *'Neanderthal'*, etc. are all simply human, and contemporary in the fossil record— alongside or even preceding 'Australopithecines'. Many human artefacts and bones are claimed from the earliest geological times, yet dismissed out of hand.

• Dakota's 'Moab' human skeletons destroy the whole idea of great age and evolution. These skeletons are buried in foetal position in solid 'Jurassic' (dinosaur) sandstones, supposedly '150 mya'![37] Just like 'Miocene man' buried in his solid limestone matrix at about '20 mya'. The evidence does not support claims that these are more recent burials.

• Ignoring the fact that apes have penile bones and humans do not, how did two completely different methods of reproduction 'accidentally' evolve from 'similar' ape-like stock, when reproduction is vital to the survival of a species? Creationists still await proper answers from the 'experts' to such questions. (Richard Dawkins has come up with the risible idea that this massive change could occur, and calls it 'honest signalling' from the males. Against overwhelming odds, amid ages of being unable to mate properly, some bone-less, incredible 'super-Apeman' impressed the ladies, and somehow managed to reproduce! He at least admits that 'the existence of sexual reproduction poses a big theoretical puzzle for Darwinians', in the first place.)[38]

• Recently, the 'Hobbit' (Homo floresiensis) from south-east Asia, was discovered and claimed to be a midget 'hairy ape-man' though, as usual, no hair was found. Their skull is very like a miniature human's, and just as the locals accurately described it—for they saw them just a few hundred years ago and knew they were human, and not hairy! They could apparently 'chatter' incomprehensibly, but that is a possible side-effect of their possible condition. Deafness often applies to pygmy types with thyroid problems, like other tiny 'cretins' living in recent historical times, again revealing devolution not evolution. (Much of this information is in Lubenow's and Bowden's books—see bibliography.)

At least the whistle has been blown on another huge evolutionary preconception and error, the famous false claims from Yale University that humans have about 98 per cent DNA parity with Chimpanzees—even though chimp DNA had *not* been sequenced. They also 'knew' that we had almost the same parity with mice, but the so-called 'junk' DNA had not been included in this count, either, and that is over 90 per cent of the total. Since then, *Nature* magazine has reported the latest research showing the genes on ape chromosome 22 are possibly 83 per cent *different* in function from human![39] And the uncounted 'junk' DNA is now increasingly known to have important functions, but, of course, none of that made the headlines.

• Reiner Protsch von Zieten, a Frankfurt university panel ruled (WorldNet Daily 19:2:2005) has forged and manipulated scientific facts over the past thirty years. They say he lied about the age of human skulls, dating them to tens of thousands of years old, even though much younger. One dated at 27,400 years old was actually an elderly man who died in 1750! A few years ago, a top Japanese archaeologist was covertly filmed burying old artefacts so that he could 'discover' them, and cheating is now admitted to be widespread in science, because of the huge competition for funds. It is frequently as subjective as any human pursuit, and often cannot accept the slightest challenge to its theories. None of this inspires much confidence in wild genetic guesswork—remember no one had properly looked at an ape's DNA when the wild claims of similarity were made. Nor can we have any confidence in a palaeontologist's fossil 'reconstructions', when bits of bone have frequently been 'mixed and matched' to suit their preconceptions. There are many claims of dishonesty in all branches of science, as in any human activity, such as those recently reported in the *Washington Post*, (9:6:2005).[40]

The geological column

The geological evidence used by both evolutionists and creationists is the same. It is simply based upon a rock or fossil's position in the geological column: the only difference is in the interpretation. The main disagreement is over the *speed* at which the rocks and fossils were formed. Geology shows that over three-quarters of the earth is covered by a massive thickness of water-laid, sedimentary rock, crammed in places with trillions of catastrophically generated, rapidly buried and jumbled fossils. The facts clearly indicate that this was formed in huge flooding and catastrophism. The same geological record also shows massive amounts of volcanic ashes and rocks, which rapidly covered huge areas. That would explain the many anomalies, like the fact that the fossil record contains some 99.9 per cent of sea-bed creatures, like fish, algae and plants, obviously mainly water formed.[41] Evolutionists have always known their theory must rest upon actual fossils, but as they blindly deny the biblical Flood, their elastic, non-falsifiable theory must be moulded to explain a slow scenario. So now they boldly deny the need for links, like Oxford's Mark Ridley, claiming they never based evolutionary theory upon the fossil record anyway, contrary to Darwin's own statements.[42] Or, like Gould and Eldredge, they say that the absence of linking fossils proves that evolution is so rapid that it could not be recorded in the fossil record.

This is the largely Marxist idea of *'Punctuated Equilibrium'*, probably the only scientific theory based upon a complete *absence* of evidence, because no true transitional fossils have ever been found! The idea was that short bursts of evolution, like revolution, 'punctuated' millions of years when nothing happened. This is the exact opposite of the necessarily slow accumulation of trillions of mistakes in Darwinism, as they were not fast enough for Soviet scientists to base their Communism on. Their mutually contradictory notion was that both evolution and revolution are necessary to move from a capitalist society to a classless one, and change must occur rapidly, like the bloody overthrow of the Russian government. It was no coincidence that Communist scientists like Oparin were also involved in fruitless experiments to try and produce life from non-life. Marx had said, 'spontaneous generation is the only practical refutation of the theory of creation'.[43] Like Lyell, he unsuccessfully tried to 'remove Moses' from science. Like others' experiments, real 'life' has never been formed in the laboratory.

Yet another major problem for evolutionists is the reliance placed on *radioactive dating methods*, the only 'real' criteria they have for dating the rock layers, and there is an awful lot of circular reasoning involved. Palaeontologists and geologists know that rocks are usually only usually datable by their 'index' fossils, which in turn are usually dated by the rocks, which are dated by their fossils, ad nauseam. Sedimentary rocks—the majority—cannot be dated unless they contain fragments of non-sedimentary rocks, and only sedimentary rocks usually contain fossils.

The next problem is that a fossil should only be in such and such a place according to theory, when many are 'out of place', and the conventional 'Geological Column' barely exists at all in any one place on earth—'millions of years' are often missing. However, there is a regular, sequential order in the rocks—and it is largely global. Such extensive layering shouts of massive *global* catastrophe: erosion, deposition and rapidity. The violent, almost global 'unconformity' at the base of our rocks, the Precambrian/Cambrian boundary, the rapidly laid and massive thicknesses of limestone, sandstones and mudstones above, clearly point to such a catastrophe. Above these layers are lessening, but still massive, coal seams stretching from Kentucky to China, together with limestones and sandstones almost universal and crammed with trillions of fossils, then stupendous amounts of chalks, etc.

The inferences should be obvious. Complete, violent and watery inundation ripped the rocks down to the roots, wiped everything out, rapidly laid new rocks, eroded many of them again in still almost global fashion, and finally settled down as the new world emerged from catastrophe. Only the global Flood of Genesis, plus its inevitable aftermath of watery, volcanic and tectonic activity, and a brief glacial period, can generally explain the speed and distribution of fossils and rocks.

There is another evolutionary problem. How could random *geological* gaps possibly explain systematic *biological* gaps? It cannot be coincidence that all their vital missing links just happen to have fallen in the chance geological gaps! Different radioactive dating methods are often unreliable too, because they do not take into account the many factors that so greatly accelerate the processes. They can all distort the age of the rocks. We cannot know the original, starting values of the elements in the rocks, as all rock is permeable to some degree and elements like uranium can wash in and out. Hence they often come up with totally contradictory ages from the same sample. In fact, most laboratories will not test unless given an evolutionary age estimate of the rock *first!*

Thus, *recent* lavas are radio-dated to millions of years old, whereas in some cases the trees *beneath* (or sometimes in them) were more reasonably aged by carbon-14 dating to just a few thousand years. Some of the lavas thus aged were in New Zealand, yet the Maoris' recent ancestors had witnessed the eruption of the 'mya' lava. They also left their footprints in the rapidly hardening ash, as probably humans, not apes, did at Laetoli in Africa. That is why the ape 'Lucy' is dishonestly given human hands and feet so as to fit the Laetoli footprints: the prints are supposed to be too old for the humans that probably made them. Scientists have recently discovered that differing chemical conditions can accelerate certain radioactive decay rates by up to a billion times.[44] Then EM (electromagnetic radiation) from lightning and volcanic action is also very common on earth and also greatly accelerates radio-decay, as apparently exploding supernovae also do. Some also admit that radiocarbon 14 (^{14}C) levels have also varied widely in the past, making even their 'recent' age calculations extremely unreliable. This method is usually used only on 'young' samples up to '50,000 years old', and other radioactive methods, like uranium into lead, used on the very 'old' rocks. However, many 'millions of years old' fossils retested for ^{14}C show them to be just thousands of years old! In the same way, atmospheric ^{14}C and radiogenic helium exhibit youth by not yet reaching equilibrium, when they should have done that in just 10,000 years or so.[45]

Meanwhile, back in the real world, solid rock, massive canyons, oil, coal, gas, diamonds, opals, stalagmites and even fossils can form in only hours, days or months, both in nature and/or the laboratory. This has recently, and most dramatically, been demonstrated by the eruptions of *Surtsey Island* and *Mount St Helen's*. Iceland's Surtsey Island appeared suddenly out of the sea in 1963, yet its rocks had eroded to cliffs, screes, rounded boulders and even sand in only a few *months,* giving it the almost instant appearance of great age. When *Mount St Helen's* (Washington State, USA) volcano literally blew its massive top in 1980, it swept millions of trees into Spirit Lake. When they started to sink, many were buried upright in different layers, and stripped bark sinking to the lakebed is already turning to peaty coal. The eruption, mud flows, huge remodelling of the lake, and subsequent 'dam burst' also deposited up to 600ft (200m) of finely graded sediments, identical in appearance to 'millions of years' old cliffs, in days. The massive dam then burst and cut canyons through hundreds of feet of both new sedimentary and solid rocks in times as rapid as one afternoon.[46] The Grand Canyon was probably formed in the same way, for only huge water bodies could cut both laterally and vertically through the still soft and uprising Flood deposits. Today, only lowland rivers cut serpentine curves, and only through soft sediments. Many small rivers are infilling, not eroding, canyons: again the opposite of evolutionary theories. Creationists are still debating different theories of fossil and rock distributions, especially as they relate to any post-Flood boundary, but be assured, speed and catastrophe are always the basis of their ideas. I personally think the whole column is probably a record of less than a thousand years, from the Flood's dramatic beginning to the end of the Ice Age—at very roughly 1600BC, when many peoples were still spreading world-wide with similar tales of creation, catastrophe and a lost 'Paradise' (garden); or similar concepts like the Elysian Fields, Tir nan-Og, Atlantis or Shangri-la.

Earth—old, or just tired?

There are many other factors that dramatically show the comparatively young age of the earth and universe. Of hundreds of estimates for the age of our Earth, only *one* gives the 4.5 billion years age usually used by evolutionists; the rest are enormously younger.[47]

Many other 'proofs' of a young cosmos and earth exist, but we must be very wary of not falling into the evolutionist's trap, and claiming factual evidence from our little understood cosmos. Nevertheless, here are just a few indications of a youthful universe:

- The comparatively rapid rate of recession of the moon from the earth;
- The weakening of the earth's electromagnetic field;
- The maintenance of the spiral arms of galaxies;
- The connection between 'Quasars' and galaxies;
- The sun's low neutrino count and apparent shrinkage rate;
- The tiny size of Mercury, which should have both lost its magnetic field and cooled down, long ago;
- The *light-time-travel* problem: often said to be a problem for biblical believers in a young universe, is also a big problem for 'long-agers'. New, theoretical measurements of the size of the universe show it to be far larger

than it 'should be'. So it 'must have expanded much faster than light in its early stage'. All these problems merely highlight our ignorance and wild guesses about the real Genesis. God 'stretched out the heavens', *then* created our light (though he is light)—a mature cosmos, as mature people, planets and animals were created, yet evolutionists regard this as cheating!

• The controversial observations of the slowing down of the speed of light, a largely creationist theory[48] now being accepted by some in mainstream science. It could explain 'Red Shift', and would drastically affect and lower all age and radio-decay calculations, possibly reflecting initially high radio-decay. So such radio-decay *units* are not necessarily *years* at all—see the work of R.A.T.E., etc.[42] Evolution demands *'Uniformitarian'*, or very slow and reliable processes—the real world provides few. Today's apparently slow radiodecay rates do not necessarily equate with the past, and cannot be taken as proof of great age—especially when we recall how many factors distort them.

There is another Creationist theory to try to account for a young earth in an apparently 'old' universe: in Russell Humphrey's *Starlight and Time* book.[49] As far as I understand it he has a young earth emerging out of a 'white hole' into a 'mature', bounded universe—because the earth is at an 'event horizon' where gravity distorts time, only six days pass on earth while billions of years flash by in the outer universe! *It is important to remember that such ideas are largely only theories relating to a one-of, unobserved, and unrepeatable event: our faith rests on Jesus.*

• The very rapid erosion, volcanic activity and catastrophic events that we observe in the world today, but which are as nothing compared with the huge events of the past. The world has just witnessed the tragedy of the Indian Ocean tsunami, in which over 250,000 people died very rapidly, yet little geological evidence was left. There was nothing remotely Uniformitarian about that event. The indications of a young earth and cosmos contained here are quoted in many, mainly creationist publications (see bibliography), with Henry Morris' *The Biblical Basis of Modern Science* being particularly useful.[47]

Dinosaurs or dragons?

Only an Evolutionist needs *time*. Our history is dramatic and recent, our 'civilisations', languages and artefacts all springing into the world, virtually fully formed, a few thousand years ago. The so-called 'Cambrian' or 'Cenozoic' explosions of animal life, which are only naively extrapolated from fairly random layers of sedimentary rocks and their many fossils are demonstrably young. We now know that most rocks can form incredibly rapidly and in huge thicknesses. Our magnificent mountains scream *'speed'*. Their incredible contortions of both thick and thin rock layers must all have been still soft when those peaks rose and twisted, or overthrust and eroded. We, and most of Creation, have always been here together: just look at the beautifully accurate engravings of dinosaurs on Bishop Bell's fourteenth-century tomb in Carlisle cathedral,[50] or the many dinosaur or 'dragon' rock paintings, engravings and sculptures worldwide.

Australia's Aborigines have long painted very convincing 'plesiosaurs' upon the rocks, insisting, that like their 'global flood' stories, that they predate the influence of Christian missionaries. In literature like the Anglo-Saxon epic *Beowulf* there are great water monsters or 'grendels' (we have a Grendel Mere, or lake, in the UK, and other lakes named for their dinosaurian monsters, as here in Wales), and medieval Italian literature bemoans their lessening size and probable extinction (many of these examples are gathered together in Creationist books, magazines and pamphlets, e.g. *Creation ex-nihilo* magazines, Bill Cooper's CSM, or CRT's leaflets. See bibliography.) One of our greatest artist/scientists, Leonardo da Vinci, drew dragons/dinosaurs in his natural history notebooks, alongside the usual creatures—were they all from life? The 'myths' of all peoples worldwide tells of some sort of 'dragons'. What of the massive swamp and marine dinosaurs of Job 40 and 41, the 'greatest of God's creation'? Remember, dinosaur is a comparatively new word, and some modern Chinese dictionaries still call 'dragons' 'extinct dinosaurs'! Red blood cells and DNA in dinosaur bones, and many unfossilised dinosaur bones also shout youth. As do unfossilised ammonites and shells still popping out of Swindon mud springs, shells pearly, ligaments intact.[51] I realise that many 'dragons' had six limbs whereas birds or dinosaurs only have four; but our imaginative memory could account for that. The Amerindians had their pterodactyl-like 'Thunderbirds' and as for a dragon's tendency to breath

Fig. 119: VARIOUS 'DINOSAUR' ROCK DRAWINGS. A: MOAB, UTAH 'SAUROPOD', 1ST MILLENNIUM AD. B: HAVASUPAI CANYON, ARIZONA, 'DINOSAUR', 1ST MILLENNIUM AD. C: 'DINOSAURS', CARLISLE CATHEDRAL, 14TH CENTURY AD. D: 'INCA OR PRE-INCA DINOSAURS'. (MAINLY AFTER *CREATION EX-NIHILO* MAGAZINE, VOL. 19, NO. 2.) E. CRETACEOUS 'PTEROSAUR', ALSO MOAB.

fire, some *could* have had similar mechanisms to the Bombardier Beetle. This startling little creature can actually store and then precisely mix volatile chemicals and fire them from its rear, in staccato bursts of blistering heat! Again, little room for trial and error there.

Times up!

Many of our top evolutionary geologists, like Derek Ager, recognise that all rocks form rapidly, and he famously downgraded the formation time of certain South Wales limestones from about '5 mya' down to a few hours, on 'a Tuesday afternoon'![52] They easily recognise that the earth's tortured surface is a record of very rapid formation, though still try to insert the needed millions of years into the 'gaps' between the catastrophic events, even with little evidence for these gap periods. If those 'gaps' represented thousands or millions of years of seabeds or land surfaces, then there should be lots of evidence of burying shellfish and worms, or plant roots, as well as water and wind erosion. In fact, some twentieth century seabed sediments are completely eroded away in only a few years. There are comparatively few of those *'hardgrounds'*, and they indicate little more than a couple of dozen years, nothing remotely like the millions needed. Many layers were laid consecutively and rapidly, with sharp, clean contact surfaces: many have studied Ager's famous limestone layer full of broken corals and other debris—and it is clearly not a record of growth and time. We only have to look at some of the many examples of neat, uniform, rapid layering in mountains or canyons to realise the constant and fast rate of deposition. From the Grand Canyon to the Welsh Brecon Beacons, or from the Chinese 'Loess' cliffs to the Pyrenean Ordesa Canyon—we mainly see massive water action and neat layering, huge erosion and redeposition: in other words, catastrophism, none of which requires millions of years. Remember that fossilisation or petrifaction only requires the correct chemical conditions—not time. Some springs like Yorkshire's Knaresborough still turn soft things to stone in days or months, as an abundance of modern 'fossils' exhibits well.[53] Anything can be turned to stone or rapidly trapped in modern 'growing' rock, very quickly.

There are also many examples of large *'polystrate'* fossils interpenetrating many supposed geological periods. Think of the many frail birds, 40ft (13m) tree fern trunks, or huge dinosaurs and whales (one upright!) that are claimed to have lain undisturbed for thousands of years while very thin layers slowly built around them. Speed is essential for such excellent, detailed fossil preservation, but it must be away from the many factors that rapidly disarticulate dead creatures and plants. A few of the many trees appear to be in growth position, but were all rapidly washed in and quickly buried. This is seemingly demonstrated by the strange angles of trees apparently caught in mid fall and actually fixed in rapidly hardening sediments.

Just think about how all those trillions of fish came to be so rapidly preserved, including skin, soft tissues, eyes and all. Some were actually fossilised giving birth and many are even eating others! That is speed—

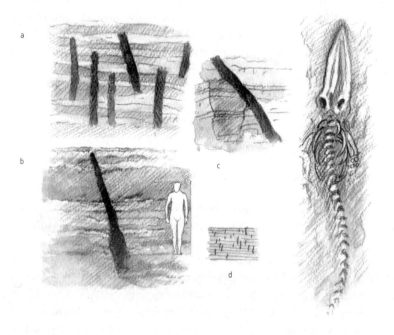

Fig. 120: 'POLYSTRATE' FOSSILS INTERPENETRATING SEVERAL ROCK LAYERS. A: FOSSIL TREES, ST ETIENNE, FRANCE (AFTER BOWDON, 1991). B: FOSSIL TREE, USA (AFTER SNELLING, IN MORRIS, J. 1997). C: FOSSIL TREE NR EDINBURGH, SCOTLAND. D: CALAMITE REEDS (FROM DESCRIPTION IN MORRIS, J. 1997). E: UPRIGHT WHALE IN DIATOMITE, PERU.

whereas under the conditions we observe, most creatures float and everything is quickly eaten or breaks down. Only instant burial during a massive catastrophe will create the conditions necessary for fossilisation. In the Grand Canyon, for instance, some 10 billion nautoloids were captured in just one very narrow band of limestone.

The Bible seems to express many of today's scientific insights, though in more poetic yet more accurate terms. Many think that our universe is finite, non-random, digitally programmed and self-correcting, like our DNA.

This points to the first words of the Bible: 'In the beginning God created the heavens and the earth.' The Bible goes on to tell us not only that everything had a beginning, but also that it was instantly created out of nothing. The first words of John's Gospel are: 'In the beginning was the Word.' The Greek word *logos,* here translated 'Word', means, among many other far more important things, 'Information' and 'Intelligence'. DNA is the information and intelligence on which the living cell is formed: without it, there is no cell and vice versa. Information is the first vital ingredient for life, *before* matter or energy. Just recall the many 'living fossils' that obviously always needed the same DNA from the beginning; what we mainly see is loss of genetic information, loss of size and of function. 'Information Theory', 'Message Theory' and 'Intelligent Design' all recognise the obvious—a complex code absolutely demands an intelligent coder. This must both precede it, and yet be separate from it.[54]

Life can only begin at conception, with the pinhead-sized fertilised egg instantly containing a massive encyclopaedia of information: about 6 billion 'chemical letters'. However, a DNA molecule has no more 'brain' than a water molecule, and although life is *made* from 'just' sugars and phosphates, etc., it is obviously much more than that. A newly dead body still has all those things, but vital and intangible life has already left, because 'the spirit will return to God who gave it' (Ecclesiastes 12:7). Only God's Holy Spirit can '(pierce) even to the division of soul and spirit' (Hebrews 4:12) and help us discern the truth about the eternal destination of our souls: heaven or hell.

Physics tells us that light pervades and affects our very being, and the miracle of water confirms our specialness, but it was the Bible that first told us everything was made from light, water and 'invisible things'. It also tells us that everything wears out, except our spirits; that He is 'upholding all things by the word of His power' (Hebrews 1:3); and that the 'round' earth 'hangs upon nothing' in space 'stretched out', where 'the sun circuits the heavens'. This is the real science, and many other scriptures confirm it: as Genesis 1; Hebrews 11; 2 Peter 3; Isaiah 40; Job 26; Psalm 104; Psalm 19, etc. Job 38, particularly, is laden with wonderful, not yet fully understood science: 'Where does light dwell?'

All creation was enormously complex from the start. As creation was finished on Day 6, it must have had latent variety and individuality miraculously allowed for, in an otherwise orderly universe. Every face, leaf and feather is slightly different, but all follow underlying order and design. Though all animals are unique and are living beings, only humans were given a special 'spirit' and charged, through Adam, with the care of God's creation. Mankind has failed to obey, and therefore does not recognise either the Creator's qualities or the effects of the Fall upon us and all creation. That God created EVERYTHING in six literal days is the first to go.

Evolution is today's creation myth, with believers worshipping at the blind altar of Time and Chance. It reduces mankind to mere chemical accidents and tries to destroy the meaning of life, the truth of eternity and undermines the morals clearly 'engraved upon our hearts' (Ecclesiastes 3:11; Romans 1:20; 2:15). It is little wonder that, after 150 years of evolutionary teaching, that many see life as nothing but a cheap accident in a 'blind, pitiless, indifferent' universe, that abortion, racism, murder, drug abuse, euthanasia, eugenics, cloning, sexual perversion, teenage suicide, downright nasty behaviour and family breakdown are so common. The Scripture's awesome prophecies about our deeply troubled 'end times' includes the prediction that many would follow 'profane and idle babblings and contradictions of what is falsely called knowledge *(Latin: scientea)*' (1 Timothy 6:20).

Just two of evolution's actual facts should alone be enough to destroy it and vindicate the biblical view. Firstly, entropy: everything is breaking down, especially over time, heading from complex to simple. Secondly, 'mankind has stopped evolving because DNA copies itself more or less perfectly'—to once again paraphrase evolutionist Steve Jones. The fact that scientists like him can actually think they are now in control of 'evolution' both shows their folly and clearly vindicates the Bible account. However, the real problem is that evolution will not be discarded while there is only one alternative and unacceptable view—that God exists and creation is true. The fossil record is clearly one of rapid destruction of many discrete forms, not slow development—and the Scriptures warn us that judgement is due again soon upon the unregenerate earth. When our Lord returns, our days will be 'just like the days of Noah and Lot' again. Most would be carrying on as usual, uncaring for the future, with evil, perversion and blasphemy abounding (see chapter 7).

It has been misleadingly stated that 'the medium is the message', but everything around us speaks, nay, shouts, 'Creation!' at us. Even fashionable 'Chaos theory' or the 'Anthropic Principle' grudgingly admits our specialness. Both of these ideas realise the incredible evidence for perfect intelligent design beneath all 'natural' processes—the true 'Matrix'; and the universe and life could not possibly exist without such fine tuning, from atom to neurone, galaxy to gravity, earth to eye. This means that evolutionists have to say, on no evidence at all, that there must be millions of 'parallel universes' without our perfect conditions, and therefore none of our 'accidental life'. In other words, we and our cosmos are a just a lucky, one-off accident! But to hear a Lyrebird's almost unbelievable display of mimicry, or watch an evening Barn Owl floating over a gilded meadow, a Peregrine's 175mph stoop, or a tiny Wren positively vibrating with passionate song, is to partake a little of the divine, and has nothing to do with vain imaginings of chance explosions. Our glorious, diverse, complex and spectacular kingdom of birds perhaps demonstrates divine creation better than anything else, except of course the mind-blowing sacrifice (2 Corinthians 9:15) of the very Creator himself, for any who care to turn to him.

Notes

1 *New Scientist,* 22:5:2004. And for the problems with quasars, *Astrophysical Journal,* 10:2:05.

2 **S. J. Gould,** *Wonderful Life—the Burgess Shales and the Nature of History* (Norton, 1989).

3 See especially *National Geographic,* 8:1998, and other issues.

4 e.g. *The Life of Birds,* BBC series and book by David Attenborough.

5 a—**Dr J. Durant,** 'How evolution became a scientific myth', *New Scientist,* 11:9:1980. b—**Prof. L. Bonoure,** 'The Advocate' 8:3:84. c—**Dr. R. Tahmisian** (USA Atomic Energy Commission), 'The Fresno Bee', 20:8:1959. All quoted in RBQ, p. 5.

6 *Philosophical Transactions* of the Royal Society. London B, 1991. Issue 332.

7 **Jensen.** Science News, 24:9:1997.

8 Material collated from **Lockley et al.,** *Origins* journal, Biblical Creation Society, no. 22, 3:1997.

Chapter 6

9 From Factsheet no. 28, Creation Resources Trust (address in bibliography)

10 'Smooth intermediates between Bauplane are almost impossible to construct, even in thought experiments; there is certainly no evidence for them in the fossil record *(curious mosaics like Archaeopteryx do not count)'* **S.J. Gould and N. Eldredge,** *Paleobiology,* 3:115–151 p. 147 1997. Similar quote in **S.J. Gould,** 1983, *Hen's Teeth and Horse's Toes* (Harmondsworth: Pelican, 1984), p. 181.

11 P. Shipman, *Taking Wing* (Weidenfield & Nicholson, 1998) p. 256.

12 Alan Feducia, *The Origin and Evolution of Birds* (2nd edition, Yale University Press, 1999).

13 *New Scientist,* 4:1997, p. 13.

14 A. Feduccia, lecture at the San Diego Natural History Museum, 11:2004.

15 *Science* 278 [5341] 11:1997, pp. 1129–1130.

16 M. Denton, *Evolution—a Theory in Crisis* (Adler & Adler, 1985), p. 212.

17 *National Geographic,* 7:1998, pp.75–99.

18 Factsheet no. 37, Creation Resources Trust.

19 Paul Garner, Origins Notebook no. 14, Biblical Creation Society.

20 *Creation Update* no. 33, Spring 2000 (Creation Resources Trust).

21 *Birds of the World,* Vol. 9, p. 2859.

22 *Science,* 24;10:1997, pp. 666–686. **Feduccia,** *op. cit.,* pp. 382–385.

23 Charles Darwin, *On the Origin of Species,* etc. (London: Dent, 1971), pp. 292–293.

24 David Tyler, *Origins Notebook,* no. 17 (Biblical Creation Society).

25 M. Behe, *Darwin's Black Box—the Biochemical Challenge to Evolution* (Simon & Schuster, 1996).

26 John Keosian, paraphrased, from *Origins of Life* (1978), pp. 569–574.

27 S. J. Gould *The Panda's Thumb* (Harmondsworth: Pelican, 1983), pp.150–151.

28 F. Hitchin, *The Neck of the Giraffe.*

29 R. Milton's best-seller *The Facts of Life* (Corgi Books, 1992). Now republished in the USA under its subtitle 'Shattering the Myths of Darwinism'.

30 L. Sunderland, *Darwin's Enigma* (Master Books, 1984), p. 89. RQB quote 35.

31 J.A. Coyne, *Nature,* 396 (6706). **J. Wells,** *The Scientist,* 5:1999.

32 For a good general explanation of the capacity of Noah's massive Ark and re-establishment of rapidly varying life, see **John Woodmorappe's** 'Noah's Ark—A Feasibility Study', ICR, 1996.

33 Dr A. Jones, 'The identity and nature of the created kinds—speciation among Cichlid fish', *Genesis Agendum* paper no. 7, 2002, pp. 9–11. **Jonathan Wells'** book *The End of the Genetic Paradigm* addressing the same sort of subject, is due out 2006.

34 Williamson, *Religious and Cosmic beliefs of Central Polynesia.*

35 C. Stock, *Rancho La Brea—A Record of Pleistocene Life in California* (L A County Museum of Natural History, 1972).

36 Cuozzo, J. 'Earlier Orthodontic Intervention', *Journal* of New York Dental Association, vol. 58, no. 4, 1987.

37 Joe Taylor, *Fossil Facts and Fantasies* (Mt Blanco, 1999).

38 R. Dawkins, *The Blind Watchmaker* (Harmondsworth: Penguin, 1986), p. 268.

39 *Nature* magazine, 5:2004.

40 http://www.washingtonpost.com/wpdyn/content/article/2005/06/08/AR2005060802385

41 J. D. Morris, *The Young Earth* (San Diego: ICR, 1997).

42 M. Ridley, *New Scientist,* 25:6:1981, p. 831.

43 D. A. Noebel, *Understanding the Times* (Ass. of Christian Schools International, 1995), chapter 16.

44 *Creation ex-nihilo* Technical Journal—Summer, 2001. *Creation ex-nihilo* magazines, especially vol. 26, no.2, 2004, summarised or referenced several important breakthroughs by the R.A.T.E. group of creationist scientists on many radiodecay problems.

45 Richard Milton's *Facts of Life,* and many creationist publications, noted in the bibliography.

46 Dr S. Austin, 'Mt St Helens' video, CSF. Address in bibliography.

47 H.M. Morris, *The Biblical Basis for Modern Science* (Grand Rapids: Baker Book House, 1984), pp. 477–479.

48 T.G. Norman and B. Setterfield, *The Atomic Constants, Light and Time* (SRI International, California, 1987). For an extensive review of this and related material, see http://www.lDolphin.org

49 R. Humphreys, *Starlight and Time* (1994).

50 *Creation ex nihilo* magazine vol. 25, no. 4, 2003, and **Professor Andy Macintosh's** coming DayOne book on *Flight.* The photographs were first published in a CSM journal. Addresses at end.

51 *Creation ex-nihilo* magazine, vol. 19, no. 2, 1997.

52 D. Ager 'A reinterpretation of the basal "Littoral Lias of the Vale of Glamorgan"', Proceedings of the Geologist's Association, 97, pp. 29–35. See also his book *The New Catastrophism.*

53 See many *Creation ex-nihilo* magazines, e.g. vol. 24, no. 1.

54 Werner Gitt, *In the Beginning was Information* (Christliche Literatur—Verbreitung e. V., 1997).

Birds, man and religion; or the eagle and the serpent

A giant eagle's head hewn out of solid rock still stares impassively out over the high, windy plains of Asia Minor. Next to it stands an equally large head of Apollo, both supposedly erected by the Seleucid Greeks of the fourth century BC onwards, yet the eagle appears far older. Its meaning certainly is.

Similar monolithic statues of eagles were a feature of the first Mesopotamian religious cultures. Raptors have always been important symbols for mankind, long before the Greeks assigned the eagle to Apollo's father, the 'chief of the gods', Zeus, whose name supposedly came via India, meaning 'sky', 'day' and probably 'light bringer', yet very like *Deus*, the Latin for 'God'. To accurately trace back all the earliest meanings of birds to man and 'gods' is rather difficult, and outside the scope of this modest book. *Yet birds, winged spirits, firebirds, phoenixes, fiery serpents, doves, eagles, falcons and gods have long been intertwined, like other varied creatures with eagle's or dragon's wings. Why?* From the very earliest times mankind has used birds, and dragons and serpents, to symbolise spiritual aspects of life. This is reflected in the obvious links between the birds and the heavens, as Genesis 1:20 says: 'let birds fly above the earth across the face of the firmament of the heavens'. After mankind fell from grace, it was a divine, winged 'watcher', or cherub, that guarded the way back to the Tree of Life.

The Spirit of God hovered over the waters at the creation of the world, as the Spirit of God also hovered as a dove above our Lord Jesus at his baptism. 'Born from above' is a truer meaning of being 'born again', and the second birth is absolutely essential for anyone seeking to be a child of God, and survive the unfolding Apocalypse. That is why we have had to endure six millennia of confused, distorted, deceiving and counterfeit 'ways to God'. Every possible occult, supernatural or shamanistic 'New Age' way has been promulgated, and never more so than now. We are currently being besieged

Fig. 121: APOLLO and THE EAGLE, ASIA MINOR, fourth to first century BC.

by more 'winged angels', and modern 'winged sun-discs' (ET crafts), than ever before, all supposedly bringing us divine, if somewhat contradictory, revelations from 'god' and the spirit realm! We already have all the basic prophetic revelations we need, 'God-breathed', in the Bible: 'Forever, O Lord, your word is settled in heaven' (Psalm 119:89).

Some of these false religions have involved our feathered friends supposedly bringing down that divine knowledge, or at least on their wings. Winged sun-discs and eyes are common to many early religions, with falcons worshipped as the 'the Distant One' of salvation, or Huru, later Horus the falcon-headed god of the Egyptians. Vultures have also figured heavily. It seems we have always had an insatiable and indiscriminate appetite for 'heavenly revelation', whatever brings it down. It is no coincidence that sun worship is tied not only to its physical role in sustaining life, as evolution also 'worships', but also to its mythological status as 'light bringer', in the spiritual sense. Prometheus supposedly stole 'fire', also interpreted as 'the knowledge of good and evil', from the sun. It is no coincidence that his wife, Pandora, opened her box of evils to afflict mankind—she is the Greek Eve, and Prometheus based on Adam. Icarus also 'flew' too close to the sun and got 'burnt', as did Phaethon. The whole confusing pantheon of Greek 'gods' can be cleverly explained by their astronomical and astrological significance, demonstrating considerable knowledge. It cannot be coincidence that in the *original* meaning of astrology, the zodiac or Mazzaroth begins with Virgo the virgin and child, has Aquila the eagle, formerly wounded in the heel, slaying the accursed dragon, Draco, and ends with conquering Leo the Lion (of Judah) annihilating the serpent Hydra!

It is almost impossible to sort out the many interpretations of actual cosmic events from actual divine revelations and their subsequent distortions. Satan has always used, or helped invent, local 'gods' and demonic messengers, or occult customs to spread his message. His purpose has always been to get us to worship him and not the only true God, and his pitch has never changed: did God really say that? (Genesis 3) The devil alone is responsible for the incredible array of counterfeit gods and goddesses that have 'enlightened us'. As God warned Adam and Eve that the 'tree of the knowledge of good and evil' was off limits and would lead to death, Satan had to contradict him and say, 'You will not die', and therefore bring us all down in the process. Well, his time is nearly up.

Just as macro-evolution is the opposite of creation, so reincarnation is the exact opposite of resurrection. 'Flying' up to be with the gods, or stars, and regularly reappearing as winged 'angels', or being 'reincarnated' is an essential part of Satan's false cosmogony. If he were to convince us that we could obtain eternal life outside of Christ and God, then reincarnation needed to be established as a belief. The obvious links between his ideas and evolution and reincarnation are legion, and well covered in Roy Mahon's book, *Cosmic War Survival*.[1] The Scriptures easily refute reincarnation, telling us: 'it is appointed for men to die once, but after this the judgement' (Hebrews 9:27). The whole battleground has always been centred on the first creation and future eternal life, which is why so many today, even within the Christian church, deny the message of Genesis. Yet the Lord

Jesus died to conquer death and sin, only brought in by Adam and Eve (Mark 10:6, Romans 5:12), and we cannot have had millions of years of death before Adam, and therefore no long-age evolution. All the Bible writers quoted Genesis as fact, for 'All Scripture is given by inspiration of God and is profitable ...' (2 Timothy 3:16)—it is not 'poetry', myth or mere Mesopotamian fables. Meanwhile the battle continues, both here on earth and in the 'heavenly places', against a diabolically clever adversary who 'transforms himself into an angel of light' (2 Corinthians 11:14).

Fig. 122: THE DOVE and THE OLIVE BRANCH.

To return to more material matters, birds do not figure significantly in our history again until the end of the Flood. Firstly the Raven was sent out, and went restlessly 'to and fro' (Genesis 8:7) above the drying lands, followed by a dove. The dove returned because it could not find any dry land, so was sent out again after seven more days, later to return with a freshly sprouted olive twig. Olives, like other trees, can grow very rapidly from torn-off branches stuck into the ground, but there is also spiritual meaning here for both Jew and Gentile. It is significant that the dove would later symbolise the Holy Spirit and innocence. The Raven from then on had a mixed reputation. It was 'unclean' in as much as it was a carnivore and not to be eaten, yet was divinely appointed to assist Elijah by bringing him food when he was outside the boundaries of Israel, in the wilderness. Once again, there is a deeper spiritual meaning here outside the scope of this present book.

After the Flood and its aftermath, birds of prey and 'winged gods and goddesses' begin to figure heavily in myth and legend. The first world dictator, Nimrod, was usually pictured as the 'Master of the Animals' and sometimes depicted with two or three feathers (horns) in his head-dress (the origins of both heraldry and the fleur-de-lys). He was known as the mighty hunter, defiant 'in the face of God', and probably hunted people, too. His wife, Semiramis, was later pictured as Eve/Holy Spirit dove, bringing God's blessings down to us—as a so-called 'mediatrix'. She also deified Nimrod as the counterfeit 'Seed of the Woman' (Jesus), thus becoming the 'Queen of Heaven', Melkat-ashemin. This how she 'became' both Nimrod's mother and a goddess, thus eternally 'rebirthing' and promoting him to an ever-reincarnating god. Genesis tells us they built the astrological tower of Babel, erected for false worship 'to the hosts (stars) of heaven', and how God scattered the disobedient peoples across the Earth. Thus their stepped ziggurats, or pyramids, were exported to Egypt, Asia and the Americas, and often involved serpents and birds in one form or other. Falcon gods would sit astride them in India and Egypt, and in the Americas, serpents were cleverly represented by the moving shadows up their stepped sides, as the sun set or rose. Serpent earth 'barrows' dot the earth from Europe, Asia, the Americas, and New Zealand, and doubtless elsewhere.

The eagle and the serpent

Eagles were often shown with serpents in their claws, denoting both their mastery of them and what they stood for.

Firstly, reincarnation, because serpents shed their skins and were thus 'immortal,' as the sun. Secondly, a serpent with its tail in its mouth was also 'endless' and circular, like the sun, rolling across the earth each day. This is how the incredibly tangled myths and stories of serpents/dragons, eagles, feathered serpents, seraphs, winged sun-discs, winged bulls, sphinxes, cockatrices, griffins, harpies, etc. became part of so many people's histories. 'Serpent' and 'dragon' are interchangeable meanings of the same Hebrew word, *nâchâsh*, in the Bible, also standing for Satan (Genesis 3:1). Flying, 'fiery serpents' (*saraf*) are also mentioned, as when Moses was ordered to make one and set it on a pole as a sign of healing, and especially to point ahead to Jesus—the ultimate sacrifice for all evil, shamefully hung upon a 'pole', or cross (Isaiah 53).

Add in the fact that many of the 'spiritual' creatures were also based upon dinosaurs and huge, winged, flying reptiles—and 'here be winged Dragons', and similar. Just ask yourself, why should the Chinese, for instance, use eleven ordinary creatures for their zodiac yet have to invent the twelfth, a dragon? Why do we find so many of these strange mythical beasts pictured alongside normal creatures in our mediaeval bestiaries? Then add in extinct dragons (dinosaurs/'thunderbirds', etc.) to our human propensity to mutate and adapt stories.

Thus 'Zeus' commanded the eagle, which with the serpent (Typhon) in its claws was the controller of, and mediator between, heaven and earth. Eastern religious ways further pictured the positive (heaven/eagle) and negative (earth/serpent) forces as the eternal battle, or the balancing act of 'Yin-Yang' in Chinese philosophy. *Thus evil is again misrepresented as equal with good!* The eagle/serpent image could also be seen as controlling or balancing the earthly serpent power (Satan), of false 'eternal life'. Geo-electromagnetic forces are often depicted by coiled and spiral 'earth energies', or symbolised as 'serpent/dragon paths', known in the West as 'Ley-lines'. Babylonian creation and astronomical myths confuse further, entangling bloody, warring gods and a winged serpent (Tiamat), somehow birthing the world from their conflict. This clearly shows mutation from the original Genesis account, which contrary to the claims of detractors, could not be re-hashed from the later 'Gilgamesh Epic'. Early sources, like the Ebla tablets (c2300BC), generally agree with the biblical account of creation—not the later distorted fables.

Many ancient religious practices used snake-like wands, lightning bolts or the sun's rays to signify heavenly wisdom brought down to earth. This is yet more intrigue from the Devil, as virtually every false religion and belief elevates him to equality with God. New-Agers promote him as Lucifer the misunderstood 'light bringer', or the 'star of the morning'. But the Devil,

Fig. 123: 'THE EAGLE and THE SERPENT'. A: GOLDEN EAGLE and ADDER. B: SILVER COIN, GREECE, c400 BC.

or first 'dragon and serpent', often 'transforms himself into an angel of light' (1 Corinthians 11:14). He also has 'great wrath, because he knows he has a short time' left to work his deceptions, since his defeat at the cross. He has always fought, and even briefly 'bruised' Jesus, the true 'seed of the woman' at Calvary. However, his head will be completely 'crushed' when he is thrown by Jesus into the 'lake of fire' for ever (Genesis 3:14, Revelation 20:10). That battle is the basis for virtually all mythology and false religion from the very beginning, Michael and the Dragon being yet another common manifestation. History is replete with false 'seeds' or 'branches', as in the 'Golden Bough' legends beloved of the Druids and others. Hence also the many other false gods who have supposedly died for us, and ongoing but futile animal sacrifice, which was to point only to Christ's sacrifice, and then cease. (Cannibalism is another gross distortion of Christ's shed blood—which was only 'once for all time'.)

Remember that the animals' fear of us only arose after the Flood

(Genesis 9:2–3), hunting and animal husbandry also became very important. Bulls with wings and human features also arose as an important part of myth, once again showing both the influence and distortion of biblical teaching. Fading memories of the divine, winged 'watchers', or Cherubim with calf's hooves (Genesis 3, Ezekiel 1) that guarded the way back to the Tree of Life after mankind fell from grace, undoubtedly contributed. Varied combinations of man and bird or beast, sometimes with six wings like the biblical cherubs (*kerub/karibu*) are very common from Mesopotamia, Babylonia (and Egypt) onwards, where virtually all our religions/myths,[2] genetics, languages, astronomy, and farming practices can be traced back to. One of the twentieth century's most eminent archaeologists, William Allbright, called the Table of Nations of Genesis 10 'an astonishingly accurate document' in its 'remarkably modern understanding of the ethnic and linguistic situation'.[3] He was talking of the dispersion from Babel into today's many varied peoples of the world, just as flora and fauna rapidly spread and diverged into many 'varieties'. Once again the Bible demonstrates true, supernatural knowledge.

Post-flood man and birds

From the Flood onwards, recorded history testifies well to the world-wide spread of mankind's common origins and religions, from the 'fertile crescent' of the near East. Birds continued to fare both well and badly from our activities during these tumultuous times. Although revered for many reasons, this often meant that sacrifice or mummification was required of them, as the Egyptians did to many falcons and Sacred Ibis, and American Indians did to eagles and condors. Grey Herons (or sometimes egrets) became the sacred 'Benu-bird' (Phoenix/Fire) birds of Egypt, for some obscure reason seen as the creator or constant resurrector of the pile of mud that became the world.

This was known by the Egyptians (and Celts) as the 'Isle of the Blessed', from which they originally came, and to where all their 'Book of the Dead' rituals were hoped to return them. They clearly linked falcon god Horus, to fiery serpent creator god Ra, or Atum-Re.[4] Birds did not always have to die, and to this day certain South American tribes keep and revere Harpy Eagles

Chapter 7

Fig. 124: 'CHERUBS', WINGED SERPENTS and 'DRAGONS' ETC. A: ASSYRIAN 'GODMAN', OR GOOD 'GENIUS', c7TH CENTURY BC.. B: KARIBU 'CHERUB', ASSYRIA c7TH CENTURY BC. C: WINGED SERPENT IN THE UNDERWORLD, EGYPTIAN FUNERARY PAPYRUS, c 5- 6TH DYNASTY. D: WINGED ASSYRIAN SUN-DISC, c300BC. E: CHINESE STYLE DRAGON (VERY LIKE THE BABYLONIAN ONES ON THE ISHTAR GATE). F: NORSE DRAGON-SHIP PROW. G: WELSH-STYLE DRAGON. H: SIGURD SLAYING THE SERPENT, ISLE OF MAN, 11TH CENTURY AD. I: NAZI STANDARD.

or Andean Condors, for 'luck', although condors have sometimes died in the bizarre rituals associated with the Indians, and their conflict with their murderous Spanish conquerors of old. It was not only their spiritual symbolism but also their wonderful physical properties, like far-sightedness, strength and aerial mastery that ensured raptors continued in our affairs and thoughts.

Some of the first cave art included birds, usually edible species like Ostrich or crane, but more rarely than creatures like bulls, horses and bison. A beautifully carved mammoth tusk from the 'first humans' in Europe shows a goose or duck in a very dynamic pose, plus other creatures

208 The design and origin of birds

and man; again confounding evolutionary thought.⁵ Yet it was the eagle that was placed on top of totem poles and European war helmets, or was rendered down into eagle war bonnets, or similar. Imperial Rome, especially, used both eagles and dragons on her standards, leading to their adoption by other countries, like the later Welsh Red Dragon (it supposedly represented British Celts defending their land against the 'white dragon' Saxons). It was no coincidence that 'Christian' Nazi Germany used an ancient pagan, winged sun for a standard, or an eagle above a Buddhist swastika sun-disc. They were simply incorporating old pagan symbols as the establishment church long had. Double-headed eagles have especially impressed peoples from earliest times and represented expansion and dominance; worryingly, post-Communist Russia has recently readopted hers. This particular scarlet flag brings the *Eagle and Serpent* theme full circle—it even incorporates Michael/St George and the Dragon within the eagle's breast. Could this possibly be coincidence, as both 'east' and 'west' face each other beneath their eagle standards, possibly for the final showdown—when the real Archangel Michael casts the original serpent, Satan, into fiery Hell?! On a much lesser note, another 'spread eagle' still represents one of our biggest banking groups, proclaiming their desired economic dominance of the globe.

Dead Golden Eagles are still to be seen hanging dustily and pathetically on Moroccan 'folk medicine' stalls, and Himalayan vultures are still fed human corpses to help 'liberate' human spirits to heaven. The Mayans and some Africans revered or used vulture head-dresses like their Egyptian counterparts, and the genocidal Aztecs believed the sun itself was an eagle: 40,000 people had their living hearts ripped out at one temple dedication, alone, as recently as the sixteenth century! It was not only raptors though, for many tribes from south-east Asia to South America still bedeck themselves with colourful bird of paradise or parrot feathers, or buy and sell with them. All manner of animal parts and decorations were, and still are, used in 'shamanistic' practices worldwide. They have various functions, like attempting to become one with the creature, or using it to divine the future, to heal, or to ensure successful hunting. Whether combined with various psychotropic drugs or not, such pagan practices are currently making a comeback in the post-Christian West, though it has to

Fig. 125: A: 'BENU-BIRD', OR PHOENIX, C19TH DYNASTY EGYPTIAN TOMB, WITH HORUS SYMBOL and SUN-DISC. B: 'FALCON GOD' HORUS/RA c12–10TH CENTURY BC, WITH 'ETERNAL LIFE' SYMBOL OR ANKH.

be said that real eagle's feathers or other uncommon animal parts are no longer used by most. This is not so with eastern medicine, alas, although birds are fortunate not to be as widely used as tigers, bears or Musk Deer, for instance. Strangely enough, for one of the most brutal folk superstitions involving bird sacrifice still hanging on today, we must look to Ireland. 'Wrenning Day', on the 26 December, is based upon a very ancient pagan festival associated with Satan, 'the 'Lord of Misrule', yet adopted by Christianity and used as an excuse to beat little wrens to death! The sacrifice of various creatures in mid-winter, to somehow reignite the dying year, is a common feature of our history. Clearly, various creatures symbolise many different aspects of human life in both the Bible and folklore, and there are far too many to go into here.

Falconry and husbandry

Once more we turn to raptors to enlighten our past, as used in the popular phenomenon of falconry. The earliest evidence seems to go back to around 2000BC in China, but man has probably used them to hunt since the times of the great Babel hunting revolution and dispersion. Interestingly, many of the earliest Chinese pictographs were all undoubtedly based on Genesis concepts of creation, sin and fall.[6] Dogs, and even big cats would have also been used in the chase, sometimes alongside raptors. A most elegant pairing of Saluki and Saker Falcon is occasionally still used in the Middle East for game as large as gazelle. Other hoofed animals were kept mainly for food or transport, though most of their bodies were used for other purposes. Clothing, weaponry, utensils, tools and other artefacts were made from their skins and bones, or would be used for engraving or painting. This leads us back to bird imagery, as in statuary and heavily decorated tools, ornaments or religious artefacts. For instance, owls were depicted as wise by the Greeks, and assigned to the goddess Athena. At one time or another, various birds have been represented or symbolised on many of our artefacts.

Most early peoples hunted, kept or hunted with many animals, and then used them for decoration, both sacred and secular. The early Egyptians painted everyday wildfowl hunts, as well as the winged 'Ka' (spirit) ascending to heaven, after the weighing of the 'soul' by Anubis and ibis-headed Thoth.

They also mounted falcons on the high prows of some of their boats, as later Norsemen would terrify with their 'dragon boats', another hangover from Babylon. Crows, and fabulous, fiery 'Rakh' (Roc) dragon-birds feature in many Western, Muslim and Oriental fables, which are mainly based on the influential earlier work of Aristotle. This part-fable, part-natural history manuscript would later heavily influence Western medieval 'bestiaries', and even our own beautiful illuminated Bibles, like the Book of Kells or the Lindisfarne Gospels. These highly decorated Gospels took biblical and Celtic wildlife iconography a step further. By associating the four Gospel writers with the 'four living creatures' of Ezekiel, Matthew typified Jesus the Man; Mark, Jesus the 'suffering servant' or Ox; Luke, Jesus the resurrecting Lion; and John, Jesus the ascending Eagle. Jesus had already arisen 'with healing in his wings', and they knew he would return to confirm it, eternally (Malachi 4:2; Acts 1:11). Going back to the giant 'Rakh' bird, it looks suspiciously like another famed, fiery 'feathered serpent' from the other side of the globe, the South American 'Quetzalcoatl' (also based on that beautiful emerald green bird, the Quetzal that hangs its long tail out of the nest hole—which just happens to look exactly like two tree ferns!). This strange beast is somehow linked with God's fiery cloud of the Exodus, or a comet, or even Venus—a frequent guise of another falling 'morning star', Satan. A spiritual yearning to fly to our heavenly home has obviously never left us, and this can be seen in many other fables from across the Earth, however distorted. They are mostly linked to ideas of getting there by our own efforts, often assisted by various spirits; contrary to the clear teaching that only Jesus is 'the Way, Truth and Life'.

More biblical birds
As for other birds of the Scriptures, there is sometimes a little confusion over the exact meaning of some of the Hebrew words used. Doves, and especially eagles, have been well covered here and are fairly straightforward, but such words as 'Ossifrage' perplex us. It is claimed to stand for the Bearded Vulture, as the root word *peres* means to break, divide or breach (Leviticus 11:13). You might recall that this huge and impressive bird, formerly known as the Lammergeier, drops bones or tortoises to crack them open. There are a number of raptors mentioned in the Scriptures, but it is not always clear which one is referred to. Storks and cranes have happier associations, and although the stork myth of delivering babies is naturally not biblical, it does have a good reputation for looking after its young. Job 39:13 compares her broad wings to the Ostrich's, and calls her 'kindly', and Psalm 104:17 describes the nesting habits of White and, especially, Black Storks. They still regularly nest in 'fir trees', as the psalmist said, but the White Stork now largely nests on our buildings.

The Bible also accurately remarks upon two habits of the Ostrich (Job 39:13–18). Firstly great speed, as 'she scorns the horse and its rider', but then it badly contrasts her parenting skills with the stork. This is probably because she lays on the ground out in the open, and several other females

Fig. 126: IBIS-HEADED THOTH RECORDING THE WEIGHING OF A HUMAN SOUL BY JACKAL-HEADED ANUBIS. EGYPTIAN BOOK OF THE DEAD, C1100 BC. THE 'KA' OR SPIRIT RISING, APPARENTLY HOLDING AN ANKH.

also lay their own eggs in her nest, and then abandon them to her care. As for the cormorant or pelican, most Hebrew scholars agree that the *shalak* (Leviticus 11:17) is a seabird, and probably a cormorant. In another passage, Psalm 102:6, a different word is also often rendered cormorant, but this is seemingly the pelican. It is still a bird 'of the wilderness', possibly because its fish eating habits have seen it persecuted, though now it is not at all averse to Israeli fish farms.

The annual migrations of birds, especially storks, were mentioned in the Bible long before many scientists realised it (Jeremiah 8:7). Two of the other birds are harder to place, but not the Turtle Dove, sometimes wrongly rendered turtle, whose voice could scarcely 'be heard in the land' (Song of Solomon 2:12). Swallow is probably another one of them, the bird of 'liberty' or 'freedom' as the Hebrew word *deror* suggests. Without casting any doubt upon the Bible, this highlights a common human misconception—that birds are free, whereas we are not. They are even more tied to 'instinctive' behaviour than we are, coming and going, mating and breeding like clockwork, unless blown off course or otherwise jolted out of their routine. Yes, there are some still spreading around the world, but driven by instinctive need for more living areas, as they are filled in or destroyed behind them. The other word in Jeremiah is *sis,* variously explained as swift or crane, yet the idea of a 'chattering' bird used by Hezekiah (Isaiah 38:14) more suggests the swift than a 'bugling' Common Crane. Common Israeli wintering birds, cranes still drift in long, picturesque skeins along the Hula valley against the imposing snowy peak of Mount Hermon.

Staying with migratory birds, we come to one of the most famous biblical birds, the Quail. There is some doubt over this bird too, but it best fits the descriptions given (Exodus 16:13, Psalm 78:27, Psalm 105:40). They certainly do 'rain down' in large numbers from off 'the sea' when on migration, and fly about '2 cubits' (3ft) above the ground. Then the old Arabic word for Quail is *selaw:* very similar to the Hebrew *selâv.* Another gamebird, the partridge, occurs in Scripture to describe David's lonely and hunted existence among the desert hills (1 Samuel 26:20). I have sketched See-See Partridge running and hiding among the mountains of the Dead Sea, well camouflaged and dodging from rock to rock, as David must have done from King Saul.

One of our prettiest birds, the Hoopoe, was unclean to the early Jews and not to be eaten (Leviticus 11:19). That could be explained by the foul odour, emanating from tail glands, which characterises its nest hole. The other explanation of the word *dukiphath* as Lapwing, or Green Plover, does not sound right, for as far as I know waders were not proscribed. Let us finish with two of the humblest and best-known birds of all: the hen and the sparrow. 'O Jerusalem, Jerusalem ... how often I wanted to gather your children together, as a hen gathers her chicks under her wings, but you were not willing'—so spoke our Lord to his first chosen people, the Jews (Matthew 23:37). The apostle Paul, however, gives a timely warning to us Christians: 'Do not be haughty, but fear. For if God did not spare the natural branches, He may not spare you either' (Romans 11:20–21). Peter for one would probably never, ever forget the cock's crow. I have already mentioned how we are 'of more value than many sparrows', and 'not one of them falls to the ground without your Father's will (knowledge)' (Matthew 10:31,29). The bird referred to here is not necessarily a sparrow, but any small, 'clean' bird commonly found for sale at the market for 'a copper coin'. The final birds mentioned in the Bible are the raptors of

Matthew 24 and Revelation 19, as the cleansers of this earth: 'then the end will come'.

Renaissance, Reformation and 'Enlightenment'
From the Renaissance onwards, all of nature came under physical and artistic examination. Birds, especially, were increasingly studied and more accurately depicted, though Egyptian statuary was hard to beat for its economy of line and power, as was much early Eastern art. Their religious significance would surface in many paintings of European Goldfinches and Robins, and pelicans, all depicting the blood of Christ in some way. Carel Fabritius' captive 'Goldfinch' was painted life size in 1654, yet its powerful simplicity and unfussy approach has hardly ever been bettered. Along with Dürer's life studies of the natural world, they heralded the dawn of a more scientific approach, and a parallel decline into florid and pagan religiosity, more often based on Greek myth than the Bible. For example, Raphael's 'Ganymede and the Eagle', where his beautifully painted immature White-tailed Eagle carries the youth up to dark, Babylonian-style 'gods'. The Reformation naturally followed the Renaissance of early Greek Bible texts, and released us from the 'Dark Ages' of the establishment church. All of this generally launched a more naturalistic and enquiring approach into the worlds of both spirit and matter, both for good and bad: good for the true scientific understanding and global missionary work that arose from it, but bad in the divorce of spiritual values from earthly enquiry. Clever scientists and philosophers like Bacon, Newton, Descartes and Voltaire, gradually broke away from the stranglehold of Church-dominated thinking, and gave birth to a strange hybrid of Christian/Occultic/Humanist science (not dissimilar to the 'new-agey' hybrid many are now returning to, after a century of dead materialism). Those turbulent centuries of travel, excess and enquiry overturned the old medieval worldview for ever.

Many exotic birds were among the large collections of flora and fauna brought back to the West from the voyages of discovery. Private zoos sprang up, and museums and individuals started the work of collection and classification that continues to the present day. The most important pioneers in this field were Bible-believers: John Ray and Carl Linnaeus, who soon came up against the main problem of classification, still with us today, that of *'speciation'*. I have already mentioned the erroneous idea of the fixity of 'species' being a biblical one, but this was only because Jerome wrongly translated an old Greek word into the Latin Vulgate Bible. The original Hebrew *min,* or 'kind', allows for much more flexibility than 'species', as do other descriptions of animal 'families' in the Torah. Unfortunately, all this discovery and general scientific 'enlightenment' also resurrected old Greek and Asian errors about evolution and atomic decay, misinterpreted as a great age for the earth.[7] Then Darwin's 'explanations' concerning the Galapagos Finches helped to kick-start it again. Nevertheless, this spirit of enquiry ensured that beautiful and fairly accurate bird books gradually emerged in the expensive, hand-printed and hand-coloured folios of the eighteenth and nineteenth centuries. They are wonderfully exemplified by the hand-coloured engravings in Audubon's life-sized 'Birds of America', and the folios of wildlife from many countries by British and European artists like Gould, Lear and Wolf.

Fig. 127: HOOPOE.

Another irony is that Darwin largely inspired the work of Bruno Liljefors (1860–1939), considered by most authorities to be the greatest wildlife painter ever. Taking Darwin's one self-evident truth, 'survival of the fittest', Liljefors went on to depict many raptors and predators in the chase on huge, freely painted canvases. These caught the 'zeitgeist', or spirit of the age, well, which was often about the 'fittest superman' and the dissolution of Christian civilisation, yet paraded as advance and 'freedom'. Protestant-based colonialism certainly had its faults, but you only have to look at the ex-colonial countries today that have lost that base, or those that never had it, to see mass poverty, suppression of basic rights, ignorance and hopelessness (though materialism is not the answer to these problems). By the twentieth century, Darwin and Nietzsche had demoted God; Freud and Jung had dissected the 'soul' and 'freed' us from religion; science had split the atom; technology had freed us from much toil; and colonialism and travel had broadened our horizons. Rousseau, and later Mead and Gauguin had also reinvented our so-called 'innocent savage' identity: 'freedom' beckoned on eagle's wings! This heady freedom of 'Prometheus unbound ... cursing God' (Shelley) rapidly took us into the twentieth century, but quickly dissolved into destruction of just about everything we had ever held to be good. What has that to do with birds, you may ask? Well, as one modern songwriter put it so well: 'The eagle and the serpent are at war in me, the serpent fighting for blind desire, the eagle for clarity.'[8] In other words, nothing much has changed since Zeus and his eagle! We still do daily battle between flesh and spirit, always needing to balance earthly and heavenly needs. Denying the spiritual, as most science now does, leads only to a lop-sided view of life—and eternal disaster.

'An eagle for an emperor'

Going back to falconry and more Imperial days, we continued to associate raptors' qualities with ours, and by the Middle Ages had established a hierarchy in the West. With shades of the 'Divine Right of Kings', it started with 'an eagle for an emperor', through 'a falcon for a king', and all the way down to 'a merlin for a lady' and 'a kestrel for a knave'. Hunting with raptors for food provision became a popular sport, and also led to social/spiritual segregation. Nowadays, the doggerel could be rendered, 'a Gyr Falcon for a Sheikh', as unscrupulous international oil companies vie for business in the Middle-East, by smuggling in endangered species from the polar north to languish in baking desert heat. This not only threatens white Gyrs, but other local prey species like the Houbara Bustard. Yet such Gyrs have long been sought after, and local, acclimatised species like the Saker or desert Peregrine Falcon are far better employed for hunting in hot countries. White Gyr hybrids are now commonly bred by many falconers, and Houbara Bustards are also captive bred for release in places like the Arabian Gulf States. Pale hybrid Gyrs raise another interesting 'evolutionary' question, for Gyrs might have only recently split from Saker

Falcons anyway, as confusion over the Saker-ish, Himalayan 'Altai Falcon' possibly shows.

Golden Eagles are still flown from horseback to hunt Red Foxes in Mongolia, while various eagles hunt smaller prey for us in other lands. Coming down the scale, falconers use buteos like the Ferruginous or Red-tailed Buzzard to take rabbits and Ring-necked Pheasant in the USA and Europe. Similarly, Goshawks, and now Harris Hawks, regularly take the same sort of prey, plus Brown and Mountain Hares, in the West. Sparrowhawks can be trained to take Eurasian Magpies, or Quail in the case of the Turkish or Middle-Eastern falconer. Just about every raptor has probably been used at one time or another, and even Common Buzzards are capable of overpowering more than worms and moles. The pinnacle of the sport is Red Grouse, or similar, hawking with a Peregrine. Here the bird is 'cast off' to 'ring up' and circle downwind over the heather moors, while the dogs sniff out the prey below. Then the dog freezes, 'pointing' to the hidden grouse, until sent in to flush it—and down hurtles the falcon. Whatever the rights and wrongs of falconry, the action is exhilarating.

Conservation

From the point of view of conservation and modern attitudes, falconry and shooting have a mixed press. On the negative side, some UK falconers and shooters continue to take nationally endangered birds or mammals, like Skylarks, Rooks and Brown Hares. It is probably because numbers of such 'prey' species are still locally common in some places, like the thousands of Eurasian Woodcocks that pour into the UK each winter from the cold north. On the positive side, responsible sportsmen have contributed much to conservation. They are often knowledgeable landowners who deliberately keep some of their fields and woods wild for the prey species, where such habitats are often otherwise in serious decline. Western farming and suburban building practices have devastated the countryside of formerly common flora and fauna. Falconers, on the other hand, have shown conservation bodies like the RSPB and NCC (Royal Society for the Protection of Birds and Nature Conservancy Council) how to gradually introduce birds back into the wild. The successful reintroduction of both White-tailed Eagles and Red Kites to parts of the UK has benefited from falconers' patient 'hacking back' techniques, which provide protection and food stations until the birds are established. Falconers' captive breeding expertise is helping other rare species, like the Seychelles's Kestrel, Pink Pigeon and Hawaiian Ne-Ne Goose, to survive and be reintroduced, and falconers *should* no longer need to take wild birds illegally.

Nowadays they can earn their keep a different way by clearing airports, rubbish dumps or town centres of gulls, waders or pigeons. This highlights another aspect of our failing relationship with creation. The most successful birds and beasts are the ones that can adapt to our messy habits, like open garbage tips and discarded take-aways. Gulls, corvids, kites, Red Foxes, Racoons, bears, Brown Rats, cockroaches and others are among the benefactors, while people are often the losers. In centuries past, we persecuted these creatures—now the tables are being turned!

Farmers and game-rearers especially, have long been the enemy of raptors and corvids who dared to take their produce, whether grain, lamb or chick. Man has destroyed many species for much less. Giant Moas, Dodos and Great Auks (all huge, flightless birds) were not alone in being completely wiped out for food, for the fate of the American Passenger Pigeon was absolutely staggering. Their flocks were still so large in the nineteenth century that they literally took days to pass by, estimated at 5,000 million, but within 100 years they had all been shot, and the last one died alone in Cincinnati Zoo in 1914. We have already looked at the paradox of falling numbers of some finches and sparrows in the West, while millions of them ravage crops in the Third World.

One of our most destructive modern attacks on birds and other wildlife was not actually intentional. During the 1950s and 60s, naturalists started to notice many distressing events involving mass death of birds and fish, eventually traced to various industrial and agri-chemicals (end note 1, chapter 5). DDT, especially, was found to have appalling effects on wildlife, while other organo-chlorine chemicals caused egg-shell thinning or fatal toxicity. Naturally, predators at the top of the food chain would ingest more of the poisons from prey like Wood Pigeon or mouse that had eaten the dressed seed or the sprayed crop, or dipped sheep in the case of some eagles. Although many of the chemicals were banned, more intensive agriculture and the removal of hedgerows, field margins, woods and waterside

Fig. 128: PEREGRINE STOOP.

vegetation have continued to play havoc with wildlife in the West. It is not just birds, but all the other rungs on the vital ladder of life: flowers, trees, butterflies and other pollinating insects, small mammals, bats, fish and amphibians. Ironically, the greater the number of predators, the healthier the natural world. So, the recent loss of some 96 per cent of all India's vultures to farm chemicals should alarm the nation greatly.[9] Should we all be concerned? Of course, but a Christian's most vital function is to tell of the Creator of everything, and just why the whole world is in such a mess in the first place—and the only way out of it, into the coming 'new heavens and new earth'.

Travel, the Renaissance, 'Enlightenment', commerce, science, industry, technology and population growth—the last millennium had an enormous impact upon us all, let alone wildlife and landscape. They played an important part in our expansion, which meant retreat for many birds and beasts. Many creatures were simply eaten, or eradicated because they were seen as a threat to us, and our farming or game, whether real or imagined. Land and forests were cleared, marshes drained, coasts reclaimed, while the air was finally blackened and many waters poisoned. As all this was happening some creatures or plants were almost expunged by scientists and egg collectors for their collections. The last British Osprey went that way, actually shot by a 'Reverend' scientist. The final straw for our awakening conscience was the millions of birds killed mainly for fashion. Hummingbirds, Great-crested Grebes, Great and Snowy Egrets are just some of the many birds slaughtered for hat decoration or muffs, as Sable, Beaver and big cats died for our coats (not including northern indigenous peoples who still need furs, small scale). Egrets, especially, played an important role in bird protection, and the first conservation society was formed in the late 1800s to help protect such birds, by the very British ladies whose hats had been adorned with egret ('aigrette') feathers and hummingbirds. This has now grown to the million-strong RSPB, with similar societies in the USA, and smaller organisations elsewhere. However, that was only the start of an uphill struggle, which is still being fought to protect the world's dwindling wild areas and life.

The dirty technology of the Industrial Revolution gradually gave way to cleaner, and although many wildlife revivals followed, the poisons are now often invisible. Crystal clear waters after 'acid rain' mean no aquatic food for dipper or loon; farm or factory run-offs empty waterways of fish; tiny lead fishing weights poison and deform Mute Swan's necks, as shot gun pellets similarly do for other wildfowl. Now another dramatic turn, for 'global warming' is all the rage, supposedly caused by our greenhouse gases: however, temperatures have varied before and the whole scenario is not properly understood and probably distorted by political concerns about oil. Ironically, current global temperature increases are claimed as spurring glacier growth—just as a probable warm sea and volcanically-dimmed atmosphere produced a rapid Ice Age after the Flood. As for rain forests, the Third World replies to the protests of the West, 'How dare you tell us what to do, when you have largely cleared your own trees and gained your riches?' 'Riches' means many more cars among other things, and apart from being dangerous, and major polluters, they are the main killers of birds: 12 million yearly in the UK, with domestic cats in second place. Natural predators only take a fraction of that number. Now we have added wind farms to the problem. Some 5,500 birds was the yearly toll of one USA wind farm,[10] and large numbers of wind turbines at Tarifa, south-western Spain, reportedly slaughters large, slow raptors like Griffon Vultures, on their main western flyway to Africa.[11]

Game, farming and fishing

Game preservation and lamb protection is still a problem for some raptors, as we try to balance our consciences and bankbooks. Northern Harriers and Goshawks do take some game chicks, and some Golden, Bald, White-tailed and Wedge-tailed Eagles can take a few live lambs—but nowhere near the numbers claimed by some farmers. Like Red Foxes, they are often a convenient scapegoat for bad farming practices. The vast majority of predators are perfectly happy with all the afterbirth and dead lambs left out on the hill or range, or to take weakly ones that would often die anyway. Studies of carcasses in eagle eyries clearly show most were dead when taken; and studies of many raptor carcasses clearly show farmers and game preservers poisoned them. However, the conservationist's, gamekeeper's and farmer's last wild places are themselves now often under threat from new demands of society like housing, wind farms or fish farms. It can be argued that such things are needed, but what of our new leisure society, hell-bent on enjoying itself whatever the cost? Thoughtless 'leisure vehicles' and activities particularly threaten much of our landscape, waterways and coasts; little space is left for wildlife to breed in peace, or even exist. Birds cannot always adapt to our noisy and messy society, and many must go to the wall. Seagulls and many garden birds might be managing, but the alarming fact is that over 50 per cent of our birds now breed in our gardens and towns—the countryside is dying. Tidy, yes, but that is part of the problem. Birds, insects and mammals all need so-called 'weeds'. They also need 'lesser' sea life in massive numbers too, as the

Fig. 129: 'AIGRETTE' DECORATED HAT.

decline by over-fishing of sand eels is currently demonstrating.

Many seabirds of the Northern Hemisphere are badly affected by such fishing, added to possible changes in warm sea currents by 'climate change'. Puffins and other auks, terns, and Black-legged Kittiwakes traditionally depend upon the huge numbers of these glittering little fish, and others like smelts. To watch large fleets and factory ships hoovering up these shoals for animal feed is a bit galling, especially when we contemplate the problems inherent in force-feeding vegetarian cows with animal protein. The outbreak of BSE in the UK was one consequence. Moses warned the Israelites of such dangers when sinning against God (Deuteronomy 28:31), and our farmers had to witness the slaughter of their stock from BSE and Foot and Mouth. Also, should we blame 'coincidence' when Foot and Mouth disease, twice, quickly followed the passing of anti-biblical laws in the UK?

Birds and 'civilisation'

Some birds have adapted to our ways by using buildings or other man-made structures to nest on or to hunt from. Peregrine falcons and Black Vultures now nest on city buildings here and in the Americas, finding them perfectly good substitutes for natural cliffs. Black Kites wheel around the 'canyons' of Hong Kong and other Asian cities quite happily, and White Storks are even thought to bring good luck to the Eurasian buildings they nest atop.

Nests will be maintained and shored up while the birds are absent, as we do to some UK Osprey nests, as Americans fix old wagon wheels to utility poles for them to nest on. Swifts, House Sparrows, European Kestrels, gulls and even Black-legged Kittiwakes also like our roof spaces and ledges. In fact, the American Purple Martin, and our House Martin and Swallow, now nest virtually nowhere else but in our buildings and nest boxes. Many American towns and gardens boast whole cities of nest boxes for Purple Martins, which even allow themselves to be winched up and down to monitor progress, like human high rise blocks fitted with elevators.

Nearly everything humans have ever built or made has been used by birds to nest in or on, though the strangest must be functioning tractors and moving ferries. We have assisted many water birds (loons, grebes, Common and Black Terns) by constructing floating nest platforms in situations where water levels rise or fall too drastically. Uncaring, speeding watercraft regularly cause nests and eggs to be swamped, and they also badly erode the banks or shores. Likewise, man-made materials now dominate in the nests of some birds—often to their cost. Seabirds can end up strangled in the pieces of discarded fishing net or line used in their nests, or even dive into them when fishing, as Atlantic Gannets have. Think of those miles of baited hooks, trailed behind southern fishing boats that are still killing many albatrosses. In fact any diving bird, cetacean and seal, can end up drowned in our nets or lines. Eiders and Grey Herons are still shot by fish and shellfish farmers, as are Goosanders, Cormorants and Red-breasted Mergansers for daring to take game fish. Perhaps if the numbers of Atlantic Eels eaten by such birds was compared to the huge numbers of game fish eggs eaten by the eels, this practice would stop. As usual, mankind looks no further than his (fallen) nose.

This is not to pretend that birds should be given carte-blanche rights to all our food. Living alongside mankind is, like conservation, a two-edged sword for both. Starving Third World peoples need protection for their vital crops from millions of weavers and finches, as well as locusts. The large increase in garden nest boxes and feeding is definitely needed in the West as we continue to raze their former home, the countryside. On the other hand, we must not be influenced by evolutionary ideas that our relationship with wildlife is only recent; for historical evidence shows we

Fig. 130: PURPLE MARTIN 'CITY', USA.

have always used and enjoyed wildlife in many different ways. Conservation is even dangerous for some peoples, when it is allied to Darwinist ideas that demote us to the status of just another animal. Some 'primitive' folk are thrown out of their lands or forests for daring to use them as a resource for survival, so that rare birds or beasts can survive instead! Such behaviour clearly shows we are well out of balance with just about everything, physical or spiritual. Along with many well-intentioned 'Green' ideas, paganism has revived, promoting not only awareness of, but also reverence for, the wild. This erroneous worshipping of 'the creature rather than the Creator' (Romans 1:25) demonstrates how badly the Church and science has let down the world we were supposed to look after. And our eternal state is even more threatened by a fog of 'spiritual pollution', or the endless distortions and wild reinventions of Scripture, as predicted by Jesus and his apostles.

There are traditions surviving today which place us no more or less in harmony with wildlife. Chinese and other Oriental fishermen still use Great Cormorants for fishing, placing restricting rings around their lower necks to prevent swallowing of the catch. Although flightless Rheas literally lose their rears for feather dusters once per year, at least they are not killed but reasonably farmed in South America. A bird's pride is soon healed. The Eider Duck's dense and discarded breast feathers still make the best duvets. One of the most wonderful of all bird and human relationships must be the Honeyguide of southern Africa, and its endearing habit of deliberately whistling to attract the Ratel, or Honey Badger, to a wasp or bee nest. But it goes much farther than that, for the bird also used to 'whistle up' a bushman to assist the opening of the nest! Bushmen traditionally left honeycomb for the bird, and supposedly even the Ratel does—certainly a rather unique piece of symbiosis. Incidentally, it was thought to be very 'bad luck' not to leave any honeycomb for the bird, and certainly common sense to do so.

Nevertheless, these are rare examples, because most birds used by us are reared in the most appalling conditions, like the infamous 'battery chicken'. The dangerous 'bird influenzas' currently coming out of Asia are the inevitable result of intensive cultivation of chickens, with millions of birds helplessly massed together and overdosed with antibiotics. I have no doubt that similar conditions in the West are contributing not only to the birds' ill health, but also to our own. The large amount of antibiotics and other chemicals fed to stock animals already affects our own lack of resistance to the 'superbugs' generated by the overuse of such drugs. Once more, 'evolution' is credited to the bacteria, when in fact the rapid and growing tolerance of our diseases to antibiotics is nothing of the sort. Whatever tolerance there may be is already in-built, or stems from a lack of certain genetic components that normally allow the drug into the cell—they are often 'superwimps' only thriving in antiseptic, hospital conditions, and unable to survive with normal bugs outside in the real world. Certain viruses and bacteria can exchange genetic information to help them fight our drugs, but that is only existing genetic information: nothing new. In south-east Asia, some storks are being indiscriminately destroyed, because they are thought to carry domestic hen viruses. Disaster on all levels looms large, for both man and wildlife. Interestingly, the symbolic prophecies of Revelation

6 are applied by some to wildlife large or microscopic, turning on us in our deeply troubled 'Last Days'. (John Mackay explains well how many 'good bugs' are just in the wrong place, post-Fall.[12])

Gamebirds like pheasants continue to be 'humanely' reared for release into the wild, and many do evade the guns each year, and live as natural lives as possible in the woods and fields partially preserved for them. Following our often-bizarre dietary fashions, 'low cholesterol' Ostriches are now farmed commercially for their meat. As for wild songbirds, and other life forms, populations have plummeted alarmingly in the last forty years or so. Fairly natural wildflower meadows used to be left for cutting until late summer, when baby birds were not so vulnerable, but now farmers scrabble to 'silage' it at least twice per summer season. After harvesting, grain stubble and root crop fields would have been left over winter to fertilise themselves, and incidentally provide seed and tuber gleanings for the likes of finches, sparrows and wildfowl, but this is now very rare. Demands grow on farmers to produce constantly, even when much of their produce merely goes into 'mountains', stored for economic reasons to maintain prices, while millions starve in the Third World. Growing desertification around the tropical zones is not the only problem for their farmers, for when they overuse agri-chemicals alongside clearance of ground cover; any rain washes the soil away. Thus the deserts grow larger, floods downstream grow much worse, and offshore sea life like coral reefs are swamped in sediments. Deforestation of mountain areas is especially bad for worsening downstream flooding, let alone wildlife, as we now see annually in places like Bangladesh, or even Cheltenham, England. God has provided superbly designed ecosystems like upland bogs to conserve and store the rainwater, like giant sponges. They only slowly release the waters so as not to cause flooding downstream, and maintain year-round waterways. Yet we not only clear the tops but drain them, and then even 'tidy' and straighten the rivers downstream. The inevitable result is faster rivers, more erosion and flooding and less wildlife. Better winter floods downstream for visiting wildfowl, yes, but that cannot balance loss of rich upland breeding areas.

On a slightly lesser scale, chemicals specifically aimed at snails and slugs by both farmer and gardener are killing Song Thrushes, and to further complicate matters, Blackbirds appear to be dominating and supplanting

Chapter 7

them in many British gardens. Magpies are currently unpopular in the UK for their habit of raiding songbirds' nests, but Greater-spotted Woodpeckers, Tawny Owls and Red Squirrels also do that. Greater predator numbers are merely the inevitable side-effect of successful garden bird numbers. This is a comparatively new phenomenon, and it will take some years to achieve balance in the new 'urban jungle'; but do we have the time?

Birdbrains

In the second half of the twentieth century, Great and Blue Tits learned that the foil tops of British milk bottles concealed a real treat. The habit of pecking off the tops of freshly delivered milk to get at the cream quickly spread. This raised the old question of intelligence in birds, and other creatures, of which many can be taught quite clever tricks and tasks. We now know that birds (and dolphins) can go beyond 'mere tricks' and even solve fairly abstract puzzles, or at least answer questions beyond 'yes' and 'no'. If parrots or dolphins are tested with colour-number-shape combination questions, and the tester deliberately asks for answers not taught, the creature can respond abstractly, that is, show the tester that he is wrong, or even invent a new category beyond the simple yes-no response. Tits and Grey Squirrels are quite capable of solving complex maze-type puzzles to get at nuts or other rewards. Pulling strings up, or matchsticks and drawers out, creeping through pipes—virtually every task set was achieved by TV's 'Birdbrains of Britain'.

Asian Baya Weavers have long been famed for their ability to thread up to ten beads, using a needle and thread! That shows how their dexterity can be utilised for 'entertainment', and reinforced by rewards of seed. However, Scandinavian Hooded Crows have taught themselves to pull up fishing lines, foot over foot, left by hole-in-the-ice fishermen, to get at the fish. Apes can be taught all sorts of things, but the intelligence and rapid adaptability of parrots and corvids provides yet more problems for evolutionary theories about our supposed 'closest cousins'. Chimps can use tools, but so can finches, and only crows deliberately bend and shape them to suit.

Deliberate or accidental introduction of non-resident wildlife to foreign parts can be a real problem. While egrets and others are still naturally spreading globally, man has made some pretty drastic mistakes in the creatures and plants he has exported to other lands. It has already been mentioned that many land birds have been wiped out by us, and our cats, dogs, mink, mongoose, and pigs, or had their habitat destroyed by grazing beasts or crops. As we increasingly blanket the earth and destroy the natural wetlands and forest, the birds and beasts will have to adapt or die. Many European Kestrels have benefited from motorways' wide, grassy verges replete with voles and other small mammals, but are depleted in the wider countryside. Barn Owls, also driven to grassy road verges for rodents, often become victims, their lightweight bodies tossed helplessly against speeding vehicles. Birds like the large Philippine Eagle cannot live in drastically reduced forests, as surely as Dicksissels or Yellowhammers cannot live in the sterile, 'weed-free' countryside of the USA or UK. Balance is once more the keyword. Even the sea is not safe from 'development', as demands for tidal barrages to produce 'clean' electricity in our estuaries occasionally succeed, to the detriment of the tens of thousands of birds who depend upon them for food and rest. On the other hand, escaped Ringed-necked Parakeets now form dense flocks up to 6,000 strong—around London! Nevertheless, at this tempestuous time in human history, my main aim is to inform of the Creator, and hope that true knowledge will also assist folk to look after his creation, as and when they can. This should be the inevitable side-effect of our greater responsibility to people and planet, as 'good works' naturally follow personal salvation.

A life of birds

You will have realised that birds greatly impress me. I have spent most of my life watching them, and they have often intervened when I most needed peace and reminding of God. I shall never forget the first turquoise streak of a kingfisher flying by as I paddled with my child's fishing net, or looking down in wonder as a beautifully camouflaged nightjar arose from my feet in Anglesey heathland. Then about the same time, 1960, a gorgeous male Hawfinch dropped to the ground right in front of me, and I was hooked! My first view of a soaring buzzard over the Welsh hills was as exciting as the many eagles I would later watch over distant mountains. What little I knew then of the wider world of birds came mainly from books, and the likes of

a

b

Charles Tunnicliffe's illustrations, but I would increasingly search out the real thing—then naturally, their Creator. This book is a celebration both of them, and more importantly, that Creator. Real science is not at all incompatible with the Bible, as the Christian faith of men like Newton, Kepler, Ray, Linnaeus, Pasteur, Kelvin, Faraday, and now Sir Ghillean Prance of Kew garden, and others, more than ably demonstrate. I am obviously not a scientist but an artist, yet trained to observe carefully. Remember, real science is about observing, thinking and testing—so we should all be able to do that to some degree or other. God has given us common sense, as well as putting 'eternity' (Ecclesiastes 3:11) and 'law'

Fig. 131: 'BIRDBRAINS OF BRITAIN'. A: GREAT TIT HAULING UP PEANUT. B: BLUE TIT PULLING OUT STICKS TO ALLOW PEANUTS TO DROP FREE.

(Jeremiah 31:33) in everyone's hearts—remember: 'no excuse' for not believing in creation (Romans 1:20).

That testing should also be applied to any idea that opposes the Scriptures. I hope this book has demonstrated that most evolutionary theory is not only bad science, but also very bad philosophy and theology. No one could possibly be an 'atheist', for to know there is no God means you would have to know everything! We can clearly see the roots of failing Communism in evolutionist S. J. Gould's super-evolutionary propaganda. As for the likes of Hitler's, Stalin's, or Mao's 'ethnic cleansing', this was also given credence by Darwin's cousin, Galton, and his *Eugenics* ideas. Recall part of the overtly racist sub-title of Darwin's *On the Origin of Species* was *'and the Survival of the Favoured Races'*! Strangely, Gould regretted that Haeckel's completely theorised 'ape-men' were shown as small black Africans, yet over a century later, in his own day, nothing much had changed.[13] Little black 'ape-men' still adorn most evolutionary books, or grunt their way through programmes like the BBC's disgraceful and unscientific 'Apeman' fantasy. Such are the desperate, racist and subjective ideologies that result from the mental and spiritual poverty of evolutionary scientism. When unscientific ideas like Dawkins' 'Selfish Genes' or, 'we are only here because millions of other parallel universes have not accidentally evolved life', can so rule education and the media, the end of the biblical 'last days' draws ever closer.

The two books—tortured geology and tortured soul

We are usually told there are two books for us to study: the Bible and the 'Natural World'. This is true, but the centuries have seen them artificially separated until they are now thought to be incompatible, as spirit and body have likewise been severed from each other. We are, in fact a trinity of body, soul and spirit, and any 'knowledge' that denies creation and the eternal Spirit is just that, *knowledge* but not *wisdom*. Truly, 'the wisdom of this world is foolishness with God' (1 Corinthians 3:19). The Holy Bible is the only book accurately to explain creation, the Earth's tortured crust and our own tortured souls. In the symbolic words of Revelation 11:17–18: 'We give you thanks, O Lord God Almighty ... (who will) destroy those who destroy the earth.' That might or might not refer to the physical Earth as well, as Isaiah 24:5–6 also records we have 'defiled' our planet, and because we have 'transgressed the laws' the earth is 'cursed'. That primarily refers to the

Fall, which could only be temporarily expiated by the sacrifice of doves and other creatures. Most importantly, such acts pointed forwards only to our Creator's ultimate sacrifice on the cross of Calvary. 'Natural selection', 'red in tooth and claw' is no more all history than the Bible is just the 'New Testament'.

The Bible is the only book to dare to prophesy relevant history in advance, and leave an accurate outline of our deeply troubled 'end times'. What is often misconstrued as the 'end of the world' is in fact a glorious new beginning, for believers in Christ's loving sacrifice for our sin.

I am fully aware that so many have wrongly interpreted biblical prophecy in the past, especially in attempting to set the date for our Lord's return. Yet he held the Jews responsible for not knowing the exact day of 'their visitation', at his first coming, and likewise warned us to 'know the season', if not 'the hour', of his return (Daniel 9:25; Matthew 19:44; 16:3; 25:13; 1 Thessalonians 5:2). Our Lord left us a host of warning signs to decipher, some obvious, some not so, before the great assembly of raptors overfly the final battlefield of 'Armageddon'. These signs include: (1) the miraculous preservation of the Jews and the restoration of Israel to the land at an exact time, (2) the re-establishment of the Roman Empire (EU?), and the rise of Islam and Globalism, (3) the increase of false prophets, false Christs and church apostasy from biblical truth, (4) moral and family breakdown, evolutionary humanism, increasing ecological disaster, earthquakes, famines, sexual perversion and disease. Everything we are increasingly seeing was predicted centuries before the Lord Jesus came to this Earth, or by him and his apostles. This can only be a rough outline, but we are warned 'be ready', and 'lift up our heads' as we see these happenings (Luke 21:28; Matthew 24).

Of course we do not know the full meaning or timing of these prophecies yet, but, I must stress, we are warned to 'know the season' of His return and to avoid the many deceptions, both scientific and spiritual. We urgently need to look into these things with both microscope and prayer. For the Bible shows the only way out of the inevitable and tragic mess mankind's disobedience has caused into a glorious, almost unimaginable future, all through the greatest story of love and sacrifice the world will ever see. It was indelibly written in blood on a wooden cross some 2,000 years ago, by the only 'Way, Truth and Life', our Creator, Lord Jesus Christ himself. He was 'crucified on a cross of wood, yet made the hill on which it stood'. This is the greatest mystery ever, for our very Creator emptied himself and took a slave's form: 'For God so loved the world that He gave His only begotten Son, that whosoever believes in Him should not perish but have everlasting life' (John 3:16). The message is clear and simple, as surely as creation declares the Creator.

The Bible not only clearly prophesied that mankind would be avoiding the obvious conclusion that life could only be deliberately created, but also that many would deny the historical truth of the global Noah's Flood. The Scriptures tell us: 'For this they wilfully forget: that by the word of God the heavens were of old, and the earth standing out of the water and in the water, by which the world that then existed perished, being flooded with water.' (2 Peter 3:5–6). It is much more serious than that, for in the same place, it is also predicted: 'scoffers will come ... walking according to their own lusts, and saying, "Where is the promise of His (second) coming? For ... all things continue as they were from the beginning of creation"' (2 Peter 3:3–4). This is the prevailing attitude of our times—'uniformitarianism'—everything is slowly happening as it always has. No supernatural and rapid happenings like global floods or second comings are going to interrupt our existence, thank you very much! However, they ignore the verifiable facts of both geology and biology, and that every prophecy in the Scriptures is totally reliable and has already been, or will be, fulfilled. The first coming of Jesus Christ fulfilled hundreds of prophecies; impossible for a mere human. These predictions were made by the Old Testament prophets centuries earlier and recorded at the very latest in the Greek Septuagint Old Testament (c250 BC). The Dead Sea Scrolls and other documents confirm that the prophecies currently being fulfilled have not been changed, contrary to sceptics and the claims of all other religions. Some are ordered to slay and make war on all 'idolaters', whereas Jesus said, 'Love your enemies' but expect persecution. Martyrdom is still a reality for believers: a Christian is killed every few minutes, somewhere in the world, every day.

There is no doubt whatsoever that 'the whole world lies under the sway of the wicked one' (1 John 5:19), a fallen angel so diabolically clever that he has persuaded many to follow his teachings, at the same time denying his very existence. Yes, it is 'Satan' (resister) or 'Devil' (slanderer), the original serpent of Genesis, who is even behind macro-evolutionary teaching. This fallen angel currently persuades many to 'worship the creature rather than the Creator' (Romans 1:25). This deeply atheistic evolutionary science, especially when aligned with politics, often deliberately undermines, or tries to destroy, virtually all of our God-given certainties and morals, including marriage, heterosexual sex, normal family life and all objective truth. But real, objective truth will out, and relative 'truth' will be destroyed at Armageddon, when the world attacks his people, both believing Jew and Gentile together, in the 'Israel of God'. Then all will witness His return, when they look upon Him 'whom they pierced (crucified)', and 'every eye will see him', 'as lightning flashing from east to west' (Matthew 24:27) and 'all the tribes of the earth will mourn' (Zechariah 12:10; Revelation 1:7; Matthew 24:30).

There is no need to look through a microscope or telescope to 'see' our Creator, for his qualities are clearly present, albeit in much diluted and degraded form, in ourselves and all creation. We all instinctively want more than mere existence, for God has put eternity, and morals, in all our hearts (Ecclesiastes 3:11; Romans 2:15). We should all know that death is unnatural, and only brought in by the Fall, yet our spirits are eternal. A newly dead body still has all its biochemistry for several minutes—but something vital, immaterial, undetectable by science, has left. At death, there are only two possible destinations, heaven or hell: 'choose this day whom you will serve'. Faith in the finished work of the Saviour, Jesus Christ, is the only way to glory—He is the only Way. The Holy Spirit hovered over the waters at creation, descended like a dove upon Jesus at his baptism, and at the new creation, that same Spirit will cause us to 'mount up with wings like eagles' (Isaiah 40:31) to be with God, eternally. Hallelujah!

Notes

1 **R. Mohon,** *Cosmic War Survival—The True Gospel distinguished from the Global Apostasy by reference to the early Ages of Man* (Truthzone, 2004).
2 **Hislop's** *Two Babylons* is a masterly exposition on the history of religion and myth (Partridge & co. 4th edition, 1871). Now reprinted.

3 **W. F. Allbright,** *Recent Discoveries in Bible Lands* (1955).

4 **D. Rohl,** *Legend, The Genesis of Civilisation* (Century, 1998).

5 *Nature,* 18/25. 12:2003.

6 **Kang and Nelson,** *The Discovery of Genesis* (Concordia Publishing House, 1979).

7 **Rene Noorbergen,** *Secrets of the Lost Races* (New English Library, 1980).

8 **Joni Mitchell,** 'Don Juan's restless daughter' (c1980).

9 **RSPB,** *Birds* (Autumn 2004). This tragic situation highlights yet another human error: treating cattle as sacred. Starving Hindus will not eat this vital food source, but just allow them to die and be eaten by vultures! Yet, they still care for the cows with expensive but deadly farm chemicals, like Diclofenac, which then slaughters the scavenging vultures.

10 *Natural World* magazine, Spring, 2004.

11 Personal communication, Spanish ornithologists, Andalucia, 1996.

12 **John Mackay,** 'Did a Good God create Bad Bugs?', DVD (CR Australia, 2005).

13 **S. J. Gould,** *Ever Since Darwin* (Harmondsworth: Penguin, 1977), p. 214.

Website: http://artofcreation.org.uk

Bibliography

(Warning—even some Christian authors can present dubious theories as fact, or try to combine speculative secular science and the Bible—always check!)

Creation science

H. Arp, *Quasars, Red shifts and Controversies* (Interstellar Media, 1987).

S. Austin, et al., *A Symposium on Creation III* (Grand Rapids: Baker Book House, 1971).

M. J. Behe, *Darwin's black box—the Biochemical Challenge to Evolution* (Touchstone, 1996).

M. Bowden, *Science vs. Evolution* (Bromley: Sovereign Books, PO Box 88, Bromley, Kent, 1991).

M. Bowden, *Ape-men—Fact or Fallacy?* (Bromley: Sovereign Books, 1978).

M. Bowden, *True Science agrees with Bible* (Bromley: Sovereign books, 1998).

S. Burgess, *Hallmarks of Design* (Epsom: DayOne Publications, 2000).

S. Burgess, *He Made the Stars Also* (Epsom: DayOne Publications, 2001).

S. Burgess, *The Origin of Man* (Epsom: DayOne Publications, 2004).

H. Coffin, *Origin by Design* (Review & Herald Publishing Association, 1983).

Creation ex-nihilo quarterly magazine, Answers in Genesis: **Ken Ham et al,** global 'Creation Evangelism'. Also *Creation ex nihilo Technical Journal.* e.g. Vol. 17 [1] :03 'Destroying Bird Evolution'. www.AnswersInGenesis.org

Creation Research articles, videos and fossil digs, worldwide. (John Mackay and team/Australia etc.) http://www.creationresearch.net

Creation Science Foundation [CSF] USA. Good videos, etc., like **Dr Steve Austin's** 'Mt St Helen's—Explosive Evidence for Catastrophe in Earth's History.'

Creation Science Movement magazine. CSM [UK]. Magazine and many leaflets available, plus Genesis Expo Museum, The Hard, Portsmouth. http://www.creationsciencemovement.com

Creation Update magazine [UK]. Wide range of leaflets, etc., available. http://www.c-r-t.co.uk www.creationism.org

P. Davis and **D. H. Kenyon,** *Of Pandas and People* (Haughton Publishing Company Texas, 1993).

M. Denton, *Evolution—a Theory in Crisis* (Adler & Adler, 1986).

The Genesis Agendum, PO Box 78, Oakham, LE15 6LZ, UK. Occasional papers.

D. Gish, *Creation Scientists Answer their Critics* (Institute for Creation research [ICR], 1993).

D. Gish, *Evolution—the Fossils STILL say No!* (ICR, 1995).

W. Gitt, *In the Beginning was Information* (Chistliche Literatur—Verbreitung e V., 1997).

K. Ham et al, *The [updated and expanded] Answers Book* (AiG, 1999).

R. Humphreys, *Starlight and Time* (Master Books, 1994).

P. E. Johnson, *Testing Darwinism* (Inter Varsity Press,1997).

P. E. Johnson, *Darwin on trial* (Inter Varsity Press, 1991).

M. Lubenow, *Bones of Contention* (Grand Rapids: Baker Books, 1992).

In Six Days—Why 50 Scientists Choose to Believe in Creation (New Holland, 1999).

A. Macintosh, *Genesis for Today* (Leominster: DayOne Publications, 1997). (New book on flight due soon.)

C. Matrisciana, *Gods of the New Age* (book + video).

C. Matrisciana and **R. Oakland,** *The Evolution Conspiracy—a quantum leap into the New Age* (Harvest House Publishers, 1991). Video of the same name, Jeremiah Films, 1988.

R. Milton, *The Facts of Life—Shattering the Myths of Darwinism.* Now published as *Shattering the Myths of Darwinism* in the USA. (Although easily shattering Darwin, Milton is not a believer.)

N. J. Mitchell, *Evolution—and the Emperor's New Clothes* (Roydon Publications, 1983).

H. M. Morris and **J. D. Morris,** *The Modern Creation Trilogy* (Master Books, 1996).

H.M. Morris, *The Biblical Basis for Modern Science* (Grand Rapids: Baker Book House, 1984).

J. D. Morris, *The Young Earth* (Master Books, 1994).

M. J. Oard, *An Ice Age caused by the Genesis Flood* (ICR, 1990).

Origins—Journal of the Biblical Creation Society [UK]. e.g. no. 28, 5:2000 'Birds from Dinosaurs—A Flight of the Imagination', **A. L. Camp,** www.biblicalcreation.co.uk

E. K. V. Pearce, *Evidence for Truth: Vol. 1—Science* (Eagle Publishers, 1998).

E. K. V. Pearce, *Evidence for Truth: Vol. 2—Archaeology* (Eagle Publishers, 1999).

W. Remine, *The Biotic Message—Evolution vs. Message Theory* (St Paul Science, 1993).

The Revised Quote Book (Creation Science Foundation, 1990). Probably now reprinted.

A Rocha—Christians in Conservation, 3 Hooper St, Cambridge, CB1 2NZ, UK.

D. Rosevear, *Creation Science* (New Wine, 1991).

J. Sarfati, *Refuting Evolution 2* (AnswersInGenesis [AiG], 2002).

V. Sodera, *One Small Speck to man—the evolution myth* (Vija Sodera productions, 2003).

L. Spetner, *Not by Chance!—Shattering the Modern Theory of Evolution* (Judaica Press, 1997).

J. Taylor, *Fossils, Facts and Fantasies* (Mt Blanco Publishing Company, 1999).

J. C. Whitcomb, and **H. M. Morris,** *The Genesis Flood* (Grand Rapids: Baker Book House, 1962).

J. C. Whitcomb, *The World that Perished* (Grand Rapids: Baker Book House, 1993).

A. E. Wilder Smith, *The Scientific Alternative to Neo-Darwinian Evolutionary Theory* (TWFT, 1987).

J. Woodmorappe, *Noah's Ark—a Feasibility Study* (ICR, 1996).

Bibliography

Evolutionary textbooks/writers

D. **Attenborough,** *Life on Earth* (BBC TV and book,1979).

D. **Attenborough,** *The Life of Birds* (BBC TV and book, 1998).

Cambridge Encyclopaedia of Ornithology (Cambridge University Press, 1971).

Dictionary of Biology (Unwin Hyman, 1999).

A. **Feduccia,** *The Origin and Evolution of Birds* (2nd ed., Yale University Press, 1999).

Field Guide to the Birds of North America (National Geographic Society, 1987).

S. **Fridriksson,** *Surtsey—Evolution of Life on a Volcanic Island* (Butterworths, 1979).

Mullarney, et al, *Collins Bird Guide* (Harper Collins, 1999).

N. S. **Proctor** and P. J. **Lynch,** *Manual of Ornithology* (Yale University Press, 1993).

J. **Rawson,** *Animals in Art* (British Museum, 1977).

P. **Shipman,** *Taking Wing—Archaeopteryx and the Evolution of Bird Flight* (Weidenfeld & Nicholson,1998).

C. **Stock** and J. M. **Harris,** *Rancho La Brea. A Record of Pleistocene Life in California* (7th edition, Natural History Museum of Los Angeles County, Science Series, No. 37, 1992).

W. E. **Swinton,** *Fossil Birds* (British Natural History Museum, 1965).

Sir A. **Landsborough Thomson,** *A New Dictionary of Birds* (Nelson, 1964).

Fairly balanced history from biblical believers

Bullinger, *The Gospel in the Stars.*

D. E. **Chittick,** *The Puzzle of Ancient Man* (Creation Compass, 1997).

B. **Cooper,** *After the Flood* (New Wine Press, 1995).

M. **Gascoigne,** *Forgotten History of the Western People: From the Earliest Origins* via CSM.

R. **Mohon,** *Cosmic War Survival—The True Gospel distinguished from the Global Apostasy by reference to the Early Ages of Man* (Truthzone, 2004).

C. and B. **Wilson,** *The Stones Still Shout!* (Pacific Christian Ministries,1999).

History and prophecy, especially relating to occultism, false religion, Europe and 'end times'

A. **Close,** *The Divine Plan of the Ages.*

M. **de Semlyn,** *All Roads Lead to Rome?* (Dorchester House, 1993).

H. **Grattan-Guinness,** *Romanism and the Reformation* (Our Inheritance Publications, 1999).

H. **Hanegraaf,** *Christianity in Crisis.*

A. **Hilton,** *The Principality and Powers of Europe* (Dorchester House, 1997).

A. **Hislop,** *The Two Babylons* (Partridge & Co., 1871). New paperback now available.

D. Hunt, *Occult Invasion* (Harvest House, 1998).

D. Hunt, *A Woman Rides The Beast* (Harvest House, 1994).

A. Morrison, *The Serpent and the Cross* (Diakrisis Ministries).

W. Martin, *Kingdom of the Cults* (Bethany House, 1997).

D. A. Noebel, *Understanding the Times* (abridged ed. ACSI, 1995).

E. Paris, *The Secret History of the Jesuits* (Chick Publications, 1975).

General history, occultism and mythology

J. H. Breasted, *Ancient times—a History of the Early World* (Athenaeum Press, 1944). Conventional, uninspired history

M. Ferguson, *The Aquarian Conspiracy.* (1980s—but still one of the 'definite' books *from* the 'spiritual' 'New Age' today.)

J. Fiske, *Myths and Mythmakers* (Senate, 1996).

J. G. Fraser, *The Golden Bough.* (Monumental, classic history of myth, but all completely distorted and embroidered from that first Genesis 3 prophecy about Jesus and the Serpent!)

Gibbons, *The Decline and Fall of the Roman Empire,* abridged by **D. M. Low,** (Book Club Associates, 1974).

V. H. H. Green, *Renaissance and Reformation* (Arnold, 1972).

E. O. James, *History of Religions* (Hodder & Stoughton, 1964). Conventional, uninspired history.

W. Keller, *The Bible as History* (Hodder & Stoughton, 1956). (Although compromised by evolutionary, 'liberal theology', this is a very useful book on biblical archaeology and history.)

Larousse Encyclopaedia of Modern History (Hamlyn, 1968).

Micropedia of World History (Parragon, 2002).

R. Noorbergen. *Secrets of the Lost Races* (NEL, 1978).

D. Rohl, *Legend—The Genesis of Civilisation* (Century, 1998). (Part Two of *A Test of Time.* Similar usefulness and objections as to the Keller book, though Rohl is not a believer.)

I. Velikovsky, *Worlds in Collision* (Abacus, 1972). (Caution—both this and the next book contain fascinating insights into the sophistication of our early civilisations and their shared catastrophic experiences and 'myths', but neither author appears to have been a believer.)

Appendix

Types and classification of birds: an introduction

The world enjoys such a huge variety of birds displaying many different forms, plumages and characters. Far more than any self-respecting evolutionists should expect! They tell us that the only thing that can influence the form of any creature is the environment, and only by 'acting' upon random genetic mistakes that are themselves 99.9 per cent harmful or neutral—well, that sounds more like endless miracles than science. And if, say, the same sea has shaped all the fish, why are there so many different shapes and swimming methods? Why has the same air shaped such a huge variety of birds and flight techniques? From the tiny Bee Hummingbird to the massive, extinct Elephant Bird, they all share the same blueprint as outlined in the previous chapters, whether they fly or not. That tiny Hummingbird, little larger than my thumb, could not be smaller and still contain the organs necessary for a warm-blooded creature, as a Great Bustard or Mute Swan could not be any larger and still be able to fly. Even some hawkmoths are larger than the hummer! The giant flightless Moa of New Zealand, like the Elephant Bird of Madagascar, only perished because man recently hunted them to death. They, and their living relatives like Rheas and Ostriches, raise other questions about why the fossil record also shows a loss of size and loss of flight. Actually, it is claimed that the Moa didn't have any 'arm' bones at all. That *seems* highly unlikely, for all other flightless birds have them, however reduced. As Genesis 1:20 says, 'let birds fly across the ... heavens', and it could be argued that all flightless birds have lost flight, as most evolutionists agree.

As to the order of creation of birds, as reflected in today's 'Kinds' or 'species', that is also difficult. 'Kinds' probably refers to a sort of 'super-Family', whereby some average sort of *heron*, for instance, could radiate into a whole range of sizes and colours.

There are estimated to be about 9,000 to 10,000 species of birds (class *'Aves'*) in 27 or 29 *'Orders'*, depending upon who is counting. For example, one such Order is the *'Ciconiiformes'*, or *herons and allies* consisting of the *herons, egrets, bitterns, storks, ibises, spoonbills, Hammerkop* and *flamingos.* (Some place the flamingos in a separate sub-order *'Phoenicopteridae'*, or even Order, based upon their different and unique, filtering beak, and part-webbed feet.) Particular *Orders* are then further subdivided into *'Families'*, in this case into the *herons and bitterns* or *'Ardeidae';* and the *spoonbills, storks* and *ibises (or Ciconiidae, Threskiornithidae, Scopidae* and *Baleanicipitidae.)* Don't scientists just love impressive tongue-twisting names! Fear not, for I use such jargon as little as possible, only when absolutely necessary to differentiate between families, etc. (Actually, such jargon is useful for communication with other birdwatchers world-wide, when first languages are insufficient.) The *Family* of *Ardeidae* is further separated out into 17 *'Genera'*, such as the *day herons, night herons, tiger herons, large bitterns,* and *small bitterns.* Let's follow the day herons further down the line to one of their 34 'Species'—our familiar Grey Heron. So it is called *Ardea cinerea*–the second name from the Latin for ashes, or ash-coloured heron. There we have the lineage of one particular type of bird, or Species, up through Genus, to Family and then finally to its Order.

However, it is not only pronunciation that is the problem with this system of classification, for most bird books will arrange all the birds in an 'evolutionary' sequence. They class *Ratites* (flightless birds) and divers/loons, etc., for instance as 'primitive', and place them first—yet the first birds in the fossil record had full flight, some 30 to 100 million evolutionary years before them! And of course such ancient birds must have had the same incredibly complex sort of DNA as modern birds, as the many other 'primitive', living fossils obviously still have.

Recently, even that became more complicated, with such as Sibley and Monroe's (1990) system of classification based upon 'new biochemical' methods—introducing yet more confusion and sub-classes in the much-abused name of science. That this is being perpetrated by the same system of DNA-DNA 'hybridisation' that produced the infamous mistake of our supposed 98.5 per cent parity with apes should cause widespread scepticism. The Order of *Falconiformes* have suddenly become an *'Infraorder'* under the *Ciconiiformes*—herons, etc!

And now in 2005, recent researchers into other genes and proteins have found that many examples of birds of similar form, behaviour and ecological niche are actually divided between two rather different groups: *'Metaves'* and *'Coronaves'*. They were surprised to find that birds seemingly related because they are similar in appearance and behaviour were not in the same subgroups. They say, for example, that although flamingos and Roseate Spoonbills are both wading birds with long legs and similar heads, wings and plumage, flamingos are in the *'Metave'* category and spoonbills in the *'Coronaves'*. (That doesn't surprise me at one level, as a flamingo's whale-like filter beak is rather different to a spoonbill's.)

In fact, both groups had representatives in most types of birds. The researchers were then forced to consider them to be examples of 'convergent evolution', i.e. living creatures evolving similar form and behaviour because they inhabit similar ecological niches. One researcher commented: 'People have been trying to classify birds based on their appearance for hundreds of years. It is valuable at some levels, but when you get to really deep divergences, you just hit a wall' (*New Scientist*, 11:12:2004). Creation scientist John Mackay, reviewing the evidence, predicts that classification will ultimately show there is as many separate 'kingdoms' as there were created Kinds. Creationists understand that each kind of bird is a unique combination of non-unique components. This has resulted from the fact that each Kind was created separately, and biblical Kinds are biologically ('evolutionarily') unrelated. The best way to classify living creatures is to group them together on the basis of number of similar characteristics. This is what traditional taxonomists (people who classify living organisms) have been doing since Ray and Linnaeus. Trying to work out evolutionary relationships by comparing individual molecules has been tried in the past, and generated nothing but confusion. Analysing individual genes will probably not produce any more coherent results. (Creation Research Evidence News, 19:2:2005).

Before I nerve myself to tackle individual bird Orders, let's also look at their division into two main groups—the *non-Passerines* and the *Passerines*. Passerine simply means perching bird (i.e. on a branch), non-Passerine—non-perching bird. Simple? No, for many non-Passerines perch in trees, others on rocks, etc! I will only use this separation for convenience, and to demonstrate yet another flaw in evolutionary thinking. Then there is always the vexed question of '*species*' being an inexact term anyway. Species are usually described as having breeding compatibility and producing fertile offspring, only among themselves. But if two very similar birds like the White-headed Duck and Ruddy Ducks can interbreed and produce fertile offspring they cannot be separate species. There is great concern from some ornithologists at present because the vigorous Ruddy Duck, which was only recently introduced into the UK from the USA, has crossed to Spain and is now interbreeding with rare Eurasian White-headed Ducks. My own view is that since they obviously came from the same 'Kind' of duck in the first place, then the Ruddy can only reintroduce its lively genes back to the waning White-headed and help to save it (although loss of habitat is also a big factor). Then we will have three 'sub-species' and more variety. It is strange how so many 'red in tooth and claw' scientists so vigorously oppose the extinction of any life by our interference, yet constantly cry that extinction's are common and necessary for blind 'evolution'!

I have already pointed out some of the problems with classifying birds, but for convenience I will roughly stick to the order and many of the groupings proposed by ornithologists. This does not endorse their beliefs, for it is obvious that their hierarchy from 'primitive' to most 'evolved is completely skewed by Archaeopteryx, for instance. Ostriches and divers are only found much later in the fossil record, yet they place them first.

A speculative list of the 27–30 Orders, and typical families of all the birds of the world is available on request from the author. Warning: it is both a very difficult and very controversial task!

INDEX OF BIRDS

Index

Index

Index

Index

Index

Index